D0389946

the velvet lounge

the velvet lounge
on late chicago jazz

gerald majer

columbia university press / new york

columbia university press
publishers since 1893
new york   chichester, west sussex
copyright © 2005 columbia university press
all rights reserved

The author is grateful to the editors of the following publica-
tions where chapters of this book first appeared: *Brilliant
Corners: A Journal of Jazz and Literature* "Batterie" and
"Monstrosioso"; *Georgia Review*, "Stitt's Time," "Dreaming
of Roscoe Mitchell," and "Le Serpent Qui Danse"; *Quarterly
West*, "The Velvet Lounge"; *Shenandoah*, "Jug Eyes"; *The
Yale Review*, "Proxima Ra" and "Intuitive Research Beings."

library of congress cataloging-in-publication data
Majer, Gerald, 1953–
The Velvet Lounge : on late Chicago jazz / Gerald Majer.
        p.   cm.
Includes discography (p.   ) and bibliographical references.
ISBN 0–231–13682–X (cloth : acid-free paper)—ISBN 0–231–51012–8 (electronic)
1. Jazz—Illinois—Chicago—History and criticism.   1. Title.

ML3508.8CSM35 2005
781.65'0973'11—dc22
                        2005042104

∞

Columbia University Press books are printed on permanent
and durable acid-free paper.

Printed in the United States of America
c 10 9 8 7 6 5 4 3 2 1

For Val, Ka, and Malcolm

. . . reverberating, eke out the mind
On peculiar horns themselves eked out
By the spontaneous particulars of sound.

—*Wallace Stevens*

We've again been apprised of an echoic whir,
warned against pre-emptive equivalence.

—*Nathaniel Mackey*

Music excavates heaven.

—*Charles Baudelaire*

contents

the velvet lounge

Gene Ammons *Photo by Don Schlitten*

jug eyes

1969: The Boss is Back!

The Boss is Back! The album was on the Prestige label, the first Gene Ammons made after being released in 1969 from Stateville Penitentiary following a seven-year term for heroin possession. With Junior Mance on piano, Buster Williams on bass, Bernard Purdie on drums, and Candido on conga, it's a hell of a record. Ammons's tenor holler breaks loose over the hard funk backing, out of the horn something like a contagious fire catching on the fills and slides and the stuttering beats. At times the music almost sticks, suspended machinelike, Ammons's horn a lyric, swaying juggernaut on the verge of overwhelming it, chopping off a phrase with tensed menace, collapsing an arpeggio into a broken staircase, bursting through the octave with a stabbing slashing roaring. It's the sort of music that recalls the power of words like *bad, mean, e il*—corked inside it all the flocking spirit tongues of jazz, all the flaring red devils of the blues.

The infernal idiom comes naturally when speaking of Ammons. In the old music reviews and liner notes, he's forever framed in flames—hot, blazing, turning up the fire, inhabiting a realm where the tenor sax and the musician who plays it merge into a single hybrid creature, a burning birdlike monster who dips and soars, swoops and flutters, and dives to the attack. He's a powerhouse, a smoker, a cooker; the thing is blistering, bristling, raw, muscular, carrying a torch, punching out phrases; he brings the house down, he takes no prisoners: the Boss is back! Listening to the record, I have to admit the justice of the language. Here's the first cut, "The Jungle Boss," Houston Person and Prince James the guest brass section and Ammons's horn doing exactly what the writers describe: charging, surging, heating up, roaring out, the rest, a series of further glosses irresistibly emerging—shouted party talk, the fight at midnight, a crazy sex boogie waltzing through a mirrored room, Magic Markered asterisks and handwritten notes under the song titles on a battered DJ copy: *Mellow Boss*; *Jugs Down Hard*; *Kicks Royal Ass*.

Yet I hear one thing more. It *booms*—yes, the horn echoes and booms like it's down in a tunnel, some effect of Ammons's playing or Rudy Van Gelder's miking. I've heard too that the sound was a commercial move, one of those bids for radio play like Sonny Stitt's Varitone a year or two later. It booms: the verb opens out a street, a Chicago night, the world is big, big (another Ammons epithet); it's the sound of a giant heartbeat, the sound of the cannon and the gun, the sound of a fate that hangs over you and one day drops, boom, or a fate that brings you to the top, boom you're there, sound inside the body a fast-jump pulsing of love or hate, boom I'm yours, you're mine, or boom you're dead, a blessing or a curse. It booms because it's touchy, it's hair-trigger, it's explosive, not spoiling for a fight but hauling a weight, a critical mass that's building toward a chain reaction, that smears across the clouds of a fall Chicago sky some eruption of a tear in the face of a cold wind, some laugh out of a warm loaded belly, some hard rush off the end of a sax or a bottle or a needle. *Boom*—I don't hear Ammons from anywhere outside, horn sounds off a stage or drifting from a window, but from inside, inside the tenor itself, a bright blind world of warm slicked brass and a rumbling, vibrating shaking. A twisting phrase. A touching. Man it hurts, it feels so good, rattling hide stops of the pads under invisible fingers and shadows telegraphing inside a hearted chamber where all I hear is you and me. A touching.

In the pressure of that sound's opening I hear the passional bottom ground of philosophy, *primum* of love and hate, the foreboding brooding of the Anaximander fragment—*things perish into those out of which they have their birth . . . for they give reparation to one another and pay the penalty of their injustice according to the disposition of time*—as the horn gruffly erupts upward and then sweetly swoops back down, within that interval the surge and the gravity and the exposure of a world's becoming. *Jug*—Ammons's best-known nickname, the fifth of Seagram's at his side during recording sessions, the word titling scores of compositions, those free-blowing or deep-down tunes where the promise is one of everything pouring out, Ammons offering again his all, yet at the same time a sense that the vessel he becomes still holds a reserve, the echoing and the booming, the debt and the payment and the love and the hate going around so there's never a final settling-up, there's always more to take and more to give. The Jug: inexhaustible.

The Boss is Back!—in the cover photo, Ammons is disembarking from a small airliner. He stands at the top of the stairs, a bulky figure wearing a tan overcoat, underneath it a plain black suit with a wide-collared gold shirt. He has his sunglasses on, and one hand is raised in greeting. It's a confusing gesture, that wave of the hand, sign of a new freedom, a happy sense of finally coming home, yet hinting as well at anger, at violence, the arm raised and the broad palm and fingers poised as if ready to slap something down or to shape into a pounding fist. By art or by accident, the photo's mise-en-scene underscores the duality. Dissolving into or looming up from the iron stairs, the lower half of Ammons's body is nearly invisible, like he's conjuring himself or perhaps struggling to escape from a dropping shaft of darkness. Above it, his upper body is framed by the plane's heavy-duty airlocks and latches, the free-waving hand seeming fettered, fixed to the door's white steel border. On the fuselage alongside, a fragment of the airline's logo appears: the letter *A*, almost perfectly sliced in half.

1970: "Laughter Echoed Softly"

1962, a Chicago street, Gene Ammons arrested, jailed—to tell the full story of the events that led up to 1969 and *The Boss is Back!*, to Ammons's second career or his resuming a career interrupted, one would track down the newspaper archives, work through the interviews and the comments from musicians and agents and friends and relatives, all the words spoken by those who knew Ammons and knew of him. My account will only be a partial one—the version of the story I heard and have remembered and imagined for many years, the story that called me to attempt to speak of another's life, the life of a man who was a stranger to me, a distant hero or celebrity but mostly a commanding, disturbing presence, a power in my world.

It's hardly a story, really, only what I heard from one person, who said he'd heard it from Ammons's wife when she was in his cab one night. It was around 1970 that Chuck Andrews told it to me. He was a friend, a man in his mid-thirties I'd met a year or so before when I discovered the secondhand bookstore he owned on the Northwest Side. The place was an overloaded small storefront, the books in chaos, Chuck hauling in stock from resale shops and estate sales, opening for business between his shifts driving a Checker taxi. Though I'd been haunting city bookstores for years, he was the only proprietor who'd ever bothered talking to me, a kid obviously without much money, not a real buyer or a serious collector. He asked me questions, spoke about everyday things, mentioned his old lady he was split from, smoked a lot of Viceroys with his feet crossed on the desk. Talking with Chuck I forgot the chronic feeling I had at the time of being younger and thus suspect, awkward, and uninformed, a confused hanger-on among the stacks of books thick with words and ideas. I wandered from shelf to shelf with only a vague sense of what I was after. I looked at his face—he had an uneven mustache stained with smoke and already turning gray, large eyes gazing directly at you but without any pressure, eyes that just lightly touched upon yours, a voice that said things in general like it was fine if you didn't have a reply—and I saw kindness.

Kindness may be the right word for what I felt there in the little bookstore. In the gentlest way, Chuck made me believe I was his friend but there wasn't any pretense of establishing a point of identity or resemblance between us—after all, he was twenty years older than I was and had lived through a world of things I knew nothing about. The sense was that it didn't matter: you were whoever you were. Nobody was going to cling to you, pull your sleeve, make you look at something he thought you should care about. That was how I came to the music, Ammons and the rest—it was just there, itself, lightly touching the air through the speakers buried among the piles of books under the desk. Chuck lived in that music, played it all the time he was in the store, varying it occasionally with Bartok or Debussy but soon going back again. It took a good while before I could hear or could attend to what I knew was called jazz—it seemed a strange word: so scrappy-small, so oddly unhooked—and today I can only imperfectly reconstruct when it happened, when what had sounded like a whirling piping, something fast and scratchy whispering mysteriously through the air, suddenly resolved itself into the nervy jump phrases of Charlie Parker's "Out of Nowhere," Chuck with a cigarette looking out the window and listening to the music in an ecstatic silence. He let the silence stay for a long time, long after the record had ended and the traffic sounds were drifting in from Cicero Avenue, my own breath audible along with his sounds—a slight shuffling of his feet, the record sliding into its sleeve, another crack of a wooden match. I understood I didn't have to say anything. What mattered, what didn't matter, was so light on the air that it scarcely existed. It was whatever happened to be there without my searching for a word or a theme; it was the stain on the cover of a book, the gray color of the afternoon on the store window, the indifferent murmur of the passing cars and buses on the street. It was Chuck and I looking at each other, the brightening stirring of the music shining for an instant across our eyes and our faces and already passing somewhere else, nothing you could claim or capture. The one word we could speak was the emptiest and the fullest—mere cliche, nonsense, dumb affirmation: *Yeah.*

Though he didn't know Ammons, Chuck had been around the Chicago scene in the 1950s. He was a young zoot-suiter, baggy slacks pegged down around the ankle, a slouching, tailored member of the original Harrison Gents, a West Side gang. He was close to Ira Sullivan and other bop musicians in the city. Like many of them, Chuck was using heroin, an addict for most of those years. It had damaged his heart: he struggled now going up stairs and got winded lifting the boxes of books. He told me once that he'd seen a man die, shooting up in a bathroom stall. It had been really good shit: too much, an overdose. The man's face had turned blue, he was cold as ice. But he wasn't cool, Chuck told me. He'd been too hungry, too greedy. Cool was another thing entirely. Cool was the whole idea of heroin that people didn't understand: you were in front of the stage hearing Bird blow at the Club De Lisa and you didn't move. You didn't interfere with the spirit in the air, get your hands on things, shouting and clapping like the drunks or snapping your fingers like the so-called beatniks. Cool so you might even look like you were asleep, and it wouldn't matter if you were because you felt the velvet hand of the music touching you everywhere; it turned you inside and out like you were its soft glove. Chuck wrote poems, words I never saw but there was one phrase of his I heard later, a favorite line of his wife's: "Laughter echoed softly / through hand-held gifts." I thought for a long time that the language was merely pretty and not true to the passion of the music it was describing. Now, though, I hear something else in those words—a sense of the music being a subtle kind of contact, a lightness as well as a weight, at its heart not just the love or anger I always thought was there but a passionate generosity, a laughter of giving everything away, a joy of powers spending themselves, hands offering all their gifts.

1962: Heroin Possession

The story: Ammons was in the car with somebody else; he wasn't even holding the drugs. The heroin was stashed under the seat, though, and he was the driver so that was all the cops needed. It might have been he was framed, set up. That was it: all Chuck told me.

1962, Chicago. It might have happened somewhere on the South Side, the Black Belt as they called it, maybe Thirty-fifth and Cottage Grove or Forty-seventh and State, one of the neighborhoods torn down by urban renewal by the time Chuck told me the story, a strip where fires raged and windows shattered in 1967 and 1968. What kind of car was Ammons driving that night—a Cadillac Fleetwood, red and heavy with chrome? Or a boxy black Buick Electra 225, a car like a big rolling coffin? Ammons was driving around casually, the Cadillac taking a ride over the dividing line at State or near the Ryan construction zone, the kind of car that almost goes by itself, you can forget you're driving the thing, things drifting before he knew it into the Back of the Yards or Canaryville or maybe Bridgeport, Mayor Daley's Irish neighborhood. He'd be seen right away by white people on the streets who were jealous of their territory, some of them resentful at what they saw as smart-assed coloreds coming over to show off what they had, a big fancy car. The telephone at the stationhouse might have started ringing right away after the Fleetwood was sighted, a middle-aged lady watching the street from her steps or a corner-grocery owner looking out the window and picturing black gangsters coming through his door with blue-steel pistols under their loose leather coats.

In Bridgeport, the police would respond fast. The mayor lived there, the house on Lowe Street, their neighborhood too and the power base of the Chicago Democratic machine. But the police wouldn't even need a call. Riding in one of the black Chevy sedans with red flashers and a swaying ten-foot antenna on the trunk, a pair of them could have spotted the car coming into the neighborhood or maybe not in the neighborhood at all but still over on the other side, the east end of the sector. The way Ammons was driving might have pissed them off, a big black man driving easy and fast, the Fleetwood boating around a corner off Southern Parkway, Ammons with a good high going that night and grooving on the deep power reserve of the 454 engine, on his home ground and feeling comfortable, his passenger lighting up a nice matchstick reefer out of the pack as casually as he would a Chesterfield, pure Panama Red. The police car would get right up on the tail of the Cadillac. They'd put a cramp in Ammons's styling. Show him who the hell was boss.

Ammons's passenger—his name was Pete or Ronnie, or a name like Moon or Fast Jack—started swearing, seeing the black cruiser, the white cops. He moved quickly, sliding the package of heroin under the seat. In his hurry he gave it such a push that it came out the other side in the back, riding over the transmission hump and landing right behind Ammons. The uniforms in the cruiser kept at the tail—Ammons tried to make a turn, get headed east again, the lines of lush trees along the street all pointing back toward the lake, all the neon signs seeming to read backwards, everything suddenly going in the wrong direction. In the mirror he could see the antenna on the cruiser, a thing quivering with signals, voices, plans for a roundup on the other side of the Belt Line tracks. The flashers weren't on yet, though, and he hoped it was a tease, a game like other times, at worst their ugly faces and words, a fifty-dollar bill handed over to them with the driver's license, after that a laughing cop whose voice would remind him of a clogged drain, something choking on itself.

And that might have been all. Harassed a while, worried a while, the money in hand to pay them off—that was what they always wanted, so give it to them. *Ammons, stop fucking around*, Ronnie said, *Stop this goddamn car right now*, but Ammons wasn't in the mood that night, he wanted to make them show their red, he gave them his own, touching the wide pedal on the power brakes and making the high fins glow and the Fleetwood rock, asshole Ronnie going out of his head already because he was afraid, so afraid. *Shine your light*, Ammons said to the mirror, *I'm looking to be harassed in a properly legal manner tonight*, and that was the bad magic, there it went, the Mars light flashing like a cold fire over the black hood in the mirror, cold devil faces behind it, and the more nervous Ronnie was getting the more Ammons was bulking his spirit, his body too feeling all its weight. *Could be I'll never stop this car*, he said, *just have to shoot me through the damn head*, and he felt the bullet already, saw his body on the street, the blood pouring out of the wound, and straight off from Ronnie the fear ran into him, and he took his foot off the accelerator and let the Fleetwood glide as though it was happening by itself, the car rolling over to a stop, the black doors slamming then and the cops getting out, the money sliding into position in his wallet, the sweat breaking out now across his face and his neck he thought he was saving.

In the instant when he turned over his wallet to the growling policeman, the second one's face hovering behind him with a close thin grin like he was sewing up Ammons's mouth, tasting all the words that couldn't be said, all the words that were expected—*Yes sir, No sir*, to a cop who wasn't good enough to shine his shoes, to lick the dust off his Cadillac—Ammons felt himself getting right. The cops felt it too, and saw it—the immovable way he sat in the driver's seat as though the car was his kingdom and he was suffering an insult, bearing it, his eyes staying with the cop as he fingered the money, checked the denomination, tucked the bill away like it had never existed. *Eugene Ammons? Yes that's right.* They never heard of that name, spoke it like it was nothing, a joke, schoolboy in glasses, *Hey you, Gene, Eugene*, and *Ammons*, what was that, I thought you boys were all named after the presidents, the people who got the money, hey hey.

Hey hey—Get the hell back into the car, boy, but Ammons was out the door, standing on his feet. What was Ronnie doing now? Making sure the package of heroin was as far away as he could get it, Ammons out of the car and the cops distracted so he slid it up under the driver's side? Or is Ronnie just now getting the package out of his pocket, doing what he had agreed to after his last bust, delivering over a high-profile case the DA imagined would teach certain people in Chicago a lesson: famous Negro jazz musician arrested for heroin on South Side, Gene Ammons in jail and facing ten years in prison, smug stories in the *Tribune* and regretful ones in the *Daily Defender*, where Ammons was a hero?

It was going bad—was it the cop or Ammons telling himself to keep his arms where they were?—his hands wanting to jump, it would be a heavy blow he'd land on the cop's face and then another come raining down, let it fall. *You're under arrest*: the words seemed to lose their meaning or they meant too much, everything, now there was a crazy pissy welling like tears, Ammons raining inside, and he couldn't move, it might be his own body that would fall. Up the street, he could see the railroad viaduct, the incline of the pavement going down into it. A train was passing above, even here he felt the vibration rumbling under his feet. Inside the viaduct, traffic shadows jumped across the whitewashed walls, on the vertical supports painted names blossomed with loops and flourishes and snaked themselves into secret languages. On the black-striped center pier a caution light flashed yellow. Walking through, a kid could beat as hard as he wanted to on the iron rails that leaned over the street, shout as loud as he wanted to inside the noise of the traffic. He could write his name up there under the road of the train. Listen to the booming echo of his voice. Small turned big.

Ammons smelled the fear coming off the cops, himself, and Ronnie suddenly still and collected as though the plan all along had been to drop off Ammons here and take over the wheel. *Get back into your seat.* The partner's gun was already drawn, dog-head clawed out his own and pushed it at the air like a prod or a stick, but still Ammons didn't move until the thing touched him, clumsily bumped his face and slid dumb and cold against his left ear. That touch enraged him—better to shoot him up front than to molest his face. And his ear—he had beautiful ears as his mother always said, women loved their small delicate shape, nibbling and biting and making up stories about what they could tell. Ear that could catch anything, Captain Dyett had said: key from the first bar of a song, melody off a passing fragment. Perfect pitch. Like a hunter's ear, too, tuned to the vast sounding world, hearing the littlest things down inside the house, rustlings and creaks of ghosted frames, hearing along the wind the heavy life of the leaning trees in the park, hearing the light life of human voices inside rooms and doors and windows, hearing the floating life of music rising from the body and making a system in the air, fragile bridges stretching out and elevating their spans and at their edges asking to be crossed and recrossed, spun and pulled and tensed.

With his face set hard, Ammons suffered the touch of the gun. He was waiting for it to happen, the thing to go off before he did. But he was listening so intently for the stir, the scrape, the click that would be impossible to hear because he would be dead before he could hear it, thirty-six years old and a corpse with his brains blown out from behind his temple, that he scarcely noticed the drop of the first cuff on his wrist, his other arm being pulled around behind him for the second.

All right, all right, he said then, *but keep my friend out of it*, nodding at Ronnie who didn't care and didn't need any help, maybe thinking Ammons was a joke, his ass down the river; or maybe he was saving Ronnie, whose life would be a waste from that moment on anyway, everybody accusing him of selling out Ammons when he didn't. But why did they let him off? Ronnie could never explain to them that for one minute the cops had been afraid of Ammons and so they obliged him and let Ronnie take off down the street with whatever he had or hadn't been holding. He wasn't the one they wanted anyway.

After that, the world changed the way it sounded. Ammons wasn't listening to its motions and shifts and voices but instead to an inside of things, nearly imperceptible whirling or subtly grinding sounds that accompanied a falling, a spinning, a being jerked into place like starting hard and panicky from a quiet drifting into sleep. There was nothing but air around him—the same air he had lived by, the stack of wind, the column and the pipe, buzzing breathing staff of all his powers—but it was impossible for him to touch anything, for anything to touch him. Somebody else was writing his name, writing his life, and he hung inside an icy void like one of Dante's condemned, all the reaching hands and dear faces and unbelievable walls around him draining off into some devising of a type or exemplum, the law freezing him inside his skin.

Stateville: those first days, that week, that month, he dreamed out his hunger for the syringe, the pricking needle—the bars of the cell, the perforations in the metal bed, the chug of the stinking commode and the hot voices calling *Jug, Jug, you with us too, brother*, all that cold hell pumped out like water, not a particle reaching him. Ammons sat there hard and impervious as a rock, but a thing like a hand coiled inside him, felt on its pulse a dipping plunge of his blood that made him so weak and so limp a baby could have slapped him aside. Nothing but air: November winds blowing hard across the flat Illinois cornfields outside the walls, the winded heave of his chest he sometimes caught himself waiting for or found himself trying to catch up with, the bodiless suctioning blank where the clang of the steel doors died out after a minute, an hour, seven years.

In that stilled cloud he imagined the touch of the junk, his heartbeat becoming a far-off thunder, his fingers gloved again in warm velvet, the touch like a prickling bud on the skin of the world, a slow oil distilling down into a swelling, a throaty voice. Touch that made the Boss boss, let the Jug fill itself and pour itself out.

Levered boom of the doors, uneasy fall of the dark, a murmuring then of love and hate, everything owed from the day that would get paid off in the night.

Ammons sat there untouched. Listening to the echo of an echo.

1975: Jug Eyes

A night at the Jazz Showcase on Rush Street, a bill with Frank Foster, Jodie Christian, Rufus Reid, and Wilbur Campbell. Foster was the second tenor, about the same age as Ammons but seeming so much stronger and younger, though not making a point of it. I sat there drinking my Beck's and like thousands of others in clubs and concerts over the years, watched at my leisure Ammons's every move—the poise of his fingers, the cut of his grizzled chin as he again took the reed into his mouth, the way he signaled to Christian as he approached the microphone for the solo. Even as he started, his tired face was showing the labor of it, his dark-ringed eyes hopefully going wide and then gradually closing themselves down, Foster's solo hanging still in the air over him, his own maybe an impossible thing he had to do anyway, all the room waiting on him to deliver the goods.

Working through the standard phrases, the signature lines, the hollowed booming echoing of his sound, slash of his own mark on the air, he made it happen again—it shined enough, it caught some fire, faltering only here and there, the hard applause afterward recognizing that if Foster hadn't been on the stage it would have sounded better. In the middle of it all, though, there was a small floating terror, watching the heave of his shoulders and the push of his chest, the terror that this next minute, this next phrase, this next note, we might see Ammons fail for good, we would lose him.

I had watched him avidly for years, though my own eyes closed sometimes in the wash of his power, the music's demand calling out an answering labor in the heart, the soul, the hard rollicking edge of it finally driving the feelings into something as sober as a prayer. I could watch him at my ease because he had nothing to do with me, he operated in the near yet ideal world of the music, the instrument, the intimidating superiority of his name and his art. That night, however, I felt myself drawing uncomfortably close, his gaze catching now and then on mine as though he felt its pressure, maybe resented the way I was sitting there gobbling him up, unseemly in the controlled swoon of a cognoscenti's delight. As he broke off into another solo, I felt the way I hovered, my mouth, my breath, my body leaning slightly forward in the chair, strangely blended with or strangely parasitic upon his, an unconscious sympathy or identification suddenly brought to awareness by the answering look he'd directed at me. The sensation was disturbing, a sort of vertigo in it that was like an approach of death, mine or his, I couldn't tell which as I followed the strain of his work, his labor, all that Ammons was again giving, delivering, pouring out. Perhaps it was no more than a touching between us that was made by the hours and years of my watching and listening, unmade too by that swift moment when his gaze returned mine, an intermittent and uncertain link that was of no more substance or consequence than a drifting curl of smoke across the stage lights or the rattling of ice in someone's drink at the table beside me.

For the rest of the night I found it impossible to look again, to countenance the returning gaze of Ammons's charged, tired face. I was caught out, abashed, mortified. I had been making him into my theme, my thing. Listening to the music I only stared down at my hands or closed my eyes, his face appearing anyway before me as though I were awakening from a dream. The image was at times wavering and distorted, at others suddenly as clear as a photograph. A face possessed of a rocklike solidity, a gravity of power in it like a spirit mask, eyes in their deep sockets vaulting an unrecoverable mystery. A face I saw in painful, near-hallucinatory detail, every minute line and incision and pocking of the skin, each singular marking on it of a time, a world, a life, and a death. His eyes—they were brown, dark dark brown—appeared immensely fragile, immensely strong; they lidded over, they closed in some ecstasy of making a line, a sound; they opened again in the middle of what was being offered, what was already moving off and away, time-tunnel of that great stalking booming, that delicate running echoing.

1999: Echoes

Echoes, echoes of echoes—why do I return to this almost meaningless phrase, perhaps too vacuous and too trite to say anything true? It's just the emptiness and lightness that I like, its sense of a touching that doesn't linger, that reverberates indefinitely. Each thing pays the penalty of its injustice according to the disposition of time—the echo of an echo forgets any origin or source, can't claim any patrimony or descent; there's a motion, a rhythm, a syncopation in between that only offers itself there, that doesn't settle down into being but exposes a becoming, again, again.

"Jug jug"—in Coleridge's poem, it's what the nightingales sing, alone in the wood in the dark, echoing one another's calls, somebody nearby leaning to hear. Jug, jug: sound of a joy attended by the ear, a whorled opening to the world, I with my eyes closing in the listening, Ammons stomping off like some thundering cloud, Ammons fluttering off like some stirring of evening birds, taking it all away, giving it all back once more.

Sonny Stitt   *Photo by Michael Wilderman*

stitt's time

1981: Stitt Dream

October: as if from far away, suddenly hearing you. I'd been preoccupied, distracted by my last-minute date, Beck's and Camel Filters, the little black enamel table with the ivory linen and the ballroom view on Grant Park. She wore taffeta, shiny stockings, mystery skin. (Later we went to her apartment, the baby was sleeping peacefully, the lamp on all night.) Suddenly hearing you—not with eyes closed studying whether Sonny was as great this time, measuring the speed and precision of a phrase that was pounced on and then whipped back, spooled through once more and punched up somewhere else I'd never quite be able to predict; suddenly hearing you—naked surprise of it, the music dancing off from us, breaking away, the old Blackstone Hotel with elegant blue drapes and the master in the house with his Chicago quartet, bass, drums, piano, pure blowing, the instruments polished, the music glossy, shining, nothing ragged, all smooth, oiled, shaped, passion leashed with super control. You switched halfway through from tenor to alto, brass rocket all systems go, afterburning out of the dark, fire of stars in my head and my hand on the woman and hers touching back—she'd never heard of you but was anyway moved, smiling too, taking that blast of grace . . .

On stage between songs you sipped a dark-gold brandy, Napoleon or Hennessy; sometimes after the solo you had a smoke while you stood and listened to Barry Harris or Wilbur Campbell as though considering the state of the equipment, how the machinery was running. The cigarette hanging for a minute from your mouth as you swung out your arm and snapped your fingers just once, called out something that could have been encouraging or could have been mocking, that sounded like directions, orders. *Play like Bud Powell, man . . . All right: you fucked up again . . . Do that one more time. . . .* At the same time looking into the eyes of people in the audience who might share the joke, the work, if they could hear it, another drag off the cigarette up from your long fingers resting on the keys, the thing would stay there burning as you came back riding down hard on the song's finish as if the horn was cutting through so much smoke.

Stitt: an art of the whip, the barb, the stinger, fast and easy and sharp-darted by virtue of an exacting calculation of interval, punctuation—extra pull you took on the brandy standing away from the piano laughing, extra leap across the octave into a last arpeggio pressured out like a fisting of rain. Every motion apportioned its time, its share, its cut and no more, and then the period: your stone face, your high Einstein forehead, your eyes opening wider and almost closing again as the phrase shivered itself out. Diced into bits. Scattered to the winds. The amused spectator or the wise aficionado could savor the moment passing yet feel the swift kiss of death. There was no holding it. Now was the time, but the now was always just behind or ahead, approaching or moving off, the escape-velocity of Stitt's flight precisely in the sliding and breaking apart, the instant spidering away from itself in the same work that was assembling it with such infinite care—and what came trembling before and after, time when soul would be buried in flesh or flesh in soul, blink of an eye or wavering of what the ear would hear. Everything in readiness, the crowd waiting, the band turning over, gold of the alto and the tenor harped on their stands, and suddenly you're nowhere to be found, Joe Segal nervously rounding the stage looking for you . . .

"Now's the Time"—Charlie Parker song, beat mantra, Kerouac and Cassady chasing or being chased by its paradox, the Now always dividing with every attempt to know or fix it, mortal flower blossoming forever before or after the fact, lives and motions and words going in circles or exorbitantly jumping off. Now's the time, but it's late, late, there's no catching up, the ecstatic baroque fling of Stitt's solo is already ending, it's burning up even as we're flying with it, riding on it, delectating the invisible machinery that opens like a watery hole or a winding tunnel somewhere inside or outside our bodies. Bare place of the soul. The thing that must flee and that performs so many motions in order to do so: how can it be held?

Fifty-seven years old and you were strong, but not a year later you would be gone, cancer of the throat. You were touring Japan and suddenly in two weeks it was over. I feel the fever touch of her hand, and I promise I won't forget, I won't, that night you plowed the air with shoulders high, your chest wide though you were slender, String one of your names.

The saxophone's mouthpiece levering wind, outside the trees blew, the park fountains brimmed, and in that night you gathered flesh from the dark ground and in that body you swerved around tall corners, slammed through doors where breezeway children banged and hollered, loomed down cold stairwells and in windows rattled up shadow hawk. Soul flight: crashing out ceilings in bursts and tangles, hard knots and rope ladders standing like snakes, and on the Blackstone stage you carved the moment folded in the lights, across the applause the last phrases looping and tightening a wavy shimmering net over rumbling drums and then lofting off once more, a restless sweeping wheeling through some accelerating shifting rotary that at the same time geared irresistibly down into the finish, the point where we felt it had to stop though we felt it would never stop.

You lit a smoke. You bowed your head, let the empty horn swing down. Baffling thing, still somehow alive for us—its gold shell, the cunning of keys, your long fingers releasing it.

1972: Use Me Up

Chicago, November: North Avenue and Dayton Street, just off Halsted— the Black Angus, the Clybourn subway stop, Sam's Liquors, the Ravenswood El running shadows over the red brick apartment buildings along the tracks. The Seeburg Corporation, inside a huge gray box extending the length of the block, a grimy employees' entrance and a single vertical of windows letting daylight into a broad stairwell that climbed to the third floor. I'd taken an assembly line job there making jukeboxes—a new model that year with a curving streamlined cabinet, hard black plastic hugging two extra speakers and no longer the rows of mechanical push-buttons but a small keyboard with soft-padded numbers offering all the combinations. It would be the disco machine, bassing and falsettoing in taverns and restaurants through the next several years, Donna Summer and K.C. and Bee Gees, the model with a built-in price increase from three plays for a quarter to one for a quarter and three for fifty cents.

The work paid well and wasn't very difficult because each task was so small, production broken down into what must have been hundreds of different steps. The partially assembled jukebox I was looking at, sent down to me on a long metal track, had rolled already along a series of such tracks, starting out at a distant point among fellow employees I'd scarcely ever seen. Far off on the other side of the factory, they were like people in another neighborhood. You thought about talking to one of the women there, someone you saw on break, but ultimately decided against it, uneasy about venturing into unfamiliar territory.

Yet there was an underground solidarity among us all. Simple as the work was—probably for that very reason—the atmosphere under the hangarlike ceilings often thickened with a common boredom, disgust, and at times rage. The job demanded only two things: a consistent eye and a steady arm. I had to accurately position a small metal plate on the chassis of the jukebox and then fasten it securely with three self-setting sheet-metal screws driven in full force by means of an air-compression drill. The drill was branded with its maker's name, Milwaukee, and with each screw it rattled and screeched like something from a nightmare dentist's chair. The task occupied about three minutes, after which I'd send the machine over to the next in line, Jorge. He swiftly manipulated a tangle of wires behind the keyboard and shoved off the jukebox to Sammy, who in turn attached a type of solenoid to it. In between, Jorge and I smoked cigarettes, ruthlessly gunned each other with our drills, and attempted increasingly elaborate curses in Spanish and English. We swept the area now and then, or pondered the women working at the high tables behind us, or idly whistled or sang, since it was forbidden to ever sit down on the job. We had to be ready for the next unit on the line, whether it was coming or not.

And often it wasn't, since most mornings the word went around: *To hell with them. We're slowing it down. They're not getting their hundred.* We hardly saw one another, we had staggered breaks and lunch periods to manage the large number of workers, but all of us shared the same feeling when it was a question of the bosses—the foreman suddenly behind you out of nowhere telling you to move faster or to pick up a broom, you weren't getting paid for standing around doing nothing; the shiny-suited men, the syndicate, as they were called, up above in a windowed office where they monitored the progress along each assembly line, so that any minute you might be singled out and immediately there would be John the foreman again, gray hair mussed along his brow, perspiring and red-faced as if it was he who carried the burden of all the work, swearing that you had only one more chance before you were back on the street. But if each of us slacked off a little bit—a slight languor in the arm, a screw dropping to the floor instead of being driven home, maybe trouble with the drill again, who could tell—it wasn't easy for them to identify a point of resistance, and if they did it wouldn't matter, because the point was moving, at the same time everywhere and nowhere. Sometimes the slow-down wasn't even noticed until far into the day, as if the bosses too were infected by the general spirit. For hours the suit syndicate would confer in the office, looking complacently over the plant. John would go for a coffee and finish his paperwork. Of course there was agitation upstairs and down, hell to pay, when the day's unit count was checked. But often it was too late: it would be impossible to make up the lost production without going into overtime. We'd won.

On other occasions the slowdowns were unintentional—or perhaps in the course of the day intentions became confused because slowing down was more difficult and took more thought than working normally. The word would go out but it was questionable, smelling of rumor or subterfuge. The spirit of resistance could itself be ambivalent, the sense of slower and faster a relative matter, hard to measure. A punch-drunk weariness sometimes took hold, your limbs feeling like useless things even as they were being used, and in the dragging interval from one machine to the next, from one minute to the next, there was a sense that it would be better if things moved faster and there was no time at all between jukeboxes, all of it a dizzied blur of screwing and drilling and wiring, no chance then to think. Seeming infinitely divisible, time became such a burden that even though it was self-defeating—after all, you wanted time to pass, the day to end so you'd be out of there—you wanted to slow down time too, muck up its clinging perpetual machinery. Half-pints and reefers made the rounds in the bathrooms; the bar across the street was packed during lunch. Couples wandered off to find privacy along the dark stairway that went to the factory roof, later sealed off after a fight up there. Every once in a while Sammy, who never said a word to Jorge or me, disappeared for the afternoon, nodding off in a cardboard box hidden out of the way. We didn't joke about it with him. Like a fair number of Seeburg employees, he was recently out of prison, released through a program the company operated with the state. He knew how to do time.

The spirit moved differently, however, on Friday. Payday. A few of the Latino men were already dressed to go out after work, wide-necked shirts in bright colors, cowboy boots buffed to a pointy gloss. Some of the women showed off their new hairstyles, streaked Afros or curly perms, and came laughing and dance-stepping down the lines on their way to break as though to get us in the mood. Even John the foreman had a fresh necktie and a less harried expression than usual, as if relieved the week was ending. Today we'd knock off a hundred boxes easily—hell, we could do two hundred if we felt like it. The latest Seeburgs got bumped and jolted down the line like old friends, the screws and wires plugging in effortlessly. At such times, we understood that we were all whores, the foreman pimping us to the suit syndicate, the suit syndicate pimping the jukeboxes to the world (the keyboards came in several languages, including Japanese), but it was all right. We were difficult whores. If time was money we at least had the satisfaction of being able to play with it, hold it back, give it up only after a struggle.

On certain Fridays the Seeburg factory attained a state close to the dream of bosses and corporations: a moving singing humming of people and tools and machines drawing into well-oiled unison, a contagious energy coming off all the bodies heating up with the hours. It didn't come easy, however. The morning would feel endless until the first break, then run fast all of a sudden up to lunch. A slow drag in the early afternoon, at one o'clock maybe sixty machines and the growing feeling that it was enough, they'd had their pound of flesh, a few guys down the line were suddenly sitting down, and John could go screw himself. A technician was testing speakers at full volume with the Bill Withers hit that seemed to be playing all the time somewhere in the factory:

You keep on using me

—expectant pause, bass line dropping—

'til you use me up.

There was a pleasure in the heated shout of Withers's voice, and in the tables being turned at the end of the song when the loser being walked on comes up as the winner, the servant as the master. Listening to the sardonic keyboard riff and tapping drumbeat I thought that as simple as it was—exactly the kind of thing that would be punched up a million times on the jukeboxes we were making—the song had its truth, on the smooth-rough edge of Withers's voice a taste of the elusive slippery thing called *soul*.

Soul— the company was using us. We were human tools, nonunion laborers being paid well so there would be no problems with work rules or sick leaves. Seeburg Corporation (Delaware) was consuming our souls, our hours offered up to the jukeboxes that after a while appeared as wicked plastic shrines prostituting music to mass production and mass taste, their purpose not the pleasure of sounds but the tinny clatter of coins being swallowed down a galvanized gorge, hoarded up in a stainless steel belly. But it was impossible to own the soul, soul itself an impossible thing. Soul wasn't a substance or energy residing in you that could be husbanded or extracted; soul floated outside, away, apart. It got used, but using didn't mean it was consumed, finished; it got used up, up; it went up, over the top—roles could be reversed, the tide turned, and under the weight of everything you had to deal with would come an unaccountable breeze lifting like a fresh wind that out of nowhere came blowing up a hot littered street, setting the leaves moving in the trees and sweeping the papers off the sidewalk, sending them driving and leaping along the curb. *Soul*: like time breathing the world. Coming always from somewhere else, going always toward somewhere else.

Two o'clock on Friday and John angry, expecting a lower count than usual, the suit syndicate studying the floor as if considering firing the whole factory. The last hour of a day that had started at seven, our checks handed out after lunch so we had nothing to lose if we started slacking off, but then it came, the second wind—*sure am using you, for the things you do*—as if everybody was thinking about the same thing: ecstasy in one form or another, how high you'd soon be getting, and always sex, sex, the place burning with it now, random singing and Spanish shouts, screws banging in, wires devilishly fingered, Jorge cupping the double speakers on number sixty-seven, Sammy bleakly smiling, buzzing his drill down from his crotch. In the inspectors' section below our line we could see the bank of finished jukeboxes stacking up, the machines glowing bright and seductive, vaguely tropical pinks stenciled on the smoky glass and the broad fronts edged with sly chrome smiles. Foxy ladies, ready for the night.

The twangy keyboard on the Withers song kept stringing along, the drumbeat tapping out. Precipitated from our hundreds of different ways of dancing in time, through time, out of time, under the ceiling there gathered a slow fogging together of powers, a fragile vented clouding made of sounds and smoke and the exhalations of our body heat. Soul-haze. Production was a fucking joke. A wild jumping infiltrated the motions, punctuations in time, phrasings of the hand, the arm, the leaning sweating brow and the cagey wandering eyes, the feet that wanted to lift and kick and run. We were pleasuring our own homemade machine, half the factory high already and the others taking it by contact, *sure am using you*, and William Blake in my mind singing along with Withers: *The soul of sweet delight can never be defil'd.*

Three o'clock and the usual time for us to close down, thirty minutes always killed off with brooms and smokes before quitting—but the eagle flies, the soul forgets where it came from, we slammed on until 3:25 and they had it from us, their hundred, their C, with ten or more extra, John pleased and trying not to show it, the factory then in a five-minute madness of clearing out and all of us holding our timecards on the way to the clock like tickets to heaven that would land us somewhere back in the world.

1970: Soul People

Soul. Breathing, breathless. Instant of wings before their rise. Awkward exposure, fleeting weakness, coursing pulling power and swift scissoring . . .

Float. Flight. Not inside—or letting inside outside, letting outside in. Hovering between. Shadow, mirror, name—everything that belongs to you, but by the same token is vulnerable, can be captured or used, seduced or captivated, infected or imitated or falsified.

June: Grant Park, the Cannonball Adderley show at the Bandshell, Ninth and Michigan among the elms, the brick castle of the old Illinois Central station down past the bridge and darkness along the paths, leafy places to drink a secret bottle. At the south end of the park the concert with a mostly black crowd, Chicago still feeling the heat of '68 and '69, the audience in the heat of a summer night and the Adderley brothers soul-exploding, breaking out and away, alto from trumpet, trumpet from alto, brotherly love, brothers having a tussle. In a highlight, Joe Zawinul from Czechoslovakia, the white man with soul, extending the piano solo on "Mercy, Mercy, Mercy" until people were loose and singing and shouting back to the music, swaying in long roping lines dancing across the grass.

After the concert, though the park was officially closed, my friend and I walked along a path circling a fountain that was still brimming water. The night air was heavy, fragrant, lush with the smell of trees. We talked to a middle-aged man who'd seen Adderley too, accepted the bottle he offered. No, he said, Cannonball was good but Stitt, Stitt—the way he said it, the word sounded strange and angry, outrushed air making it like *sticks* or *Styx*—he'd blow Cannonball away if the two of them were together on stage. All that soul talk, people didn't know what in the hell they were saying, Cannonball was good but he played like he was in a Sunday church, fluttering up with the angels . . .

Seventeen years old, and we were a little nervous in the dark, but I said words about Charlie Parker, Bird. *Bird*—the sound felt awkward out of my mouth, like a thing was hovering there, soul touch, because I'd presumed to speak.

"Bird," he said: "Shit, that just Sonny Stitt. Son of Bird. Bird Junior. Soul went right into him. Cannonball, he in a hurry, eat it all up. Stitt, he takes his time. It's like sex," he said, and laughed and took a swig, gave us a lowering stare, a growl maybe for the hell of it. "Or the devil."

We were susceptible enough to believe the man was something like the devil himself, and after a while we thanked him for the drink and walked out of the park toward the Harrison subway station. Traveling home that night was the first time I'd ever thought about the fact that the subway was truly underground, burrowing below tons of dirt and pavement and buildings. For years I'd been looking at the streaking walls outside the window, the abrupt green-lamped openings into the dark, the sparks stuttering up now and then under the wheels with a fitful bluish light. I didn't see any of it as significant; I enjoyed the carnival-ride feeling, terror train or ghost railroad, and made a point of riding in the first car where I could gaze into the tunnel and watch the stops coming up. Now I was suddenly aware of how I was *inside*, not looking out but instead prone to being observed, something up ahead waiting or something behind following me. I was inside a body—inside the tunnel of brick and stone I was inside another tunnel made of flesh and skin, and what I called my soul was yet another tunneling-through, like the train humming and clattering from station to station, iron wheels screeching around the long curve from Division to Clybourn. In a chaos of echoes, dank smell of the air, reflections flashing and dragging over the window glass, I for an instant lost hold of where I was going, had no idea where I was. There was a shadow-thing made of sound and light and color hanging there in the window, a ghost image of myself in the seat flickering across the glass scarcely recognizable, a lone soul clinging to its brief life like one of Pound's petals on a wet black bough.

When I was eight or nine years old, I had a fervent image of a white, glowing entity, wonderfully fragile and pure. In its delicacy it was easily soiled, tainted by the smallest of sins and sadly injured, even though I could still ask for forgiveness, do penance. I saw it as a webby gauzy creature inhabiting my chest and stomach, a dear creature of my own that I had to protect from harm. It was me and it wasn't me—*my soul*—a finer thing, brighter thing, a thing that floated and sang among the intoning of Latin during Mass, a thing I invoked by following the missal instructions: *Strike your breast, thrice* . . . As though that soul needed blood, like the shades of the underworld, as though there had to be a wounding, an opening, a way for it to get inside or to get outside—which of the two was never certain. The soul was a portable thing, would divorce itself from your body someday yet still be you.

I closed my eyes in my bed, struck thrice, and felt it growing in me like a black flood, a swelling wafer of light. In a childish version of *kundalini* belief I attempted to draw it up into my head. I would feel a kind of vibrating singing, a darkness whirling down a tunnel, my pulse murmuring a distant music, a passing then almost instantly into sleep. *I pray the Lord my soul to keep*—the soul traveled in an unknown only a god could see.

It was possible though to use the soul, to sell it for power and pleasure, which might seem a good bargain, because what was the soul after all? An insubstantial thing, maybe not even real, and besides, the payment didn't come due until the end. A popularization of Faust, a forgotten episode of *The Twilight Zone* or a Marvel comic book: after the pact was sealed in blood, the signature on the contract betraying just how empty a thing your soul really was and just how much your soul did indeed belong only to you, the story was animated by a dizzying tension. Time, which before had seemed a common and expendable commodity, now became infinitely valuable. By the same token, however, it was too late for time—what gnawed and troubled and made you dizzy was the realization that giving over your soul meant all your time was already gone and you could never recover it. You were forever the master and forever the abject slave of your fate. You'd been delivered over.

Under his own name, Sonny Stitt made close to one hundred albums from the 1950s through the 1980s. Almost seventy hours of music on record, much more if you include his dates as a sideman and the sessions with

Gene Ammons. Sonny wasn't his given name; he was Edward Stitt, born 2 February 1924 in Boston and raised in Saginaw, Michigan, his father a music professor, his mother a teacher. He began playing professionally when he was fifteen years old and was pretty much constantly traveling the United States, Europe, and other parts of the world for over forty years.

Sonny—a way of marking the son, the junior, the heir. And Sonny— wasn't he not only his father's heir but also, as many in the music world said, the heir apparent to Charlie Parker? When he met Bird in 1949, the story goes, Parker told Sonny, four years younger: *You sound like me.* In the late 1940s and early 1950s, Stitt played and recorded with Bud Powell, Dizzy Gillespie, and the other bebop masters. Yet in the Miles Davis bands of the 1950s, or in Monk's classic recordings with Sonny Rollins and Johnny Griffin and Coltrane, where was Stitt, maybe not as great as Bird but at least very close?

You sound like me—the ultimate praise coming from Parker the genius, the fiery self-consuming sun of the bebop revolution. Stitt had Bird's blessing, and when Parker passed, it might have been the road was clear: Stitt was the heir to the throne, held the keys to the kingdom, was the main man. So he went on his own, which made sense professionally and financially—why work under Miles or mess with Monk? Until 1952, Stitt had a group with Gene Ammons, then was a solo act picking up bands in whatever city; nearly his whole career carried on that way. But there was the other side: people branding Stitt a Parker imitator: *he sounds like a copy of Bird, he's not his own man. . . .* It was said he played mostly tenor in the 1950s to avoid comparisons to altoist Parker, Sonny living on under the shadow of Bird until in the early 1960s he made the classic album for Atlantic, *Stitt Plays Bird*, perhaps enough time having passed.

Sounds like. But so many sounded like Parker. Bird was the inspiration, the demanding standard—Jackie McLean and Cannonball and Phil Woods and Ernie Henry, Rollins and Griffin and Coltrane. Was it that Stitt was too early, too close to Parker? Being the heir was his glory, but it cast a heavy shadow, offered a distorting mirror. It may have been that Stitt understood Bird so well, too well, because he didn't come to Parker's innovations as the latest thing to learn so much as he developed musically at the same time, not descending from Bird but next to him, parallel. And what did Stitt do with it? He worked. That was all he did, forty years on the road, night after night—Parker compositions, the standards, his own works, a playbook with hundreds of songs. If he sounded like Bird, what was the problem with that—wasn't that what everyone wanted, what people paid to hear, what a whole generation of musicians was trying to achieve?

And did he really after all sound like Parker? Try listening sometime to Parker's original and then Stitt's "Cool Blues" solo on *Burnin'* for comparison. Bird kind of stutters, a fluid watery character to his playing along with its intense blues-fire, a sound from the alto like the phrases are getting pressured out right under the pads, spilling over, the horn and the ambient air wet, supersaturated, on the delirious edge of losing it, Bird-soul pushing and thrusting out its song. Stitt's musical idiom is very close to Parker's but there's an unmistakable difference—a tempering, a smoothing, those same impassioned stutterings distributed and managed with exacting care. What leaps and erupts and spills is measured out, under control, not the sound pressing the horn but throating further down inside, bored and barreled and tunneling, a sort of precision machining with a sustained attention to the fall and sway of the phrasings, clocking the points where they run up time, double and triple; clocking the points where they smear it across, burn time down.

Sounds like, but doesn't quite sound like—Stitt might be too perfect, too controlled. Mechanical, designed, lacking the creative imperfection of a Monk or a Miles, lacking the productive distance from Bird that powers McLean and Cannonball, Rollins and Coltrane. The machine runs effortlessly, music throating out of it so fast you often have to listen close to hear all the things that have been worked and finished in the span of ten, twenty, thirty seconds. Stitt said that playing the horn the fingers had to be like little hammers—the human hand was itself a part of the saxophone machine rather than the hand using the sax, a mechanism punching out hard eighths and sixteenths in triplet runs, a device of endless generation, creation, the instantaneous imprinting of a time and a space, a space and a time, Stitt's music a system of hydraulics, pistons in heavyweight oil, cooled tooling, a masterful administration of wind. Bird might be buried in there, a muffled grave, his sharp cry drowned in a lubricant of tears or sweat, mourning or triumph.

Sonny shadowed with a name, Sonny himself shadowing Bird as much as he was shadowed by him, shadows confused like a flocking of pigeon wings over a statue in the park, or like phantoms of lovers sliding over walls in a candlelit room while the phonograph winds through the last song on the side, "Now's the Time" and then near silence, the needle riding over the black-mirroring vinyl of the record spinning forgotten. The lovers who say exactly what they want, how they want it, just there—no, not like that, exactly right *there*, and then *there, now* . . . an infinite lubricity. Soul.

Sonny Stitt: he always swings, always has soul—the commentary on the liner notes and in the reviews, through the years of West Coast cool and the gospel-soul style, Coltrane and the New Thing, the same words. But other words, too: Stitt makes too many records, Sonny's out for the dollar, going commercial, oil on the palm, soul gone to whore. The album cover images from Roost, Prestige, and Chess might mark a decline: from Sonny the young black virtuoso with head rearing high to Sonny the bad motherfucker with sardonic gaze, and always the cigarette somewhere, smoke floating like strands of soul plasm. A low point might be the 1974 album *Satan*, on the cover a fifty-year-old Stitt wearing a turtleneck, a leather vest, and a giant scarab ring (his hand appears oversized, too, the fingers long and thick, bending with the cigarette in ambiguous code: *Come hither* or *Don't fuck with me*), the smoke lifting away from his brow like wispy horns or hovering there like an infiltrating ghost. His gray Afro like frozen smoke, under a heavy mustache his lower lip preparing a sneer or a challenge, in all the concentration of his face—being bad, being the devil for this photo, for this new album (it will be one of his better sellers)—a subtle look also of loss, of puzzlement, of *What am I doing here?* In the gesture of his other arm, the one nested near his shoulder and keeping the cigarette hand up in a vague hex sign, you catch at the same time a smoky flickering: *What am I doing here—I know damn well what I'm doing here* . . .

Show business. The image. Through it all *Stitt*—name like a pair of scissors, a blade, a knife. Stitt *cuts*. Cutting sessions in the groups with Ammons, phrase building on phrase, topping it off, one-up. Over the years hundreds of pretenders—local stars, the up-and-coming, best students—getting cut. Carving the time way ahead, coming from behind, speed, control, gears and machinery, rhythm section working like mad to keep up, Jaguar XKE in a race with a Schwinn bicycle. Ammons was the best foil because it was Bird versus Lester and both of them copping from each other, Stitt riding up and Ammons swerving off, they never got in each other's way, though you could hear sometimes where they touched, one inflecting the other: my buddy, my buddy.

Stitt—writing his signature in the air, *Stitt, Stitt,* who else could roar up out of time like that, who else could hold back so long and then let rip so you didn't know for a second what happened, surgical incision, in the middle of it all you forget and there's soul-traveling, the room lifting up and the women pressing toward the stage and the men raising their glasses and the bar mobbed with money passing everywhere, in five minutes make them five hundred dollars, in five minutes lose them five hundred dollars, make them a thousand if you're in the mood for telling a story . . . Soul people: living for once, one night, inside their clothes and their smoke, no secret about what they are—bodies: cocks and pussies pulsing like souls under their veils and vestures, their own show business for one another and for Stitt, too, the local undertaker or the politician or the bookie shaking his hand, a few words, smoke or a shot, a request for "Groovin' High" or "I'm in the Mood for Love," the owner's wife languishing somewhere backstage, a crash off the drums, chimes from the piano or the Hammond organ gurgling a prayer, bass getting to work and the machine starting up, laying down a cushion, a road, assembling a body with a throbbing heart and skittish quivering nerves and in its blood dance waiting for the run, the ride, waiting for the *stitch*, Stitt, the brass dick, the golden brain, the horn work that traces the lip of the wound it's forever sewing together, the breath labor that animates it, delivers it into time.

1982: Japanese Folk Song

Use you up but you're cutting out, cutting away, monstering a thing that has your face, and across that face the branding of your name, and in the letters of the name—S-T-I-T-T—the tongue and the teeth, the embouchure's bit, the caressing bite on the air and under it the swelling of the opening throat, the pump of the breath, forty years on the road and fifty thousand hours on stage, *So doggone good,* laughter there that dices everything up, *Yes sir, that's my baby, call that boy Sonny,* give the devil his due, I'm yours body and soul.

And I can't help imagining Stitt in that last July: flags splashing under the wind at the Tokyo airport, the breeze smelling of jet fuel and flowers,

a group of people meeting him at the gate. It seemed everybody here potentially knew him—he was well loved, one time called the highest master
of the alto saxophone, another the samurai warrior of jazz, man of the
golden sword. In Stitt's mouth the new teeth from the year before; for a
long while his upper incisors had been in bad shape, no insurance and no
chance for the dentist, though it hadn't much affected his playing. But he'd
been roaring like a lion since, the old fire burning strong, the embouchure
perfect and tight, except now there was something else, like a pit stuck in
the throat, the craw, at times the breath not drawing easy. The doctor had
gone in through his chin for a biopsy, a small bandage there now scarcely
noticeable, and Stitt was feeling decent but after the flight he was ready for
a rest, laying off cigarettes and having a drink to relax and sleep a while
in the hotel room.

Coming to him through the afternoon light, a new idea, a thing to try
with the Monk song tonight if he was in the mood. It was a simple, angular melody, the kind of tune where he could rearrange and shift tempos
while at the same time blowing the hell out of it. He lay there under the
light of Japan he thought of as a free light. In some way the sky here was
full of air, best place for him to be, the mountains and the sea around,
it was like floating in another world. They said souls lived among the
snows of the peaks, but in Japan the body right here and now was the
soul too—that was why the people loved jazz. The warrior soul fought
off its enemies, held its death at bay, claimed its own time using the body,
blood beating and muscles poised and standing inside your power. How
they could stand here—hours at the concerts, in the streets and the restaurants, standing room only and standing ovation: *Sonny Stitt, Sonny
Stitt.* It made him happy.

Stitt imagined the snow peaks far off beyond the window, the place
of souls, nothing there but clear air, clean winds blowing, source of all
the waters running down into the world, of everything's flourishing and
quickening. Souls, though, didn't really have a place, were everywhere
and nowhere. Like your own shadow on a late night, a figure accompa-
nying you along the sidewalk, sliding long up the walls of the buildings,
foreshortened behind you somewhere or looming somewhere up ahead.
You had the uncanny feeling it was leading you on its own dance, following or leading, casting your image from itself. A bold and forward thing,
pretending to life; a weak and wandering thing, dependent in its every

move. It showed a truth that fell from you, was cast by you alone. And it made a lie and an illusion, took something away from you, exposed you like an image off a camera's film.

In the clean white room, Stitt napped a while and then woke up in the dark. He switched on the lamp over the desk and the phone, thought about making a few calls. He rubbed his eyes, looked over his equipment stacked on the luggage rack, the Selmer and the Yamaha in their cases like parts of his own body waiting assembly—tubes of flight, pistons of breath packed in blue velvet. He took out a sleeve of reeds and held each one up to the light inspecting the grain, a hunger infiltrating his tongue for the taste of the shaved bamboo, the desire coming anyway for a cigarette.

The soul—it had to be invoked and coaxed, had to be waited on. He called room service and ordered coffee sent up, a light meal to come later. The cigarette in the meantime drew wrong, a little cough and then the smoke made him feel sick. The cough set something off, cut the blood flow so that for just a second there were watery stars floating in the air, a washing across the bedspread and over the bright reflection of the room in the glass of the window. Once it settled down, Stitt's gaze kept running to the shadows, not the things that were in the light standing clear, but the darknesses subtending them, patches and stains, a second world that seemed to gather more density as he noticed it: the shadow blades of the lamp, the phone, the dark halo around his own head, and the weird claw of his own hand hovering over the cradle to make a call home—a kind of heaviness there, a weighting of black.

Like a cage, a prison. And he'd spend what seemed like years in that room though it was only a matter of days and weeks. The shadows heavy, heavier from night to night as though a soul was being lustrated with black oil. But at the same time an increase of light, a knife's edge that made it shine harder off things, soul getting sharpened, defined to its maximum, right where it shaded off from itself. Shows had to be canceled; there was a question each day whether Stitt would be able to go on with the tour. He looked often at his hands in the light, his own hands, moving his fingers—they were long, remarkably long, he'd never thought about it before. The skin was engraved with a multitude of fine lines, like pieces of thread. The knuckles especially appeared strange, an intricate folding and tracing like the inside of a body or a shadow inside flesh itself.

Moving his fingers, Stitt felt the pressure of everything that had gathered there, forty-some years, all his time . . .

Those last days: light running along the edge of dark, hard shadows. Gazing out the window of the airliner on the flight home, Stitt leaned back, holding one of his hands inside the other. It was a strange gesture for him, a thing he'd rarely done: hands together as if he were consoling or congratulating himself. Off in the sky, he didn't see any shadows at all. Only the clouds, now and then shot through with blue, vapors weaving and stringing like hair blowing in strands, colors there like pearls. Pearls—he'd always liked them, things that seemed to take light and mix it with dark. He thought awhile about what they were supposed to mean: rarity and price, jewel in the muck, pearls before swine—the last a laughable image, somehow, all that snorting and snouting over beauty.

Traveling east, the hours going backwards, he was losing time. But he drifted off easily into sleep, a dream pearl globing cool and slippery through his mind, a thread being cut somewhere like a wandering finger of cloud parted by the wind. How the pearls would lay so perfect against the smooth skin of her throat in a necklace made of air. A quick pulsing where he would imprint his lips in a kiss. It would be *lingering*—that was the word. All the time in the world.

May 2000: On the Soul

Shadowing Stitt—yes, my words are shadows, words that would fix the soul and at the same time steal it away. Stitt's own sentences tell all the story: the tenor solo on "Casbah" (*Constellation*), or on "Sunday" (*Soul Shack*), the alto on "Cool Blues" (*Burnin'*), the trumpet-tunneling of the Varitone on "The People's Choice" (*You Talk That Talk*). Elaborate power charms, soul medicines: a language that consumes itself, burns itself away. Motto on an effigy, the devil in flames getting his share, but it turns into air, into breath. It leaves behind a kind of lapse in time: blank slate of forgetting, fresh slate of possibility. Gearing inside the machine, another machine. Soul technology. I can't use it, can't use it up, because it takes off its share in the very gesture by which it apportions it to me.

The soul is impossible—I think of the speculations of Plotinus and Parmenides, their troubling over how to maintain the power and dignity of a grand universal or world Soul while explaining what soul has to do with body, earth, and time. In one place, the great Soul is imagined not as something on high, but instead as a netting over the waves of the sea—as though souls are surrounded and floating and whirling, nourished by what touches them everywhere. Not a raying of emanations, a powering-down through levels and hierarchies, but a swimming contiguity. Winds moving over the waters, the lapping over of each along its borders, crossing, recrossing, tangling, roping currents and foam-stringing waves, tongued with one another.

Soul: on this wave, the next, passing. Arriving soon and already gone. Tunneling through an everywhere and a nowhere, through passages between. Leaping from the cut, its doing and its undoing.

Sun Ra *Photo by Michael Wilderman*

proxima ra

1973: Auditorium Theater

The Auditorium: a grimy Romanesque edifice running the length of Congress between Michigan and Wabash. In the early 1970s, it was a depreciating chunk of downtown real estate apparently destined for the wrecker's ball (it would later be saved through citizen efforts). It had been Adler and Sullivan's 1888 masterpiece, a brilliant flowering of the early Chicago school and for a time the world's largest and grandest opera house. Its construction had been likened to that of the Great Pyramid—a vast foundation pit, hundreds of workers swarming over the ground all day and all night, and teams of horses and ropes and tackle in a colossal labor. It was a remarkable work of architecture, an anticipation of the skyscraper of the later 1890s and an embodiment of egalitarian ideals, designed so that seated anywhere among the several floors, even in the highest gallery, six stories higher than the main stage and nearly half a block away, music lovers would be under the same brightly illuminated arches. Every man and woman would have a clear view and would be able to hear the merest whisper from the stage. Sarah Bernhardt performed there and said she could feel the quickening pulse of American democracy; at a rally in 1899, William McKinley and Booker T. Washington spoke together against racial intolerance.

The limestone and granite walls were of a monumental weight, enough to collapse the interior of its tower and topple the entire structure, but Dankmar Adler dreamed up a solution, an inspired formula that seemed to defy the laws of gravity. The lower stories were overloaded, while through the ascending floors the burden was gradually eased, thousands of tons elevated to a height of two hundred and seventy feet, the summit of Chicago's architecture in 1890. The tower's observation deck looked over the prairies for hundreds of miles. Probably imagining the run of the Union Pacific Railroad, Edgar Lee Masters said he could see all the way to Council Bluffs, Iowa.

But over the years, the Auditorium was supplanted by the Civic Opera House, and in the course of the 1960s, the south end of downtown, even near Michigan Avenue and Grant Park, had come to be viewed as a questionable area. Those were times of white flight in Chicago, with the lower end of State Street and Wabash turning into a mostly black shopping district, and there was a sense of a potential crossing of lines. It was a zone of uncertainty, a condition most people in Chicago, black or white, strove to avoid. The Auditorium building now housed Roosevelt University in the former quarters of the hotel, while the theater was devoted primarily to rock concerts—with a few thousand seats capacity and nobody particularly worried about damage, it was still a profitable space, though its days were said to be numbered.

The Auditorium, that spring or maybe early summer night, run-down and neglected, but still expansive, cavernous, soaring inside, marble staircases and a bank of elevators, eight levels in there, the seats running up in tiers to something like its own sky, a ceiling of painted arches and old-fashioned incandescent lights like candles in glass. Though it wasn't exactly a rock show, the place was hot with bodies, heavy with smoke, people here and there whistling and rattling small instruments, the crowd moving down in the course of the first act, Alice Coltrane's group, to fill in the seats on the level closest to the stage, and through the intermission, a bar serving plastic-cup beers in a hallway next to the unused cloakrooms.

It must have been a quarter ton of velvet: the Auditorium curtain washed through all its reds—burgundy and scarlet and a shimmering rose—as the lights came up again and it began to lift trembling like a mild breaking wave, the broad expanse of it luxuriantly gathering its skirts, dark puckers like ingrown stars and shadowy runners clustering into folds, along with its heaving sweep a small disturbance in the air, dust and smoke clouding the rays of the lights as though seeded with all that was fugitive and random and infinitesimal in the matter of the world.

Somewhere behind it a rumbling. Inside the rumbling, a furious battery of knocking and hammering, like a workshop of chaos. And then a swimming benison that enveloped and overwhelmed and let up again, the hard-struck beats breaking around its edges, driving over it, mimicking it, troubling its borders with backwashes and sudden turbulences. A swift arching slit now tearing up the middle of the curtain, revealing the Arkestra in the guise of fifteen, maybe twenty drummers working as if they'd been at it all day, all night, forever, though you could have imagined it was the drummers themselves doing the unveiling, levitating five hundred pounds of velvet through sheer pounding insistence, a last ruffling flourish of the drapery exposing the opera house stage under the full beam of the lights with a feeling of still more to come, another curtain to be lifted, creation never finished but always beginning again.

Behind that farther curtain: a morning before the heat of the day sets in, a morning when all the preparations for a journey are complete and it's the last moment before departure. Everyone is ready, everything called home is being left behind and home suddenly seems so good, the place you know, the place that knows you, familiar and safe, but at the same time you're already gone, it's only elegy, you're not mourning for home but seeing it once again as when you first came—empty now of your things, the doorways open freely to all the rooms, the windows open to all the light, you're offered again the promise of the new, the next encounter with another place, space.

Behind the curtain of memory, I see that night though there were others over the years and inevitably the memories drift and fuse and overlap. And the experience itself had a sort of duality. The immediacy and intensity of it would have you transfixed: in a minute, the drummers would change their positions, some of them their hats, their robes; and John Gilmore would take up his tenor and growl a keening march, Danny Thompson stab and worry with a flute, Sun Ra leave his big conga and mount the temple of keyboards for a ritual parenthesis of chromatic zigzags and electro-howls. Yet there was also a sense of everything sliding away, an unsettled distancing, as though you were hearing from far off or from inside a tunneled angle; or paradoxically were right at the point of the music so that you couldn't really listen to it but instead were struck with the entire force of an always gathering shout implicit even in its pauses and silences, its whirling hyper-body getting mixed up with your own in a helpless contact where you lost your bearings, no frame anymore for your ear that was just a ravished thing, the powers of the music moving you aside from where you could sit back and savor it, that location where *you* were supposed to be *you* seeming no more than a temporary slot, a floating function, the χ of that sound's spacing.

On occasion I'd take a friend to a Sun Ra show and watch for a reaction, because in that spacing was ample room for bewilderment and dismay, satire and irony. On the Auditorium stage: Gilmore on one side belling through a series of astringent tangents, something like the swelling and bursting of a great silver bubble; Marshall Allen and Danny Davis on the other screaming in an eccentric orbit, silk planets glowing on their vests and pointy toes on their suede elf-boots, the saxophones gripped and mocked and abused, played sideways and upside down like a mad Lester Young. The air bristling: outraged harmonics and squealing overtones so you might drift into thinking about unaccountable things—the revolt of the animals, say: every imprisoned creature taking back its color and its fangs. Or a snake winding a tree, a limb—a thing that wouldn't be banished to dirt but would shed tears that would be its speaking in a wordless voice like water: the last would be first, the wrong rise against the always right, a path like the snake's would twist up an infinity that uncoiled you across a vibrating susceptible plane, a surface always on the move, an opening space.

But a cold eye could strip away with a glance the layers and veils of sound and motion. Yes, the shrilling fire trial of the saxes was reaching its limit point; obeying a strict order, the counterweight of the brasses swung into play with Kwame Hadi's trumpet tangling inside it, a new line of motion breaking out along with a theme like a fragment of an old musical, ephemeral and sentimental, June Tyson and the other dancers winding up and back across the giant stage, so much space there in the Auditorium they were doing leaps and twirls like never before, Tyson spinning after her long shadow under the lights, her body a blazing bronze pillar. Yet the whole thing was fragile, questionable, all the wild business offering itself to the skeptical as hocus-pocus, as ruckus and noise. One time, a guitarist friend watched in a sort of trance and then laughed, shaking his head in disbelief that anyone could get away with such things. Though he sat bemused through two more hours, he dismissed it as nothing but a three-ring circus. It wasn't jazz.

I could have said he was overly attached to the proper, the technical, the dignified, all we'd learned to respect—the soloist's rigor, the bass player's impeccable time, the drummer's rowdy tastefulness. I could have argued that the Arkestra was as precise and structured in its way as the most faultless quintet. But I didn't care, I could grant that the Arkestra was absurd, I laughed too, feeling the simple delirium of it, like when you were a kid and you'd spin and make yourself dizzy—a stupid thing to do but you liked it anyway, did it again and again no matter how often you were warned. That goofy spinning gave you a different sense of your body and of the ground under your feet—the precious gravity that, cultivated and regulated since you were an infant, made you a person, made you human. As you turned and turned, you felt how your body wasn't necessarily together with itself, it flopped and stumbled, it lurched and wheeled on its own as you tried to catch up, laughing, your own existence suddenly a crazy joke. You didn't know quite where you were in the room, the lamp was swaying, the door swinging at an improbable angle, the carpet dropping off in the wrong direction. Someone would have to grip your arms, stop you before you did serious damage. You'd lie on the floor then, everything still spinning, sensing what it meant that there was such a thing as a *plane*, and how it could be multiple, multiplied, not what you stacked up by addition but what slid away into something indefinite, like a jet steeping off into a sky of clouds and stars.

One put away childish things and found one's place in the world; the spirit of the circus played with and against that world, shook it up and spun it around and made it dizzy. The beautiful woman stepping precariously on a near-invisible cable across the air, the brave tamer sporting with a pride of lions, the clowns with their phallic noses and monster feet: human energies given over to spectacle, bodies exposed to the chance of their death, bare hands trafficking with the powers of beasts, faces masked and distorted and leering in powder and paint. You were taken back to childish days when you apprehended spirits everywhere—faces in knots of wood and hands traced in water stains on the sidewalk, the rasp of a crow or the trill of a robin sounding a vague sign of your fate, the green air of a spring wind whispering in your ear indefinable things about how you and the world were making each other live.

Those powers you touched and that touched you intimated more—what were your house, your room, all your territories and possessions and even your own mind and body but a kind of cage, when outside was an invitation to some other world? The Arkestra rocking on through "Watusa" and later the players by turns chanting "Space Is the Place" ten times, twenty times, fifty times over until there was no memory of anything else, only that whirling circus that called on you to lose your position, to give up your ground, to come out from your earth. And where was that space? It was right there, it was right here, it was nowhere but it was arriving somewhere between the here and the there, and those black faces telling you to leave the planet, and those black voices saying you were wrong, you had no right, a battle was raging, angels and demons at play, the world was in struggle and travail, who controls space controls reality: white or black, you had to find your own way. The crashing exploding roar of the drums and horns that splintered and fused rhythm and melody and harmony, the leaping dancers flashing their colors in trailing wings, their hands signing enticements and warnings through the vibrating air—everything that was lifting itself off on the stage was as much a warding off as a welcome, as much a barrier as a door, as though you probably wouldn't make it, your chance was only for an instant and it was receding, in the music there was elegy and mourning, sad but resigned, too. For you, not for you, since all you knew was your slave body and your slave world, how could you ever be free? And it wasn't even freedom that was the issue, because thinking about freedom, you were already in chains. Space: not a place you could take but what took you off, spacing you you you—and what could anybody do with that?

1964: Galactic Derelict

It was a miscalculation, driven I guess by my fear of arriving home late, my parents angrily waiting in the house where I was supposed to have been for the hour and a half after school instead of wandering off to the Prairies, as we called the vacant ground near the factories and the tracks, and worst of all having ventured to the other side of Archer Avenue, a busy highwaylike thoroughfare roaring with rush-hour cars and trucks, which I was forbidden to cross.

Three lanes on each side, a black and white stripe in the middle where you could manage to stand, if necessary, testing your nerve against the big vehicles passing only inches away, their wind against your body. Living on one of the streets right below it, I'd watched the traffic on Archer all my life, running fast day and night across that angle a half-block away, in between a weedy field where there had once been stores but now were only their ruins, crumbling foundation slabs and floors of cracked tile. Nobody wanted to slow down and there was nowhere to park on that busy stretch approaching the intersection of Fifty-fifth Street.

Archer: touchstone of our days, procession of the world passing by, the dump trucks we counted by their company names—Lindahl, Palumbo,

Consumers—and the latest model cars, Thunderbirds and Corvettes, Electras and El Dorados. Everything hauling ass while we tried to tabulate, identify, create an order and a magic from it. Thirty-nine, top number, clay-colored paint, primal motto: *The Earth Moves with Palumbo.* An angel-blue Sting Ray throttling past, chrome dual exhaust, run of luck in the sunlight. And Archer, as we knew, an old Indian trail into Chicago, shooting west to the city line and becoming highway, Archer Road, down through Summit and Argo and out to the cemeteries in Justice, the Cal-Sag Channel, Willow Springs; shooting east into the city through Brighton Park and Bridgeport and Chinatown, all the way to State Street, Warshawsky Brothers store, the approach to the Loop with the skyscrapers looming up like a mountain range.

Three lanes, the traffic heading west, an evening in March so the sun was glaring bright on the pavement, on the windshields, in the drivers' eyes. I looked both ways, though that wasn't really necessary, since I only had to get to the centerline. Cars were coming, they were always coming, but I felt had enough speed of my own—eleven years old, spring in my legs—to make it.

It was at the corner near the barbershop and the State Farm agency. My friends had started out with me but at the last second they hesitated, stood back. I wanted just to fly, I guess, jump directly home like on a Monopoly board, get my key in the door that crucial minute or two before my parents' paths converged on the house and the blank appeared that would be me not there, and that blank got scribbled all over with the heat of both of them watching and worrying and suddenly everything about me wrong and days or weeks of being grounded, my friends coming to the door with the birds outside and the ball bouncing and the door closing again with me still inside.

I did fly, or at least was airborne—so I was told, since the impact of the collision wiped away any memory of it. Somebody said thirty, even fifty feet, thrown back across all three lanes and on to the grass along the Archer Avenue sidewalk. I heard later that one of the barbers, the same mustached guy who always cut my hair, came running out with the clippers still in his hand when he heard the noise. The insurance man was out there, too.

Dashing out into traffic, madly and foolishly, because I was afraid of getting into trouble—that was pretty much the description I learned to accept, embellished by my friends who must have watched in horror but made it sound like I'd gone into orbit like a Gemini astronaut, managing a trajectory over Archer in defiance of all the rules of gravity. Look both ways, yes, but I was looking elsewhere, distracted—spaced out, as in the phrase of later years. I remember anyway that last moment before the run—by then it wasn't so much the fear of my parents, although that was what had pushed me so far, but in the momentum and approach of the Archer Avenue traffic something seductive, arresting. Along the slant of the road, a speed limit sign saying 40, a few cars slowing down, others speeding up because the traffic signal was right ahead. Across all six lanes, a shifting of variable motions, aggressive or casual or impatient—drivers who looked around at what they were passing; drivers who gazed straight on, smoking; gearing trucks that seemed destined to make it through every green and braking trucks that seemed destined to get caught by every red. Across all six lanes, the tense feeling that despite the slots in which they rode, despite the safety of lanes and lines, signals and warnings, it was a shaky arrangement, where the slightest catch could be disastrous. A lapse of attention in the tightly packed traffic making the bend, coming into the full of the sun, a blowout or a breakdown, one false move and the order of it all would be thrown into chaos.

Maybe dazzled, maybe in an unaccountable way excited by such a prospect—the atom bomb, I'd read, was invented with the splitting off of a little particle that generated tremendous power, so why shouldn't I be a little particle splitting off from the order of Archer, a similar power of escape or flight coming to me?—I more or less launched myself into the road. Groping for a formula or equation, perhaps, that would prove that *here* equaled *there*, my foot down on the pavement of Archer Avenue equaling my foot on the threshold of the door at home, key at the ready, having jumped, spaced.

Beyond that, I remember only the screaming of the ambulance which after a while I realized I was inside, and telling my parents over and over again that I was sorry, I was sorry.

I wasn't grounded. Instead I found myself on the sixth floor of Holy Cross Hospital in an immobilizing traction designed to heal my pelvic bone, where I'd taken most of the impact of the car's left fender (I'd almost made it across, after all). When I look at the photo from that period I expect to see a battered kid, and I'm amazed at the smile on my face; I appear to be in a strange ecstasy, rigged up with cables and canvas and floating over the bed, which indeed my body never touched for a good six weeks. It was a regression to the infantile, in a way—I didn't have to do anything but hang there, my food coming to me and usually tasting fairly good, the television going all day and a stack of library books alongside the nightstand, brought by my parents at my command. I don't recall doing any schoolwork, though I must have; mostly I worked my way through the books.

An older cousin had started me—Poul Anderson, *Space Ways*; Andre Norton, *Galactic Derelict*. Science fiction: there was the hero, there were the plot machineries of search and rescue, there were the women in distress, just like any western, any comic book. But along with those familiar pleasures was more. It was *science* fiction—a defiant sort of oxymoron, suggesting the possibility of a knowledge cut loose from mere fact and maybe surpassing it. My parents disliked the very idea—my father insisted on calling it *science and fiction* as though denying any chance of the two things combining; my mother remarked how much better it would be if I read science fact and actually learned something. And beyond the aura of knowledge was the other thing—not a thing at all, but a dimension, an expansive unmeasured unknown: *space*. Space was the place where everything interesting happened, where the hero encountered sights and sounds and beings otherwhere and beyond: worlds of *if*, as in the magazine of that title I later would discover one day in Hayden's Drugs.

From my bed I could see out the window a view of trees and grass, a stretch of Marquette Park across the street on California Avenue. The trees were still bare when I first came but through April blossomed into flower and leaf; one day the grass off in the distance unexpectedly was brightened to a rich green. After the six weeks in traction I'd believed it would be over, I would simply get out of bed and walk but I was of course disappointed. I was indeed like an infant again, unable to take a single step without gripping the chair, months of whirlpools and the walker and crutches and a cane still ahead.

I went back to finish seventh grade in more or less good spirits anyway, but I felt immediately a change in how people viewed me. While I believed I was the same, my ability to walk and run again only a matter of time, I was suddenly marked as different. One kid (I swore I'd never forget his face and his name but I did—I had to—and he even seemed to know that I would) pursued me on the walk from school every day to drive home that image, jeering me down the streets. For the rest of the year, I was the cripple.

Every night and then all summer, restricted to the yard, the chair in the shade and the glass of iced tea, I kept on reading. I couldn't run free with my friends so I made up for it with a sort of running through pages, covering ground through book after book. Now and then, my eyes tiring, I stopped for a while. I looked at the small peach tree that grew in our yard, its spindly branches and soft pointed leaves, the places in the trunk where the bark oozed a sweet sap, on the ground the tiny fruits that were inedible, more pit than flesh. I gazed at the shiny cover of the *Galactic Derelict* Ace paperback of which I'd bought my own copy, the first book in my collection.

The cosmic firmament was a dark military blue, the edges shading toward an icy black. The pitted gray hulk of the ship hovered like a meteor-beaten asteroid, like a fossil written all over with nameless traces of orbits and light-years. Floating nearby on a long serpentine cable, a spaceman appeared to be approaching the airlock, yet through an error of his own or by virtue of some inexorable law of bend and drift, at the same time he seemed to be moving away from it. It was as though he too was floating abandoned in space, never quite able to reach the ship, himself the galactic derelict.

1965: The Magic City

If you can keep your head when those all about you are losing theirs and blaming it on you—I imperfectly remember Kipling's verse but recall drawing from that late-Victorian paean to masculinity and empire a sense of the power of detachment. What if I were alienated and alien to those others, my tormentors at school, a number of whom viewed me as a flaw in creation, a shuffling thing negotiating the stairs with my limp and my steel three-footed cane, a number of whom, with the teachers, offered syrupy sympathy and used me as exemplar for lessons in morality? Suddenly the issue was my being different, and the more the well-intentioned insisted I was the same as everyone else, the more I found myself being defined as indeed different. The visible marks of the accident were being replaced by a clinging, invisible taint that would remain long after I was back to normal. But if that was how they wanted it, I thought, it was all right with me, since as a point of pride and finally from sheer disgust with it all, I now wanted to stay different, to take that mark as my own.

If: maintaining your nerve, sangfroid, unruffled and unmoved. Even if your heart wanted to beat fast and your breath come short, you just stared off into space. What if I do, what if I don't: resisting your foes, testing your friends for their true coin. If: power of the syllogism, of abstraction, of detachment and control and cool—if all x is y and all y is z, then every x is z, irrefutable. Yet if: all the buds too of the possible clustering tightly along the branch of the given, sweet or bitter folds whose opening scented the air of the powerless, the imprisoned. The cripple under the discipline and surveillance of his parents, captive of house and routine and regimen, school, chores, food, sleep; but under the homework page, under the bedclothes later, the small glossy book, Ace paperback like I had drawn a lucky hand and the price only forty cents, the least expensive on the newsstand. Sometimes they were Ace Doubles, two books in one, two different covers, so whatever I was reading was constantly disturbed by another if. If, with only a small movement of the hand, I turned the book around and made the top bottom, the bottom top, I would be in a different world from the first, though I was holding the same volume. Everything that existed had its other side, each singular its plural.

I remember one night reading until late a Donald R. Wollheim anthology, *The End of the World*. Its cover illustration captured as if in an impossible panoramic lens the bright flaring disaster—the breakup of continents, the frenzy of teeming millions, the world gone to smoke and riot—while outside the frame, a last survivor looked on in shock or pain or joy at the planet Earth in its death throes. If the world disintegrated in an atomic holocaust—and in those years that possibility was always in the wind, backyard shelters and *On the Beach*, air-raid drills and the black on yellow like a spider's back of the fallout shelter sign on the door of the school—everything as the world knew it would be over, and by the same token everything would again be possible. Of course you would have to be a survivor, yourself like a spider or cockroach, one of the creatures who were said to be able to live through the inferno, who could mutate and adapt and be among those who inherited the earth. Or better yet would be to relocate, to escape the war and fire and madness by leaving altogether, find your way to a last rocket cobbled together by a renegade band and so blast off the blasted earth in the nick of time, watching sadly but with a sense of having triumphed over the odds, of having caught the upward arc of the if, as the world was consumed before your eyes. If you kept your spaceship toward the sun, you'd come next to Venus; if you steered away from it, you'd come to Mars; if you set controls for beyond the solar system, for outer space, the first star you'd come to would be Proxima Centauri, the closest to our sun.

After that, the infinite universe would be yours if your ship had what it took to cross the intergalactic gulfs. The ultimate engine of if: space as time, time as space, the warp drive carrying you through the gaps and interstices of creation, suns and nebulae and vast systems distantly glittering like the lights shooting past on a Riverview roller coaster at night or glowing through absolute black like blotted figures in a photographic negative.

But there were other ifs—what if the world were not what it seemed but something else, only one of many possible worlds to which dullness and familiarity made people blind? Time was the fourth dimension, tangling with, disturbing, and disturbed by space, so why not other dimensions at farther, higher reaches? My thumb and two fingers keeping open the page of the paperback book, the book itself with its smell of paper, of pulp, of desks and basements and park benches in the rain; my avid scanning eyes on the coarse-fonted text, the words not connecting to the world so much as brushing against something like it, close by, approximate, but otherwise—all of it might be the point of crossing of scores, of hundreds of thousands, of a near-limitless number of dimensions. Perhaps if I had the right key, spaceships and warp drives would appear crude instruments; I would step between worlds, I would slide through folds and puckers and tears in the fabric of creation as easily as I stepped across my room to turn off the light and look out the window at the stars, Orion standing sideways in the firmament, the Big Dipper upside down and pouring out the void.

If it were true—if the if, if otherness, were not only outside and beyond but already right where I was, coursing through or infinitely touching here and then there, coming near and withdrawing, weaving and unweaving, the plethora of its metaphors confirming just how dizzyingly elusive and true it might be—well, then, that changed everything, too. I saw the potential strangeness of my own two hands under the light on my desk. (It was the earliest avatar of the high-intensity lamp, a walking-stick thing with a little black box for its base and a tiny cowled bulb that promised the finest illumination, itself a maker of harshly exhilarating new dimensions on the walls and the book.) For all I knew those familiar appendages might be mere cutouts from an impossible space, not grasping by my order but being grasped, or what I called their grasping really a letting go, everything I did some miniscule mechanism within an incomprehensible cosmic process. Or my hands could be dictating the destiny of countless subworlds, planets and systems beyond my ken might be coming to life and dying, forming and exploding, with a twitch of my finger, an urge I indulged to chew my thumbnail.

Who at that age doesn't dream of being a god, a power, tossing and turning all the while over the pressures of sex and socialization? Maybe it was scopophilia, then, that fever to look and look I contracted from the if, that sense of dimension folding on dimension: the sun on the pavement with speckles of crushed pebbles inside it, the pattern that began to emerge like a congeries of black stars, those stars flashing for a second in the singularity of their arrangement and submerged again back into place; or the bedtime study of my face in the bathroom mirror after a while losing its composure under the fluorescent light, something startled as though I were catching in myself someone else, around my eyes and mouth an alien haze of indefinition suggesting itself as what might after all be the actual thing that was me, reflected for an instant on the slant. And at school, the girls in their miniskirts toward whom I ventured a swift arrowing glance, far above their knees the dark band of the stocking tops maddeningly near but not quite visible, impossible to distinguish substance from shadow in that fugitive dimension where the way up and the way down seemed one and the same.

Scopophilia—unlovely word, suggestive of peeping toms and mirrors on the ceiling, but at the same time the origin of philosophy inasmuch as seeing and knowing are allied, the love of wisdom founded on the avid eye, on a taste for lifting the veil and discovering the secrets behind appearances. It's said that cosmologies start with a baby wondering where he came from; science itself is a matter of learning the score, every equation and formula a derivation of the first copula which says this one plugs into that one, and from that you can make another and yet another: be fruitful, divide and multiply, from being get your beings.

The love of looking—anywhere might be that welling inside the air, that gathering in the light, that thickening in the shadows that intimated the if, a sliding running quicksilver fluttering like leaves raked by wind. Or like the composed and discomposed images of the steel bar across the top of the green leather seat, the rubber flap of the exit door and the red emergency ball dangling heavy as fruit, the *Read As You Ride* pamphlet receptacle and the *No Smoking/Spitting* sign and the passing street and traffic signals and the reflection of my face angled against the glass of the window into which I gazed while riding the Archer Avenue bus downtown on a Saturday in October of that year. It was no spaceship, but there were mysteries in that bus and that window—not just the images coming and then being wiped away, never the same one coming twice, but the murmur of human voices, tumbles of words with their own moving worlds, and the warm scents of bodies, around me a press of feelings and passions I could feel on my skin so that I wondered if everything might be the opposite of what I thought: my eyes, supposedly the prime organs of vision, were actually a primitive means of perception, while what I called looking was really a weird configuration that along with the eyes included the jumps and starts of mind and the prickling sensitive field of body and skin—precisely what tended to make me feel uncomfortable, raw and vulnerable, the world not only a blossoming garden but a spiky minefield of ifs.

In the eighth grade, Saturday was my day of freedom: housework done in the morning, and in the afternoon, the trip to the main library on Randolph Street allowed to me because I was doing schoolwork and, just as my parents said they wanted, learning about science. But my book wasn't any volume on the shelves. It was downtown Chicago, the Loop, with its circuit of elevated trains, the Lake and Ravenswood lines, like an endless iron snake consuming its tail. After the last bend of Archer below Eighteenth Street, after the warehouses that stretched to the river and the rust-veined viaduct at Roosevelt Road, after the Moler Barber College where the bus turned again at Polk, swinging through a view of the burlesque houses and arcades of South State with their sidewalk signboards running up to Van Buren and the El, and just after the clock tower and the smoke and the jammed traffic of Dearborn Station, I felt rising in me a fever, an exaltation as though I was coming into high mountains or landing on a new planet. Dearborn: a solid mile of skyscraper limestone and granite and steel, a dark tunnel of shadows and windows and red neon, lights and forms mixing up their images in reflections everywhere—in

glass, pavement, and metal, in my roving and overexposed eye. All was
height, mass, bulk, and illumination in incandescent white. A multiplic-
ity of windows, of painted or rounded lintels, of spidery iron grates and
fire escapes, a *hive* feeling like the Frank R. Paul covers of the old 1920s
Air Wonder Stories I had seen, a sublime there of too many to count
or to calculate, an unknown exponent edging off between the vertical
reach of buildings and streets where the clear blue sky seemed to tremble.
And looking at the stretch of buildings that extended all the way to Lake
Street, the buses sparking blue under their overhead cables, the theater
marquees of the Monroe and the Loop and the McVickers bulbing hot
in the dark though it was a sunny afternoon, the elevated tracks in either
direction on Wells and Wabash flashing with the motion and dispatch of
the trains, I was dazzled by something like the spirit of electricity, of what
I thought of as the essence of *physics*.

Physics: the ostensible topic of my study on those library Saturdays.
I was on the trail of cosmic rays and neutrinos, the obscure phenomena
exposed to the eye by the Wilson Cloud Chamber, the project I was supposed to be constructing for the science fair. I left the bus at Randolph
and walked toward State. Marshall Field's was at the corner, Carson
Pirie Scott down the block, the Trailways Station right ahead, and the
street was crowded with Saturday shoppers, the crossings and sidewalks
overwhelmed with threatening phalanxes, armies of people rushing in all
directions. I'd learned there was no path through the crowd, no way to
maintain a bearing or a position except to launch myself into the press of
bodies and let the motion carry me. Among the crowd, in that flocking
and clustering and milling, I felt as though every person—the man in a
blue suit, the lady with the heavy bags, the younger guy in a leather jacket
who I could tell would turn indignantly if I happened to step just an inch
too close behind him—was another world, and inside that world other
worlds, and in the crossings and interferences of their paths more worlds
still. I was being touched by the central pulse of powers beyond me, forces
of commerce and capital, history and politics, but all I knew was the ex-
citement of a contact and confusion, a raw magic.

And in that magic city, without knowing it, I might have been tracking
Sun Ra himself through some long and irregular approach, though by
that time he had moved on from Chicago to Montreal and New York. Yes,
Birmingham was the Magic City of his childhood, but along with the tide

of migration from the South it was Chicago he came to after World War II in pursuit of his visions. Years later, I lingered a while in that same city, Randolph Street with its arcades and novelty shops, sometimes bought a hamburger at the Holloway House snack shop, sometimes talked to the street photographers, young men strapped with Polaroid Land Cameras who offered an image of the city and you for a dollar and when you refused, crumpled your photo or some facsimile thereof into a ball of folds and expertly sank it in the trashcan at the corner.

One day I ventured into the Chicago Civic Tower, an imposing red stone edifice on the north side of the street next door to the Greyhound bus station. I'd noticed a sign near the entrance: Metaphysical Book Shop. I had no idea what metaphysics meant but was drawn by the word, its promise of something extra, beyond what I was going to study at the library. The shop was on one of the upper stories; inside, a group of elderly women listening to a lecture turned all together and seemed genuinely startled by the apparition of my face at the door. I lasted no more than a few minutes in there, buying the only item I could afford, a glossy newspaper called *The Occult Gazette*. Making my escape, I sat for a while on a bench near the elevators. On a Saturday, there seemed to be nobody around, the numbers on the master control panel running over and over through the sequences of floors without a stop, the red arrows indifferently pointing up or down. The pages of the newspaper were possessed of a fine silky elegance I kept touching as I tried to read the front page. It was columned with extremely fine print, detailing the esoterica of astral labor, attainments and levels and degrees of color and spheres and light. The headline illustration offered a Blake-style seraphim wrapped in a black and white crown of fire, bannered with cabalistic mottoes and pouring out rays and emanations as though in the very fullness of all its power it was helpless to do otherwise. *Maitreya*, the caption read, *Lord of the Flame of the Central Sun*.

If—the particle of magic: if you know how to write the secret names, you can gain the audience of the elemental spirits, range their powers against what you fear and toward what you desire. If—while I was supposed to be understanding the Wilson Cloud Chamber, I found myself looking for something else. On the ground floor of the Main Library, a room of high broad windows facing Randolph; and just outside, the grand marble staircase that took you to the upper floors under a flood of green-tinted sunlight from the stained-glass dome. Most of the library had the aura of a temple dedicated to learning, but the science section was stripped to essentials, packed rows of metal shelves and crowding men who seemed impatient, almost desperate. I was looked on indignantly by some of them and roughly pushed aside by others, as if I had no right to be there among the books. Others appeared to have eyes for nothing but the page in front of them as I walked by, invisible.

At my age I couldn't check out any of the materials, so I found a book and sat reading at one of the tables with a feeling of jealous eyes watching. That day it was *Elementary Particles*, a thin red volume snatched right from under a smelly trenchcoated man whose crotch kept locating itself near my head as I stooped to the shelf. At the table, I stared for a long time at the mathematical formulas on pages as delicately glossy as those of *The Occult Gazette*. The text of the book was opaque, far beyond anything I could hope to understand, but that didn't make it meaningless. On the contrary, the text seemed absolutely saturated with meaning. I thought of it as *supersaturated*, as in the mechanism of the cloud chamber where, with the thrust of a rubber piston, the atmosphere created in your Mason jar was supposed to exceed one hundred percent humidity, inside the glass a storm brewing. In that sudden clouding and dash of a miniature rain, you would make visible a random and unrepeatable event—the passage in one instant of the cosmic rays incessantly bombarding the earth from worlds and galaxies beyond and leaving their marks on the photographic paper in an asymptotic ragged pattern like the ones I saw on the pages of *Elementary Particles*. Under the bright fluorescent lights I pored over the snaky graffiti of Arabic numerals, Greek and Latin characters, slashes and sines and exponents, all of it seeming to promise the power of bombs and cyclotrons, all of it seeming to promise some other power in the crowded elegant flourish of itself as nothing but a mark on the page. The baffling of reference in elaborate formula implied an if of power itself: its failure, its disorder, and its noise, whatever was scattering and scintillating and infinitesimal that murmured in some other voice through it and across it and inside it where all the ifs flowered in black secret like something inking into my eye.

But it was over one of the photographic plates in *Elementary Particles* that I gazed the longest, transfixed by what might have been a sort of ultimate pornography or what might have been the exact opposite of pornography insofar as the secrets exposed offered nothing to the eye in the way of object or even position but only a grainy set of tracks that seemed to skate across an impossible angle, a luminous confusion there like the waste footage of a film reeling sideways through a projector. Cosmic rays: trail of the meson, a particle that exists for two nanoseconds before releasing an electron, and which the laws of physics say demands an invisible participant—the neutrino, chargeless and so neither negative nor positive, a particle that has almost nothing to do with matter though the earth and the universe are said to be traversed by it in constant storms and blasts, neutrinos penetrating everywhere and passing through all things without regard, bodies and planets and stars, as though in space there must be yet another space, spaces.

Cosmic rays: I leaned over the photograph protectively as if guarding a portrait of a face—maybe a face that I feared, maybe a face that I loved, maybe my own face. I stared and stared, feeling again after a while a mixing of perception, the eye giving up its straining after image, the mind startled and then drifting, the skin as though listening, the body becoming a whorled and hollowed space like an ear. Electric buses on Randolph spit blue light and their motors hummed outside the open windows. I could hear the joyful rush of El trains over Wabash. I could vaguely divine the arcane and fervent desires of the men in the room, one of them sighing over his book, another mercilessly scratching at his bald head as he frantically wrote on a notepad. I could almost smell the icy fire of those galaxies and suns from which the cosmic rays might have come, though there seemed no way their origin could ever be located, their position fixed. For a moment I understood how, along a grain of an if that was very close, I might one day become another of the men in that overheated room that was like the interior of a febrile, insomniac brain, something very subtle scratching right then across my eyes, into my mind, along my skin, which I was afraid to touch yet wanted more than anything to touch, touch again.

Everywhere, nowhere, somewhere born out of the flare and the outstreaming and the overthrow of suns. An infinity of ifs: in one of which I'm discharged and dispositioned, looking for a berth on Ra's spaceship, the solar ark, petitioning for my passport; in another of which I'm only following in a parallel universe Ra's track, scarcely at all involved with matter but maybe anyway saturating it, saturated with it, riding a neutrino between.

Sun Ra: in your magic city I found not you but your veils, flowering if in steel and stone and in the run of the trains, in the El the sound of joy.

Infinity Myths

Jazz—it's said the word means sex. Making love. Yes, jamming the thing, plugging it, feeling the buzz and razz and shake and jag and rag, but elegant with foreplay and game, zoning all around. Fucking, with syncope: a spacing in it, versions and inversions and perversions, baby baby this song is you, this song is us, this song sings in and out of every kind of position as though there's no more time or nothing but time, bodies laced and spaced in some infinite twisting. Jazz: maybe called the devil's music not so much for the sex but because it's about going wrong, not working, all messed up with skin and eyes and mind in a lost swoon tripping on itself, dizzy with living and dying, its charm and its spell in a singular formula always again leaving its track, arcanum repeating its piece to pieces, equation drawing its measure to the incommensurate, riff of the if. If you go there, if I go here—love, who knows where we'll be? Jazz—the body out there spaced from itself: throat of the horns, the heartvalve of the drums, piano vertebrae, bass gut. Colony of organs: it comes together each time but each time it's coming apart, too, exposed on its inside, naked in its betweens. If you can keep your head—but you go to my head like a summer with a thousand Julys . . .

1977: The Jazz Showcase when it was a cellar club on Rush Street, a disco bumping and rumbling upstairs, a long line crowding down the carpeted steps. Smaller quarters didn't make any difference: the Arkestra plunged again into peace and war, Allen and Davis right in with the chairs, inches away, testing the meaning of endurance itself, everything lasted and lasted, nothing could last, Pat Patrick's baritone this time, too, tearing out all the ground, and dressed in silk banners of the planets Tyson and the dancers wandering the low-ceilinged room, releasing shouts, whispers, cries, sometimes almost in your ear: *The universe has come to converse with you. With you. And you, and you*, the last phrase whipping past you or training in like radar, circulating through the audience so it seemed each person would be addressed, all of us, every one.

After a while I closed my eyes, whatever was my being and substance as if focused by a colossal microscope and under its lens all that was I coming undone, dispersed in a broken blossoming, space that kept dividing and raying and folding itself until it collapsed, until it gathered together again. If. I didn't need to look, to see, though I opened my eyes sometimes inside the storm of the Arkestra overwhelming the black-painted room, flash of colors and Ra's thundering console and the spit and sparkle and glow of hissing cymbals and squalling horns, throw of light across bodies and faces of the audience and the overcrowded stage loaded with instruments and music stands and costumed players, bandit's cave or pirate's grotto in a dream opera.

And then in the near dark, a sudden quiet: Ra alone at the keyboards, gold of his skullcap under a violet beam, gold of his snake bracelet as his arms came down on the scribbling Moog, sounds like machinery on the blink, ready to short circuit and explode, and rocky dashed phrases off the Rhodes. Again a sudden quiet and the Space Organ starting at nothing: a merest touch brushing or breezing the ear, answering itself from what seemed a *ne plus ultra*, farthest point. Out of an exterior plenitude or nothingness, a harsh roaring that sounded like a gargantuan vacuum cleaner sucking off the void, or the void itself sucking everything in until there came a hard chord, a mad run, a stilted stately melody where there was a cradling, cosmos and chaos indifferently mixed—*khōra*, receptacle, egg—and Ra its huge shining hen or himself the egg, first or last, position and mission impossible, a sound in that melody something like light from a sky of clouds, the sun breaking out here and there, the light over wind-pressed water slightly rippling, trees on the shore thick and smoked with buds as if in frost, a feeling of an absolute rain falling through the all, the music its scattering track.

Ra: a benevolent yet imperious presence surrounded by his controls behind the platform of keyboards, or out on the stage, out among the audience with the players and the dancers. Maybe androgynous: the brightly colored gear, the sequins and robes, an aura of billowing skirts and veils, the neutral or neuter beyond man and woman—Hermaphrodite, Tiresias. I was haunted by that face: Ra's disdainful eagle glance, his absolute sobriety in the middle of what was by his own design circus and carnival, Ra the ultimate straight man as though it was a task requiring the utmost concentration and discipline to reach what was really pure joy—say, the joy of a Wordsworth or Coleridge, eddying from pole to pole, suffused and interfused, one's own *fiat lux,* a creation always beginning again, but for Ra coupled with a joy that eased off from Romantic synchrony and synthesis, not the royal wedding to secure the family line but instead a joy out of space, spacing (El the sound of joy: run of the many-windowed trains, IC and the Jackson Park Line, radiant carriages and their silhouette faces in the Chicago night where everywhere the lines are crossing). Joy of the if, the again as again, each time, who controls space controls reality but who touches space rides the lines between and beyond and out—

In one respect closing my eyes was defensive: it was all too much, or there was a quality in Ra that made me understand downcast gazes—the congregation at the Eucharist, the apprentice before the master, the abashed feeling before what I couldn't identify with, couldn't even imagine, really, but could only attempt to participate in through an answering gratitude—applause, a passing word coming off the lips or a shout from someone in the audience I realized after a minute maybe was mine; not *jazz* as an aesthetic object of study and pleasure but something like being *jazzed*—like sex, like passion, I was floored, burned, dispossessed. I wasn't the only one at those shows who found himself saying to the air and whoever would hear: *Thank you. Thank you for this.*

Converse—to talk with, to follow a track together, a line. The *with* qualifying the agonistic *verse* and *versus*, though Ra often enough was hectoring and sermonizing. *How can you ask me what is my identity when you don't even know who YOU are? You say you want to live but if you live that means you have to DIE. Sacrifice your life. Sacrifice your death.* Listening to the verses from the songs, reading the material from Ra's book *The Immeasurable Equation*, it seems things don't quite add up. I'm exhorted to leave my body, to leave this earth for outer space. I'm told at the same time that another, better world can be made, maybe right here on Earth, if I can see things straight. On one side, a sort of Orphic heaven where we leave our bodies behind, liberated for good; on the other, a seemingly revolutionary utopia to be gained here and now, or at least in some immediate dimension, some near future.

Chicago—circa 1959, say. Sun Ra was still in town, playing the clubs, De Lisa and others, recording hours and hours of work, part of it being released on Saturn Records. The rehearsals and new compositions were going day and night in his place on the South Side, and soon would come Montreal and New York, Europe and the world. Chicago, magic city: Loop metropolis of towering number and bulk and mass, the buildings rising high in exaltation of quantity and multiplication, on La Salle Street the gold goddess–topped temples of commerce and exchange, the market floors where voices cried out options and futures. Chicago: city of crossings, railroads everywhere, grades running higher than the street, the roadways dipping low under viaducts, diesel fumes or a low-frequency hum and sometimes an electric crackling in the air, right in your windows the silver IC train mounted with its spidery racks, the El shadowing the block and sliding past rooftops, the kids climbing off third-story porches and risking the thousand volts of the third rail to ride for free. Chicago: city of bridges and boulevards, expansive parks and wide-tracked streets, Garfield and Southway and Midway Pleasance, Pershing and Cottage Grove and Vincennes and Thirty-first and Forty-seventh and Fifty-fifth. City of visions, Burnham and Olmsted, lines mapped and drawn in all directions, down to the lake and out to the horizons south and north and west—

If. And where was it, that one line, that place in space, on a late afternoon, some long night near morning? 1959, the magic city, apartheid Chicago: the race line at Halsted or Morgan, Fifty-ninth or Sixty-third, depending on where you hit the taboo, the white divide, Canaryville or Englewood, Back of the Yards or Gage Park. Ra on a warm afternoon, along South Side streets people out everywhere, springtime in Chicago with the trees in green and a cardinal with a red so fresh thrilling the eye, a world of delight touching like the light of a red planet, unknown worlds, if of an angel spirit in disguise. In Chicago always a route, always a way to another place, space, transits of riders in cars with the radios playing WVON, Daddy-O Daylie the jazz deejay as good as the Mayor. And the Chicago Transit Authority—green cheer of the CTA signs, BUS STOP, RAPID TRANSIT, joy of the roof-hugging El and the mystic echoing subway and the bus stops on almost every corner, the electric trolleys with round-moon windows down low so you could reach out and shake someone's hand on the sidewalk, and the clean-running motors that hummed up a scale almost to silence, comfortable seats and a spiriting vibration through the body like your spaceship had arrived.

And later, wandering that night out of his usual Bronzeville territory, points west, where the music led you followed, he was thankful for the CTA Owl Service—all night the buses running, every twenty minutes there on the main artery, and Ra thought of the owl—Oh, double U, EL:

the *O* like the vigilant eye open in the dark, the *W* with a sort of hook in it like the bird's talons for prey of wisdom, and the *L* his own, magic letter of the city of trains and winds, supporting trestles and safe corners, his wind-men Gilmore and Allen.

Oh double you, El: Ra is El, is Ra el; yes, wandering, exiled on this earth he loved, that one Ra; that second Ra ready to soar out of here, knowing he was on the line, something called WHITE on the other side where the bus stop sign shivered a little in the wind. He thought of walking over another block east and giving it up; he thought of how the owl spread its great wings like a cloak in the night hovering against the stars.

So cross the street. Only a street, line among lines, place in space that marks another if, and there's another and another beyond, dimensions to open like Moses with the serpent staff over the Red Sea, let my people go.

And if—the white kids out running wild, who knew where they were from, maybe not even that neighborhood where it seemed everyone was sleeping, their fleece as white as snow, but drawn to the line, lambs turning wolves. If: the rock, the stone; no, the chipped red brick, launched from where they scuffled together a moment as though fighting among themselves; the chipped red brick, rocketed out of a sudden silence among them by a bony arm, that hunk of the city their only word.

The march of the street lamps either way for miles. The store windows offering their glass to faces and shadows, with worlds and dimensions inside every reflection. Not far down the street what looked like the headlights of the bus. If: Ra in the middle of the street, on the striped dividing line, the missile tracking in its arc toward his head. He felt an urge to raise his arms to protect himself, his big hands fluttering like wings, yet he didn't turn. He stood there in the middle of the street and folded his arms. Regal. Supreme. There was no traffic except the bus still a couple of blocks away, not a car in sight, and he himself was becoming the vehicle, the ride, the rapid transit of the brick shard approaching, approaching, but where Ra was standing it would take just the smallest step to avoid (space is the place: you move in, you move aside, you dance where it divides) and the brick anyway had to cross half of half of half of half again, again, the thing would never touch him, infinity to traverse and Ra feeling its near scrape, closing his eyes just a second, time blowing like the wind, and on the pavement the strike of the brick and its dry tumble, its pink dust, the kids running and the bus humming up to the corner with its kind fuselage face of double moons, silver sparks from the power cables in back, a tunnel on wheels for his escape, electric ship of the voyage home, maybe behind him a world of if blasted black, maybe ahead of him a world of if swimming welcome in the fertile dark.

Infinity: *in fin*, the end, but in the end without any end. Infinity—the if and the N, if in its indefinite number, *n*th power. Spacing and spaced; utmost almost if. And that night at the Showcase, another time opening my eyes, last climax, June Tyson driven back and forth across the room by the powers and principalities of the horns, the keyboard armageddons and drums perpetual, her body leaping and leaping again, *The universe has come to converse with you, with you, with you, you,* her voice whooping sirenlike and then her body gathering into space, place, her arms sweeping through the air and then drawing in, pumping as though from a well inside the music, pumping as though she was its body piston, the Arkestra yearning and swirling itself into a number called "The Dance of Energy," and Tyson's long legs jumping and scissoring and moving at such speed, I swear, for an instant her feet were altogether off the floor, we had ignition, she was up.

And as the show ended and the Arkestra wound through the audience still playing—it was never over, they kept circling again though you thought they were done, and even when they'd left you could still hear the horns and the voices going on somewhere offstage, outside on the stairs, out ahead of you a minute on Rush Street, mixing with the crowd and the taxis and the noise of cruising late-night traffic—a touch, there on my shoulder. Ra's hand. But I didn't even see him reach that hand, his touch already past by the time I realized it, that hand among the audience touching another, another and another, those bodies of earth, worlds of if.

2001: Proximities

On a night in late March I walk along the lake, the stretch just below the Fullerton rocks, the line of willow trees in pale new green along the bend of the land going toward North Avenue Beach. It's a foggy night and there seems to be nobody else about, though this is usually a busy crossing point for bikers and runners and skaters. The atmosphere is thick, the air approaching rain.

Looking through the fog back toward Lake Shore Drive and the Loop, I see the distinct shapes and grids of the city distorted, foreshortened and lengthened. After a while the buildings are scarcely visible, only the white glow of lights on the John Hancock showing against cloud, somewhere farther off a pair of blinking red lights. I wonder who else I might meet out here. In the fog, I feel both hidden and exposed, vulnerable to whoever might appear, a face coming out of the rain. Running through my mind is a melody of Ra's—really, a blending or interference pattern of more than one, maybe "Fate in a Pleasant Mood," maybe "Images," maybe something else, the main thing about it a kind of haunted syncope I'm remembering as much in the way I'm walking as in my aural memory, my steps falling strangely doubled, troubled and exhilarated by some passage toward mystery—what world is this?—like Ra's compositions in their climbing through towering steps and then with some unexpected interval for an instant hanging suspended.

Who or what might I face in this space, this place? Perhaps the if of that syncope is something like infinity. I tend to think of infinity in terms of galaxies and the space-time continuum, the omniverse, but I recall too that its mathematical symbol is one of a crossing and looping, a chiasmus. Perhaps the face in the rain, that unsettling if, is like a knotting in which nothing is bound or secured but instead is indefinitely substitutable across its looping turns. The clarity of the mathematical symbol is fogged over like the grainy exposure of particle tracks in a cloud-chamber photograph.

In the fog, in the saturated air that verges on rain, I see things looming up, curving away—the wall of Lake Shore buildings, the dim lights in the windows, a human figure in the near distance. Inside my coat I feel the dampness on my skin, and in the circumambient air a sort of trembling. Suspended within that trembling as though inside a tear of the night, I am offered to the surprise of whatever may or may not happen. Myself an alien, I face the strange, the stranger. Proximate in that proximity, that wavering of position, place, space.

Rahsaan Roland Kirk *Photo by Michael Wilderman*

monstrosioso

1965: The Creeper

The fussy encyclopedic gravity of the Hammond B-3 overcome and the electric organ lofted to hard-bop orbit, still trailing diapasons of his mother's church music and the boogie-woogie tap-dance routines of his father's band—*The Incredible Jimmy Smith* proclaimed the block letters on a score of albums since the 1956 breakout recordings on Blue Note, those words celebrating a nearly miraculous mating of technology and soul. The thing had first stirred to life at a club in Atlantic City where he heard Wild Bill Davis make the Hammond roar like a big wave. It was a monster, upsurged through chocked, choppy chords and backwashed through rilling legatos, wattage enough there to power the entire Basie band. Davis was gruff, brash, gloriously loud, a bumptious lumbering attack, great swoops down on the keys and shameless ripsaw goosings of reverb and tremolo, the organ not so much singing as signaling, the music stripped to pure swelling impulse. For a piano player schooled in the overbrimming muscular lines of Art Tatum and the stabbing, nervous prances of Bud Powell, it was almost risible, the goddamned wired-up thing rocking on stage like a gurgling showboat. Fats Waller on "Jitterbug Waltz" coaxed over the organ with a percolating finesse as if running a trapeze artist up a swaying wire, but Davis almost seemed clumsy by design, as if in awe of the organ's powers yet unable to forego provoking them. A bristling, striding approach, a monster dog named Lance or Rex baited through the fence of a yard and teased into a frenzy and dashing back and forth, Davis showing a mouthful of white teeth as he shut the racket down at its very peak, a hushed arpeggio crawling down inside the Leslie speaker, Johnny Hodges's sardonic alto sniffing up the trail.

The golden gullets of trumpets and saxophones, the bright guts of the drums, the broad shoulders of the piano: music connected to the body, vibrating through the teeth, the throat, the fingers, the instruments like real organs depending on systems of breath and blood and muscle. The saxophone participates in the hands, the neck, the mouth; the trumpet is an externalization of the lungs, the throat, the ear; the piano is all phalanges, hinges and angles of wrists and elbows, strings and hammers of nerves. Fingers quivering, we play air solos as though under the spell of creatures of our device for whom we too are devices. Boundaries are crossed and confused between the instrument's body and our own—we speak of inspirations by which the saxophone comes alive under our hands, the violin does things we never believed possible, the guitar is playing us. In such prostheses our bodies seem to meld with the instruments in intense contact and immediacy. Teachers instruct wind players to relax the throat muscles so the music sounds not only through the body of the instrument but resonates deeply through the chest and lungs, the hollows of the player's body becoming an extension of the instrument. One of the pleasures of live performance is seeing the body moved and shaped, mastery seeming to demand a share of passivity, the grafting of player and instrument. Louis Armstrong's eyes open wide as though surprised but pleased to welcome the trumpet suddenly grown from his face in a brassy, cunning flower. Jean-Pierre Rampal's shoulders hunch and his head cocks, the stick of the flute a renegade appendage that appears to have the power to draw his whole body along its tangent. Riding the bench, Cecil Taylor jabs and hammers as though mimicking a piano taking stock of its own inner equipage.

Wild Bill Davis rollicking through a fast blues or laying a gush of vacuum-tube pipes under a ballad or a waltz, maybe "Stolen Sweets" with the Hammond slapped on thick, dripping, soaking, and Hodges's saxophone for all its hard cut and its languid precision sounding adjunct to greater forces. Something incredible to begin with about the *organ*, an instrument that generates sound elsewhere, not in the immediacy of contact with the musician's body but through an external apparatus. A systematization of the voice, a sonic mathexis resolving and dissolving differentials and frictions, organon and organization of sound, all the moves visible under a single gaze and spread out under the span of two hands. The cathedral organ is God's instrument, approaching pneumatic automatism and scarcely in need of a human operator, under the pipes the organist dwarfed, functionary in the service of empyrean syntheses. The majesty of the instrument of Bach's fugues and Saint-Saens' symphony is however related to organs of a humbler kind. The hand-pumped harmoniums and cranked hurdy-gurdies of street vendors and traveling entertainers, the bubbling calliopes of circuses, carnivals, and riverboats suggest what might be the innate gimmickry of the organ, its aura of a vaguely improper or mocking musical ventriloquism. Instead of a band of musicians playing together, one has the rough equivalent of their instrumental voices resounding from a box of plugged whistles. A confection, an obvious fake, but exciting wonder and admiration because it appears nearly autonomous, automatic. Still, there's an unsettling aspect to such musical auto-affection, an air of the monstrous about a thing that subsumes the vocal expressivity of music to a mechanical apparatus, redolent of the solipsistic elaborations of hermeticism and alchemy, of Gothic aesthetes in velvet-draped chambers, of spells that capture and enslave voices in jars, trees, the throats of howling beasts.

Under Davis's command the Hammond tottered and strode, the thing a gas, a ball, by turns indecorous and elephantine, frilly and elegant. You could score a movie or a baseball game with it, run skaters round in spins, quiver the asses of strippers or launch a congregation into getting the spirit. And inside the sound an almost imperceptible hum like the channel clearing for a bullhorn sermon, like a buzz of angels stunned with prayer, that hum offering the neutral and colorless sound of machinery and systems, of sound before anything was happening with it, before it was freighted with a voice, a story, a song. Objective, standardized, indifferent—the frequency of raw electric, the hot potential the Hammond operated on, capacitors and solenoids and resistors webbed under the keys and the organ droning beside itself like an anchorite resolving the dance of phenomena to an uninflected signal, a vibrating *om*.

Jimmy Smith woodshedding for a year in a Philadelphia warehouse, summer days the streets licking tar, under the wash of red leaves trains blowing off to Camden and Newark, and the slick, yielding keys—walking, striding, dancing on eggs, on water, scarcely any resistance—and learning to crawl up a ghostly wall inside the Hammond, kicking, trampling spiderlike the ribcage of the twenty-five bass pedals. Beating on the wall, singing to it, spit-words, curses and blessings, crossed scrawls. A shrill street-whistle amazed, looking through a sudden window on the traffic of the world. A sliding grip taking hold, but *hold* with a hole in it where a tentacle of space trembled, where it lashed to the left and to the right. It pawed and stroked the angel body of organ air. On the street one day the wind moved the branches of a beech tree in the same way, in the sunlight the shiny gray bark like wrinkles of finger skin.

Smith: the left hand comping with attitude, the right smashing runs, shoes marching over the bass pedals, fingers jumping off to work the drawbars, a foot shaking loose to stomp the volume pedal. Like his hands on the *All Day Long* cover, double-crossed over the keyboard, the organ offering such a road that there was a danger of indefinitely wandering or indefinitely sticking in one place. Sometimes it accelerated smoothly and overdriven, other times it was cornered, repeating, sneaking back then on its trail, creeping home and surprising itself there as if it was a new thing again. And a secret that ran inside the fingers—for all its electricity and speakers and watts, next to a trumpet or a piano the organ was weak. It didn't naturally cut through the air, lay down a weight. No chambers, no hammers, no hollow gut—nothing but wires and tubes, switches and solenoids. Though it promised an instantaneous production, music at your fingertips, there was an ineluctable lag between striking the keys and hearing the sound coming out of the Leslie. It meant working like hell to make the wired heaven of it gather mouth and teeth and bite.

The *electric organ*—the Hammond wasn't designed to be blown, hammered, strummed, or beaten. It was doubly monstrous, not only a systematization of the voice but a second-order system, like a sex device made to imitate a sex device. Smith's music is often characterized in terms of funk, grease, soul, a great boiling kettle bubbling and bursting. In one interview he condemns the thin-toned synthesizer and glorifies the Hammond, which he says has a sound you can feel in your bones. But the electric organ doesn't so much resonate with corporeality as index it, floating bodiless even as it's signaling body. The sound is coming loud off the Leslie speaker but it's detached from the keyboards by its almost imperceptible delay, and in that space, a thing wants to *feed*. An appetite that wants to feed on feeding itself—feed of the electric, feed of the signal doubled over, turning out the skin of music.

Laurens Hammond modeled his 1930s invention after Cahill's Telharmonium of 1900, an elaborate machine with hundreds of rotating metal discs inscribed with serrations and projections from which a contiguous array of electromagnets took their imprint and read off the pitches of the tempered scale. Like Freud's dream-apparatus of the same year, the thing worked by virtue of discharges firing up from a system of coded glyphs, and much as Freud also discovered, the machine was prone to glitches, the purity and stability of the tones susceptible to infections of electricity, even though regulated by batteries of condensers and capacitors and resistors. Hammond's design for the electric organ reduced the scale of the printing press–like Telharmonium mechanism, though it remained elaborate enough: a tone generator assembly consisting of ninety-one wheels, an electric motor that engaged a set of gears, those gears in turn setting the wheels spinning, inside the prim walnut cabinet of the console organ something like a locomotive's power train. And as though sublimating a taint of scandal involving the sacred music of the pipe organ being delivered over to commodity culture—the Hammond an instrument of the ultimate Protestantism, a church in your own living room, running on your own electricity—the organ was freighted, burdened, and overdetermined with controls. Not only was the full range of organ-stops replicated, but a system of 38 drawbars for the keyboards and pedals afforded an almost limitless capacity for fine-tuning and mixing, each drawbar sliding through a wide span of harmonics, with the Hammond capable of imitating most of the instruments of the symphony orchestra. The drawbars were color-coded, brown and white for what were called the consonants (roots and lower fifths) and black for the dissonants (higher fifths and thirds), the language of the Hammond suggesting you'd indeed gotten your hands on a universal encyclopedia, the key to all music. There was a host of other devices—a group of preset keys, for specific harmonic effects, which lay on the far left of each keyboard and inverted the black-and-white pattern of the others; switches that regulated the attack and decay of pitches; and, all-important for jazz players, the percussion setting that offered a mock-piano sound possessed at the same time of the timbres of winds and strings and brasses. The expression pedal, down there among the bass ribwork, could push the volume up to forty-eight decibels.

Half late-Victorian fantasy, half modernist elegance, the Hammond hummed and warmed with its load of electro-harmonics, its levels and degrees of switches and settings. Incredible, state of the art, seemingly transparent to all of music, electronically tempered and ordered and running the orchestral gamut, yet for that very reason provoking distempers and abuses. It's rare to find a parlor with a full-scale Hammond these days, but there have been generations of its later avatars, those home Hammonds and Wurlitzers and Lowrys, thousands of them now languishing in family rooms and basements, stacked with old photo albums and boxes of books. They promised a good time to mom and dad or grandma and grandpa, easy-play manuals with all the old songs and an automatic percussion feature offering waltz, fox trot, rock, or jazz accompaniment. They promised the youngsters an initiation into the world of music, everything they needed to know right there, chords, scales, the sounds of the orchestra. Those hopeful autodidact's machines have probably suffered the worst songs and the worst music-making in domestic history—I remember a book that started you with "Pennies from Heaven" and moved on to "Wichita Lineman"—as well as absorbing the cavalier and sometimes wildly experimental depredations of bored children trying, say, the oboes and violins and English horns, a nasal calliope issuing from a swoop over the keys, but more often dreaming of phantoms of the opera and with self-pleased dispatch tagging every possible switch, laying the volume-pedal to the metal. Or with both hands strafing across the octaves, elbows, arms, and even heads and feet effecting mighty crescendos in their own way as singular and wonderful as the baby wailing at the unaccustomed noise and at the same time reaching greedily with her hands to make some herself.

The incredible Jimmy Smith: wearing a flannel shirt on the cover of the album *The Sermon*, displaying his graceful hands like a workman worthy of his hire. Although from a town near Philadelphia, he might be out of Carolina, a country boy, framed as he is with dogs and livestock on *Back at the Chicken Shack*, swinging from the ladder of a boxcar on *Midnight Special*, though those records offered big-city music, sophisticated blues workouts with Stanley Turrentine and bebop outings with Lee Morgan and Curtis Fuller.

The slick teeth of the double keyboards wanting hands all over them so the air could bite down hard on itself. The thud and thump of the bass pedals banked underfoot, a crateload of tubes and wires circuited into bunched tongues, the Leslie warming like a chimney. Chockablock arpeggios, punchy two-handed heaves and throws, bass-pedal trots and gallops. A wide-chassis, comfortable expansive thing, Fleetwood, Imperial, the pleasure of smoothly tooling over a rough street, railroad crossings and potholes. Your ass in a plush seat, your hands and body sort of hanging over and sort of hanging from the steering wheel. Automatic transmission: the lightest touch and the car leaps, swings, fishtails. The squeal-track of rubber laid down fast and easy so you hardly knew you did it. U-turn coming back around, silver switches in the armrest and the electric windows up and down like spy doorways, the air pouring in.

Incredible: vehicle of nerves, sometimes a reeling eerie hornpipe like the windup of a horror film, sometimes an ominous obbligato like an episode-closing tune from the soap opera "The Edge of Night," boxed and imprisoned but at the same time master of the chambers, strumming over bones or devising refined tortures of suspense. The thing endlessly clearing its throat: glottal stops, clips and clicks, the clatter of film stock through the projector—*The Thing*, an extraterrestrial mystery stiff and impervious, figure of ice. Or the Thing of Marvel comic books, man of block and stone, the blind girl's love, clobberin' time. And that other incredible figure of the early sixties, the green-glowing Hulk, monster double of a genius nuclear physicist, a phosphorescent outlaw in ragged jeans who couldn't stand to see wrong and splashed his rage in bursts and stars across the panels. As a monster of color, he spun the wheels of the cultural tone-organ, and most wonderful were the panels where his scruffy, quasi-Frankenstein figure rose over the treetops flying. In those moments, the Hulk, shining with his radium-clock power, broke loose altogether, incredible not because of his atomic-driven metamorphosis from Bruce Banner to Hulk or even because of his just-cause anger, but because still trailing his rags and tatters he struck off into the air with one fist raised like an avenging angel though all the while he looked a devil.

"The Creeper," an Oliver Nelson composition on the 1965 *Monster* album, which also included movie and television themes: *Goldfinger*, *The Munsters*, and *Bewitched*. The home style of old Blue Note albums like *Chicken Shack* was updated in the Verve label package of cover tunes and broad jokes: *Who's Afraid of Virginia Woolf* offering Smith in wolf's-head mask, *Respect* in snow-white martial-arts gear taking on the Hammond. Oliver Nelson plays the melody on alto, the organ lines exquisite product, swift and ruthless as Sonny Stitt, sassy and sanctified as Cannonball Adderly, in certain phases as passionately systematic as early Coltrane. Along the mellow road of mile-long legato runs, skidding phrases are turned around, they hit back against themselves, the percussion setting catches up the notes with a snapped, crepitant edge. Driving home from the factory in happy paycheck traffic, coming down the hill to the main junction among telephone lines and colored signals, traffic lights and neon signs, brand names and billboards, the machinery of the world operational, switched on and ready to go. Monster, you could gobble it up, suck the fat off its bones, lick the grease off your fingers watching a little wink or blink inside the air, the flash of appetite itself.

Funk, grease, soul—a long string of organ players following him, Johnny "Hammond" Smith, Brother Jack McDuff, Jimmy McGriff, Shirley Scott, Don Patterson, Lonnie "Liston" Smith, Charles Earland, by turns lush and luscious, smoked or stunk, though not approaching the rushed velocity, the hard stutter of the bass pedals, and Smith's sound ultimately clean, almost flattened out, pure feed, not until Larry Young does anybody achieve such cold in the middle of running hot. In later years, the Varitone electric saxophone in the hands of Eddie Harris or Sonny Stitt approximated such a sound, much derided by jazz critics as inhuman, voiceless, a shameful mechanization. It stripped away timbre and reduced the sound to gesture, style without a body, ideal as the Moog and with the same naked rise of transistorized exhilaration to it. Bodiless jazz—perhaps a monstrous thing, counterclocked, a minuscule slide inside its gears, a rogue centrifugal breaking out in free play. Riding the tracks of the bebop idiom and messing with it, diverging, merging, the simulacrum of a perpetual-motion machine that doesn't give a shit about the sound of music anymore and glories in signal and pulse, consuming its own friction.

Monster wouldn't be the selection for classic Smith on Verve (*I Got My Mojo Workin'* or *Respect* would be more likely, or *The Dynamic Duo* with Wes Montgomery). There's a casually Gothic strain, with an up-tempo "Gloomy Sunday," a brightly menacing "Goldfinger," a hard-swinging "St. James Infirmary"; and there are the sweeps, the rolling repetitions, the feel underneath of a broad veering traction, the thrilling of a super-harp fingered at every stop. Signal, skin, and surface: like Goldfinger's girl, like the ghostly smoke of jinx. Everything's running over itself, offering itself, inciting itself, legs pumping high in fearful delight, the riffs fast and heart-beating like the hyperalertness of a marijuana paranoia: I'm spooked, man. The thing is a fucking monster.

The Hammond: organ with too much power in it, roaring up at the slightest touch of a key. Outcast in thick underwood, the monster roaring in travail. A tentacle reaches around a corner, the creeper leaps out from a dark spot on the road he'll always come back to again. The cover of the *Monster* album is dominated by John Henry's remarkable photo, a devil's mask in black and red made by a process that must have involved staining, painting, and overlaid exposures. It's a Rohrshach devil, in one respect saying only one thing, that the album is state-of-the-art 1965, flippantly hip, and in another saying many things, too many, the monster's face revolving through buttocks and vaginas, through rats and embryos and holstered guns, through two big fat hens facing off over the devil's head which is also them and also Jimmy Smith slitting his eyes inside a flight of wings, until the whole damn thing is flashing Op-Art style and escaping within its caves and folds, monster the running skin glowing with emblems and signs, monster the shedding of signs and skins, the howl and the shout not rage not anger not pain but shaking loose.

1966: Incense, Herbs, and Oils

Where was the shop—the blue storefront, the smoke-stained window, the words *Incense, Herbs, Oils* scripted in fading gold on the glass offering equipment for handling spirits and lovers and enemies? It might have been Peoria Street, Newberry, Thirteenth or Fourteenth, somewhere in the old Maxwell Street market, all of those buildings and the very streets gone now, converted to athletic fields for the University of Illinois at Chicago.

Maybe a few letters leaving a clue, tag end of a street name in the cover photo of the first Paul Butterfield album, in front of the shop Mike Bloomfield, Elvin Bishop, and the rest of the group young and scruffy, grease on the longish hair and sport jackets without ties, sunglasses and cigarettes, the original blues brothers. The Eastern European Jewish immigrants had moved out of the neighborhood; it was mostly black, but their sons had come back to it. In the segregated world of Chicago in the sixties, Maxwell Street was the rare place where the color of your skin didn't much matter. Shop, buy, sell—seemingly everything imaginable was displayed on door-and-sawhorse tables lining the streets, arrayed on blankets spread on the sidewalks and draped across the hoods of cars, or more or less dumped in piles on the bare ground with a casual confidence that a buyer's eye would sort it out. In that hotbed of exchange it didn't matter what street you came from or what race claimed you. Among the press of the crowd you were simplified to a creature of hands and feet and money in your pocket like a gambler's, charged with the question of what you'd spend, how you'd spend, what would be the bargain of the day, and later the shopping bag swinging from your arm with its secret weight, or the newly grown limb of whatever hammer or lamp or chair you were triumphantly carrying home with you.

Then you'd carefully negotiate a path through the shoppers, trying to avoid bumping into anyone. If you did—if you trod the heel of the man in front of you, himself still empty-handed and searching for his own buy of the morning, he would most likely stop dead, turn around to face you with a hard look. You were already apologizing, apologizing again, and that would be enough, it would simply be over. The territory around you was no longer the streets and landmarks of a neighborhood but just the modest space around your own body: how far your arm swung, how long your stride. You learned to be humble. And as you walked away with your purchase you knew that whatever bargain you'd managed—even if you'd achieved the Market dream of the steal, the stand where the guy had no idea what he was selling, he might as well have been giving it away for nothing—the bargain wasn't as important as the fact that you'd made a transaction. Along with all the others walking the street, you were a sort of anonymous hero, having affirmed the life of the thing, taken your part in the Market. When you brought the money out of your pocket, a stack of quarters or a bill held out flat so the transfer of the object of sale over to you and the price of it paid into the vendor's hand were synchronized, nearly simultaneous, it was like your hand was making an offering of your own eye. With that avid eye, you'd come, you'd seen, you'd conquered or been conquered. It was as though you'd become all eye, a Cyclops gazing dazzled into the sun while counting off his flock, contemplating the treasures of his domain. Of course, there was always the other side: the sense that even as you clutched your bag or lifted proudly your hammer or your chair, or even as you thrilled over an unbelievable steal, the story of it all running through your mind as you walked faster approaching Halsted or Roosevelt, the bus stop or the car parked somewhere near the Soo Line viaducts, there might be someone in the crowd laughing over what a sucker you'd been. Pity the fool—there was a guy on the next corner who was selling the same damn thing for half the price; last week he couldn't give the stuff away but look at that joker, he turned over good money for it.

Maxwell Street—the bargain, the deal and the steal, the business of race temporarily dissolved in a dance of raw exchange. In one respect, though, there your skin mattered more, because you weren't contained with those supposedly of your own kind behind one side or the other of a territorial line. Whatever the makeup of the neighborhood, on Sunday morning it was the Market, and in the bright sun you felt the plain and newly pleasurable exposure of your face to a world of others, though mostly those others weren't particularly concerned about you, and you needn't worry very much about them. Along those streets, cars crawling through and trying to make way, people walking almost shoulder to shoulder, heel to heel, you could feel strangely alone but in a way that had nothing to do with the alienation of the man in the crowd. You'd stumbled into a different sort of place. In the midst of the anonymous press of bodies you attained a certain height as well as a humility, your walking through indifference and hurry and the sweat smell of the man in front of you making you feel your skin wasn't so much a container freighted with meanings and desires as it was a surface where things touched you in the same way they touched your eye, where the world was not so much a collection of objects as it was a concourse of strokes and smokes and oils, bodies and airs and spirits that could catch and cling, charm and bewitch you.

Where was the street: Peoria, Newberry, Fourteenth? Sometimes early on a Sunday morning, seven or eight o'clock, the signs would appear for an instant incomprehensible, last flags of a sinking ship, the city grid overwhelmed by the market crowd, sidewalk cottonwoods and trees of heaven in the alleys fluttering down leaves and the hawkers' calls from every direction, *I got your gloves special today; Apples, apples, apples*; the universal cry of *Pick 'em out, Pick 'em out*. Often enough the calls were incomprehensible too. The message would be for a select group, those shoppers who had an ear for the particular item—unless I had a mind to it, how would I discern among all the shuffle and noise that the chubby Polish guy leaning on the hood of his station wagon was really calling *Brooms* and not something like *Spoons* or something I'd never heard of, something that sounded impossible—*Rooms* or *Moons*. Among the market stands, there might even be a seller with an item only one person in the crowd could possibly want or even understand. Maybe an item destined for one person in all the world, one person in all of time and history. In those calls there was a sound of things fateful and ephemeral—what was here today and gone tomorrow, the last and only chance never to come round again. At times, I wished I could be at the Market every day, every hour, so I wouldn't miss that call even though I heard well enough the mocking tone in the hawker's cry, that bluff and mimicry of the buyer's desire. I had no idea what I would hear, it would be something unimaginable, maybe a word I could barely decipher but once I did, I would have arrived at the point of a transaction that would change me forever or maybe not change me at all but crystallize in a single instant everything I was looking for.

My Uncle Joe must have had a similar feeling in those days. It was imperative that we arrive at the Market early; he blasted the horn of his Chevelle in front of my parents' house at six thirty on a Sunday morning, annoying the neighbors, and if I wasn't out in less than five minutes he was on his way, no time to wait. Even six thirty was running late for him; without bothering about me, he could have been there already. He tried to make up the lost time, heavy on the gas and running a red every now and then, in a matter of minutes reaching the Stevenson Expressway and then the Ryan to the Eighteenth Street exit, no radio playing and not a word to me until we had parked in his usual spot and were walking through the darkness of a viaduct from which we'd emerge into the thick of the crowd. He must have been relieved on those Sundays when for one reason or another I wasn't able to go with him. He could get there as early as he pleased, even before sunrise if he wanted. He could catch the vendors first putting out their wares, have an advantage since, as legend had it, the first customer of the day was given the best deal, it was good luck.

My closest uncle, my godfather, the uncle whose birthday was the same day as George Washington's and close to mine, Joe was the big one among the brothers, taller and with more bulk than my father or the oldest, Johnny. In his childhood years he'd been notorious for his capacity for food and especially for stealing the fresh milk in those days delivered first thing in the morning, when it was still partly dark outside. He sneaked out of the house and made a tour of the neighbors' steps up and down the block, drinking down every bottle he found. He came home with a mouth licked with rich cream, happy and sleepy. They called him Pig. Later, his equally extravagant capacity for labor earned him the name Bull. My dad helped him to land a job at the Santa Fe yard at Forty-seventh Street and Joe worked so hard and so continuously—he used to do an entire trailer-train car, normally the task of three men, by himself—that my dad was

let go while they kept his brother on. He was crazy, my dad said, Joe was
go go go.

Joe and my Aunt Jeanette didn't have any children of their own, so I
was privileged, the godson and the favored nephew. I mowed the lawn of
their long yard on Kilbourn Street and was paid handsomely for it, my
aunt spoiling me too with cold drinks, Seven-Ups, urging me regularly to
stop and take a break. Inside the house it was cool and dark, the blinds
usually drawn against the sun, the pantry and the cellar and the attic
stocked with all kinds of food and treats. Much of it was in tins without
labels or in damaged packages, fruit and chocolate and cookies of all
kinds, the pantry at my Uncle Joe's a place where I could forage at will
and myself become pig. After the job was done I'd sit in the front room in
front of a huge dish of candy, chocolate stars and nonpareils, a book from
the glass-doored cabinet on the table in front of me and the song of my
uncle's canary whistling back and forth through the house. The bird was
named Micky and there had been a series of them, dashes of bright yellow
and orange trilling loudly with the songbird record my uncle played for
their instruction until an untimely accident occurred involving the swinging door to the living room which Joe sometimes closed without remembering that the birds liked to perch on top of it. He would mourn the lost
bird for a while but there would soon be another Micky as if it had never
happened. The new bird would choose that same place atop the door, fluttering the same way to the kitchen and back, singing out its life along with
the record or urged on by the chirps and trills of Joe himself.

The books in the cabinet were mostly about fishing, along with the
stacks of *Consumer Reports* my uncle studied, researching products
and prices. *The Racing Form* and *Midnight*, an Enquirer-style tabloid,
stayed in the kitchen on a magazine rack. My dad joked that Joe would
believe anything—for him, a breathless *Midnight* proclaiming "Woman
Gives Birth to Frog" possessed the same authority as a sober *Consumer
Reports* evaluation of tire performance. My usual picks from the cabinet were books my Aunt Jeanette frowned upon my reading and that
my Uncle laughed about—dismissively or defensively, I couldn't tell.
"Let the kid see it," he'd say. "It won't hurt him." So I delved into John
George Holman's *Pow-Wows, or the Long Lost Friend* and the *Sixth
and Seventh Books of Moses,* both of them yellowed paperbacks whose
pages crumbled their flavor into the chocolate I was eating. They were

books of spells and magic, the *Pow-Wows* with practical charms for curing warts and winning at cards and overcoming enemies, the Moses book with serious incantations for raising angels and demons, pentagrams compassed by mysterious Hebrew letters and on one of the pages a strange dark glyph of a serpent crowned with stars.

I'd been up late the night before, watching a movie and then reading, and had barely made it out to the car, Joe impatiently gunning the engine as I ran out the door. Things had been changing between us, Joe and I now heading our own ways as soon as we reached the Market and only meeting up a few hours later when it was time to go home. I no longer followed him on his rounds and he didn't insist, having understood that I wanted to go off my own and probably quite content to let me.

On that August morning it was heating up fast, and along every street there were kids selling sodas from coolers with blocks of ice. I had my orientation, Dorothy's clothing stand where I could always go back and wait for Joe since he was a regular there. I set off to look around, smoke a couple of cigarettes, a pack of Salems in my pocket Joe either didn't notice or didn't care about. I was wearing my usual clothes, white Levis and black suede shoes, a Banlon polo shirt. The shirt was made of a sort of stretch fabric that I guess was beige yet suggested ugly bare flesh. I would have preferred black but the thing had been on sale, one of my parents' economies.

My own prowl would be nothing like tagging along with my Uncle Joe. There were vendors who had known him for years and who hailed him from halfway down the block when they spotted him. Years earlier he'd been in the junk business himself—he'd even changed his name to Meyers in keeping with what he believed was a Jewish dominion over the scrap-metal trade. The vendors always had a special stash under the counter they'd been saving just for him, and usually whatever it was, Joe would buy it. My Aunt Jeanette complained that the house was overflowing, but there was always room for more, as Joe saw it, and half the time the thing he bought was ostensibly for her—a dress, a painting, silverware, all kinds of lingerie and stockings, one time an expensive mantel clock that was given a place of honor in the living room and whose chimes became an accompaniment to the songs of the Mickies.

An obsession with books had first drawn me to the Market, but for the time being I'd had my fill. I suppose I was becoming more interested in the book of the world. Incense, herbs, and oils: the spelling of everything and everybody in motion down those streets. With Joe, the tour of the market had been a mad rush, punctuated by the greetings of his old pals and the glad buying of the latest gift, after a while his hands clutching bags and objects sticking out in all directions like bouquets of crumpled flowers. He was a prime target for filching or robbery but no one ever had any luck with him. Once, as he was walking back to his car, two men in the viaduct had tried to fell him with a lead pipe; he'd fought back fiercely and driven them off, never letting go of his merchandise.

On my own that morning I took a slower course. Where I walked down Peoria, the man I thought of as the record guy was playing 45s at full volume through a big radio speaker, the bass buzzing and distorted in the heated air like something desperate was trapped inside there. The music was gospel and especially blues—Junior Wells, Little Milton, Jimmy Reed, a rack of singles on Chess and VeeJay. It was he who had taught me the exception to the general rule of haggling. The 45s cost one dollar, same as the store, and that was it. He had just about chased me off from his stand when I tried to offer him less. "You don't know what the hell this is," he'd said, veiling the box of singles with his hand. And the music confirmed him though it took a while to hear. On a spring morning a month after I'd turned thirteen, I was walking past and it wasn't so much my ear that heard as my legs that felt it. A drag on my stride, making me slow down, making me consider my feet. They seemed weird things, bearing my weight across the pavement, shod bones, clumsy hooves. I stood near his stand guzzling my soda, a kid who didn't care. The bass thudding like a thick heart through the bare speaker without a grille. The harsh spinning traction of the electric guitar with the solo lines pulled out of their stitch and sewn back again needle sharp. A gruff, lowering vocal with a pressure inside it like wind, like bad weather. The parts didn't sound like they fit, a delay between them so that each seemed to be plunging along its own track. A forward motion driving apart and trying to catch itself up but never making it. Still lumbering, lurching along, its own skin clinging to it like the tangle of jelly I felt inside my legs. In the song a voice that wasn't hawking any wares but only calling out:

> I've got a good mind to give up living
> and go shopping instead.

To pick out me a tombstone
and be pronounced dead.

The rest of it had to do with the letter a woman left on the bed and the heartbreaking fact that she would never be coming back. I didn't know what the hell it was. I only quivered at its touch, like a stray dog I sniffed it along the warm air of the morning where the odors of the Market floated. Smoke of sausages grilling almost black on an oil-drum fire. Knife-stuck globes of cantaloupes and honeydews on a pickup tailgate. A slop bucket spilling out on the ground, festooned with wrappers and string and rinds and bottles. And the unforgettable human smell of the Market: sharp onion stink and a feverish sweat, as if your own body were another species of food, another slop bucket.

The record guy knew me now as a sort of regular though he didn't seem to like me much. Even paying him full price I had the feeling it wasn't enough. Today, I walked by without stopping. Seven o'clock, an August Sunday morning: down Fourteenth Street streams of people blocking the cars crawling through, the cars stopping the flow and people surrounding them like a mob of looters. A wide-bodied red Pontiac with boxes tied to the roof was stopped in the intersection, exhaust pipe smoking black, the engine sending waves of heat off the hood. Somebody crossing gave it a fist on the trunk, somebody swore steadily into the driver's window in passing. On those streets there were rarely any police even though the Fillmore District Station was close by. The driver ignored the insults. At that speed it was as if he wasn't really driving anyway, it scarcely seemed his car, he was a sort of passenger or attendant, by turns exasperated and apologetic. He waved a dollar out the window and the girl from the stand brought him a soda. The fan belt screeched and the car jumped forward a few feet, rumbling.

Closer to Maxwell, near the heart of the Market, the crowd increased, the cars still moving through. The only way to walk without stumbling into someone or having someone stumble into you was to drift yourself like a smoke bending its trail. Everything was always about to move, everything was always about to come to a standstill. The stench of the idling cars and the smell of soaking summer sweat oiled the air. I was looking for nothing, for whatever. Next to a fenced-off lot, a group of men happily shouted back and forth, having an early beer. A white rooster marched out a pattern across the sidewalk below a flatbed stacked with caged chickens, crowing over his territory. The shoppers mobbed the clothing stores and the stands, the searchers after watches and jewelry five deep in Diamond Alley, a thin man nearby flashing wrists and arms ringed to the elbow with metal. I could buy a heavy ring with a glowing stone that looked like an emerald or a ruby and make my wishes on it. I could buy a switchblade stiletto with a silver hilt to protect me from my foes. I could buy whatever booty was offered, all the truck of burglars and boosters and thieves, though I had learned after a while that most of it was fake.

Farther down the street, I saw a gap in the crowd. I had known I would see the man eventually; often I wondered whether the track I followed through the Market was determined by a desire to avoid him or a desire to seek him out. Since I had been a little kid, trailing through the crowd while my father held his hand behind his back for me to grab if I was frightened, the man had haunted me. Wherever I walked, I was shadowed by a feeling that I was about to come face to face with him as he scraped and rowed down the street, pounding hard on the pavement with his wooden sticks. He was an older man, my uncle's or my father's age. A salt-and-pepper beard, a mouth with red nervous lips always licking, an expression compounded of prideful anger and abject fear. His chest and arms were muscular, powerful, his big hands roped with veins as he propelled the wooden cart in which he rode low to the ground. He kept a folded newspaper alongside him, which he made into a visor sometimes to shade himself from the sun. The stumps of his legs were swaddled in white cotton, strips cut from an undershirt.

I knew I was wrong, I was forgetting he was a human being like me, but I reeled away from the sight of him as if getting a whiff of an absolute horror. I saw not him but a naked blank exposed in the middle of things, and in that blank not merely a sense of how things went wrong, but worse, a sense of how everything kept on, life itself the horror. Even without any legs to carry you upright through the world you still ate and shit and talked and hurt and raged. Even in the lowliest bucket of slops that seemed pure waste, someone or something would find nourishment, a way to thrive, eagerly lapping it up, hatching and feeding, the world itself a monster smacking its chops over the living and the dead.

I felt pity, too, but such feelings seemed meaningless, insulting. He had a power that made everyone get out of his way, a voice aggressive and hectoring, hoarse from shouting. If you touched him you knew he'd probably kill you with a knife he had ready there or choke you with the force of his bare hands.

My uncle once told me: drop a quarter into his cart and you'll have good luck.

People continued pressing into the street, from Newberry to Halsted now almost a solid mass, impassable though restless, moving, a thick heat building up with no release, the body stink of a greedy giant. A man was urinating against a wall in the alley with a hawker right on his heels showing off a glittering armful. He stuck out one hand to have a look at a watch, and with the other finished his pissing. Go shopping instead. It was as though I wanted something from the world but knew already that everything that was offered was garbage, worthless. All those treasures and goods being sold only proved that there was nothing really worth having: if there were, why was there always a person so eager to sell, why was there always another person equally eager to buy as if it was impossible ever to be satisfied and have enough?

To pick out me a tombstone and be pronounced dead—I sang it under my breath, trying to imitate B. B. King's reading of the last word, the vowels stretched and broken and doubled. From looking for nothing in particular I turned to looking at every single thing, each item offered in piles or stacks or heaps or jumbles over the ground. A rusty wrench with a length of pipe still clamped inside its jaws. A pair of wooden mousetraps nested on a clean pink blanket. Trailing sockets and wires, a television picture tube with the word GOOD scrawled across the screen in Magic Marker. On one table a spill of hundreds of flashlight batteries, along with a skeletal wire and bulb to test their juice. Some of the piles were indistinguishable from the trash the vendors and shoppers left behind in the street. At one point I delved into a discarded miscellany of rags and boxes, seeing damaged but promising items in there—the black rim of a record without a sleeve, a water-stained book. A boy younger than I was came along and asked me what I thought I was doing. I said it was just garbage, but he insisted it was his. He stood there ready to fight for it.

The man was wandering from stand to stand offering words, gesticulating and then being mollified or distracted, moving on to the next. A skinny guy, a shambling sort of walk like he was lost, asking for directions. He was bold, though, walking right inside the vendors' zone, behind the stands and up to the windows of the cars, the back doors of vans, places where people escaped the crowd and took their breaks, places where money was counted and stashed. He was waved off casually, sent on his way, a man in a cowboy hat selling stacked cans of Pennzoil watching him go, laughing with his buddies. A woman trailed uncertainly behind, his girlfriend, I guessed. She waved back as if to say don't worry about it.

The first thing I noticed about him was his eyes—they were reddened, bloodshot. I thought he might be high but wasn't so sure, it could just as well have been weeping and moaning, a terrible thing that had happened to him. When he stopped in front of me, the girlfriend hovering behind, I anticipated being asked for money, a request I usually handled by saying I had nothing on me, my defense that I was only a kid.

"You got matches?" he said instead, his face close to mine, his breath blowing a sour wind that might have been from wine, might have been just his own heat.

"Yeah sure," I said, the easy question making me feel generous, my hand going to the pocket of the shirt where I had my Salems.

"No, no," he said, and pushed down my hand. "I said do you got matches."

I looked at the girlfriend but she was gazing down the street as if yearning to get away. She attempted to move him along, pulling at his shirt.

"These are matches," I said, showing the book again.

"Goddamit, I said do you got matches."

"What?"

"*Matches, matches, matches,*" he sang louder, moving back now and swinging a wiry arm as if he was winding up for a punch, the repetition of the word slurring and distorting it, so it seemed to no longer match itself.

And then I understood that what had been so far a simple exchange, the word *matches* to be answered by the book of matches in my hand, had suddenly turned impossible.

"Sure," I said. "I got a mattress," giving my voice as tough a sound as I could manage. "So what?"

I was still hoping to get the joke, grasp what code or reference was involved. A mattress? It mixed up with the song lyric about shopping for a tombstone, my thought itself buried under a blank slab. I looked for a clue in his face but he was only serious, aggrieved, and becoming angrier by the second.

"You got a mattress?" he said again.

"Yes," I said, trying to move away but afraid of what he might do.

"Well then go home and get it."

"I can't do that." I knew I should have laughed him off as the others had, but instead I found myself having wild thoughts of traveling across the city, carrying the thing on my back across streets and empty lots. I imagined the shiny quilting on the bare part, the sheets trailing from it, myself appearing an awkward lumbering creature without a head or a face, my legs caving under the weight. I would deliver it to him right there and I supposed he would lie down on it with his girlfriend. Or maybe I was the one who was supposed to be laid out, subject of a bizarre ritual.

"*I told you to go home and get it.*" Now he was shouting, pointing off in an indefinite direction—the projects to the west across Morgan, the bus stop on Eighteenth Street, the sky, the sun.

I said leave me alone. He grabbed the pale flesh-colored neck of the polo shirt and started to twist it around my neck. I pushed him away but he took hold again as if he imagined he would pull me right out of my skin. I stared at him as he twisted once more, seeing every detail of his face—he was probably not much older than I was, maybe nineteen, twenty, and his skin was a dark brown, roughened and freckled by being out in the sun and the streets. There was something haughty and disdainful in his gaze, as if he found the smell of me unpleasant. His mouth tightened hard into a grim line, his reddened eyes lighted up manic and insistent.

I saw that it was impersonal, it had nothing to do with me, yet it was immensely personal. Out of all the others he'd approached that morning, I was the one who had to answer to him.

One of the cowboy-hat guys called across the street, warning him off. He let me go, looking confused. He circled for another minute. Then he wandered away. The girlfriend said she was sorry. He was out of his head.

To pick out me a tombstone—my legs felt weak, halfway down in the ground, and I supposed everyone in the street had witnessed my humiliation. I felt wronged, not by his hand or his words or his touch but by the sheer impossibility he'd posed, all the rules of exchange breaking down. You got a mattress: what was that? It was monstrous, that idea of something nonnegotiable, an exorbitant claim for which he'd found in me the chance though perfect addressee. I had the thought I'd never feel at home again, home suddenly a place fatally compromised and tainted, not really mine anymore. I imagined the roof of my parents' house open to a sky and a weather where anything could happen, mattresses levitating out of the bedrooms and tombstones sprouting in the front yard, the guy and his girlfriend lurking there, making incomprehensible demands or just wandering in and out at will. As though my world would become a vast open-air cinema where reels would clatter and shadows run and lights flash and flicker, an unaccountable event about to happen and my gaze captured by the cuts and dissolves and trackings across the screen, *you got a mattress* the aperture through which I absorbed the bleak fact that to live meant to wander everywhere, looking, even when you'd forgotten what desire drove you in search of a bargain, flying back and forth until one day an indifferent door banged shut on you.

I could have made for Dorothy's stand, waited out the hour until my uncle came back. I would have the comfort of sitting there among people I knew, somebody bringing me a cold soda while I told the story of the mattress guy. But I was sure they'd either laugh over it or cast it as an instructive drama, and that I couldn't take.

Instead I started walking, back into the press of the market crowd, into the very thing for which a hot hate was flowering inside me like a poison herb. As I headed again for the center of the Market, every face became the face of an enemy. The limping old guy contentedly carrying a wooden box of nails, whistling to himself as if he was the luckiest man in town. The lipsticked woman struggling with a bundle of glossy magazines wrapped with twine. A sweaty white kid like me wandering through the crowd empty-handed, trying to look wise. We were all dirty, grubbing creatures, rioting in our own stink. I was overheated, stumbling, but I wouldn't buy another soda because I couldn't bear the thought of the hand that would mechanically pass it to me in return for the greasy coin from my pocket, couldn't bear the thought of how the liquid would be sucked into me, laving down my throat and sloshing its sweet juice into my stomach.

The avid set of a haggling mouth. The raucous trolling of a hawker. The stubby fingers of a grasping hand stashing merchandise into a bag. Faces like the masks of a monster feeding itself through them, all the goods mixing in a vast belly, a churning sickening factory. I felt the bitterness of being born, of being flesh—pick out me a tombstone because it was there you could rest, the cool of the marble your mattress, nothing of your body left and only the carving across it of a word, a name, pronounced dead.

Dullix ix ux: Yea, you can't come over Pontio ... I chanted in my mind the words from the *Pow-Wows* book, a spell for overcoming your enemies. I might have called upon the spirits of the cabalists to devastate the unholy earth, to cleanse it with water and fire. But I didn't feel any spirits answering. There was only a fever through my body, the cars and the crowd pushing, pushing, until it seemed there was nowhere left to move, no path anywhere.

It carried me along, not even a drift anymore but an immersion, a swim. I felt among the crowd the gazing and searching, the incessant swiveling motion of a thousand heads. I felt among the crowd the quickening frantic rhythm of a thousand hearts. A multitude of words spelling out their chains, a multitude of deals in the making. In that sea of sweat, that pooling of greeds, I helplessly fled like a little child from a monster inside whose mouth he is already being chewed up, consumed. I wandered into a memory of the inscriptions on the hide of the cabalistic snake in the Moses book, the star-jewels that crowned its head, the magic writing hatching inside every available margin and space. For an instant I felt my skin was made of those same indecipherable marks, a skin not just the flesh on my bones but the surfacing skin of the world from which I was being born together with the others as though breathed with their body smoke and sweated through their body heat. As if inside an impossible crystal, outside all proportion, there was a monster with whose legs I shambled, with whose feet I stumbled, with whose tongue I tasted an herb harsh and sweet.

1976: Kirkatron

Roland Kirk out of Ohio, Columbus, green land and the rivers, the railroad bridges and the burial mounds in the humid dark. Later, Rahsaan Roland Kirk: like so many things, the name came to him in a dream.

Frantic. Chicago in the fifties, the crowded streets, the cars and buses and trains, contagion of blasting horns, one blaring hot and the others right away taking it up, short taps and gruff toots and then long-drawn wails, the sound traveling down the line of traffic as though the least idea that motion might come to a stop was unbearable, an insult and a crime, chains of angry shouts now and the revving, rumbling engines, stink blown out in the air like an incense of oil, the monster-sound spreading in an ephemeral plague, he heard it wandering back and forth between noise and song, in that interval he too felt the itch in the throat, the press and the swell, the need to roar.

(In the movie: the creature made man but whom the master then abhors. He can't bear the sight of the patchwork thing showing all its threads, a thing that isn't covered but instead is exposed by its own skin. The flower and the little girl and the running stream. The mob of villagers hunting him down, an abomination. Trapped in the burning windmill, the monster frantic, keening and wailing, perishing finally with a harrowing cry that skins together its sound with the roar of the consuming flames.)

Chicago: the Loop and Bronzeville and Sixty-third, space to move but at the same time a multiplication in that space of tracks, paths, trajectories—room to trip and stumble, flat on your face; room to bump, slide, and collide. Excuse me, sir. Where the hell you think you're going? Hey buddy watch your step. Move.

Frantic. Everything moving, hotel to rooming-house, doors slamming down the hall all times of the day and night, bang up the window it's hot, bang down the window it's cold, Drexel Boulevard there was sheeting rain, there was feathering snow, there was wind rattling against the panes and there was stalled summer air, the city soaking its bones, the sky gone deaf. At the bottom of the hottest night of the year, unbearable stop of the room, burn box from ceiling to floor, not the slightest touch of a breeze on the shade, stifling mound of a premature burial. Four o'clock in the morning on the Jeffrey bus and the clarinet without a case, in Jackson Park a little wind off the lake and across the lawns the groves and grooves of breathing wood, the hawthorns and elms leafing a green silence, on the Boulevard and the Drive the city running its ghosts and he was keeping the monster awake, nothing to be buried there but all to come bright out of the dark. To come bright in the angle of the shadow dance where he walked like he was staggering, to come bright out of a shadow where for an instant he forgot everything and in the low throating of the clarinet heard the voice of what was coming, a sound like a swimming skin of sun tiding over a night-black wave.

Ira Sullivan presents, album on Argo. Andrew Hill, the Freeman brothers. In Chicago, plenty of work. But at times a silence from the audience, comments in the front row or backstage. Learn to play one horn right instead of sticking two in your mouth. Somebody messing with him, sound of a hand in front of his face waving, a shoe across the path of his cane. *Freak show shit* he heard in a junky whisper one night at Club De Lisa, and though he was blind he could see the smug whiskered face, cool with being high and hanging out with musicians, sure of his fix, fixed on his for sure, for sure; certainly, my man.

Not cool, those sighs, those grunts, those ejaculations when he was slinging a horn aside, taking up another; or coming off a double or triple barreling, heavy ordnance, the vibration there like being in the middle of Ellington's bandstand or Basie's tenor section, shouting for joy inside a hard throttle of delight. Talked to himself in between because he needed to hear his own throat and the hot sob in his voice, body flank from which to next attack, and maybe talking to the others, too, commentary, defense, exhortation. Going down deep for breath, for wind, surfacing like a whale. Had to vent, blow his top. In the suit, necklaced with horns, slogging through buckets of sweat. A fat clown with big wet feet. In the wind and the whirlwind, where were all you all?

Sweat in buckets. Standing inside a river of it. Around the river, a fire like Chicago burning down, O'Leary's cow. A panicked stallion trying to break out of the stable, whinnying in terror and rage, aware of the fatuity of its imprisonment: all it would take was a hand, the merest finger, to raise the latch and set him free. At the last, a tearing bellow, a sound itself like a whipping flame. A burning church, the heat cooking the varnish off the pews and lead-fuming the stained-glass windows, images fogging and shattering and the pulpit catching in a roar together with the frantic voices of the men and the women and the children in a scream sermon, hell hymn.

The truth shall make you free. The ones who raised the glass, the ones like someone in love, even the ones hung cool in junk who thought they could safely disappear. Furnaced all. Without their faces their words their clothes, excoriated, flayed, boned out to smell of food on the mouth and sweat under armpits and fond-self stench of the crotch. Sound of breath inside the throat and down in the lungs, how the holies of the air were welcomed, how the fogged evils warded off. Sound of the skin in its catching and rustling and folding under clothes, touch of the skin in its radiance and its obscurity, its secret heats and colds.

Up in the air they're nothing but skins, no more than a disposition of surfaces. They hang like drapes, fluttering and flapping and freaking against and across and among one another. Skins palpable, impalpable—sometimes a greasy jelly hoping to gobble another and go quivering on to the next score. Sometimes foamed on a shaky wave, bobbing and swimming and eager for overwhelming. Sometimes riding in air, and while the eye wanders in its sleep, the ear stays always awake, even in dream. Furors, cries, songs.

The ones who brought him ears. Friends, Romans, and clergymen, I only ask for a loan and not a gift. And in return pay you a pearl of great price. In the middle of tumult and noise, Babsy shrieking and Donna Mae getting pissed off, Jimmy talking up another woman and his man Sonny laying out the last bill from his wallet, he could hear the sound of listening itself. Like a dream drifting into him, a crazy rubbery cartoon of a huge ear sitting on a wooden chair. All skin and folds and orifices and caving echoing canals, aura of the naked and obscene about it, organ of an ultra sex. Crossing its legs, contriving a smile or a pout or an arch frown, every motion provocative, revealing, inviting, the tiny follicles an exquisite susceptible fringe, don't you want me, want me. And the dream-coupling of the lascivious ears: tease over porch and vestibule, the room in the back in the steamy dark, long peeled stocking and the subtle convulsing hammering across a sort of opening where what you called bodies was only what happened between the stretch, the tract and traction of blanked trembling skins, echo attending echo.

Audience—noise of the world, the traffic horns, the huffing buses and the swooping cars, the gurgling drains and the doors banging and sighing and the footfalls, the footfalls: soft shoe, scraped heel, glide and march and stride and stumble and stomp. The crowd in the seats, the talk and the laughter, snap of the match and the sucked smokes, clink of glasses, sloshed liquor. Audience: a solid wall, a roar: don't interrupt me when I'm speaking; listen, listen to me. Haw haw haw.

And audience—wasn't it also a perfume and a fragrance? Her nostrils flared as she heard his words. Insulted, he sniffed haughtily. Her scent intoxicated his senses. The sweating jubilant crowd called for an encore.

Smell of oil in the bore, clean edge of brass, fresh wood of the reed.

Freak show shit. Words trying to smear his fingers, trying to slide inside his throat, trying to cheese his wind. Placard on his chest: Blind Boy from Ohio. Amazing Negro Plays at Once Three Saxophones.

Roar that shit down. Turn out the fat lady to plop herself on a giant mattress under which the needling bugs are crushed and around which her gargantuan lovers deliver crates of candy and flowers. Turn out the two-headed cow to a double pasture where she grazes on sweet new grass and then turns and munches on big fluffy clouds that sometimes look like two-headed cows. Go into business for yourself. Your own owner, your own shop. Your own company, corporation. Head of heads, cap of your capital. Branches and networks, distribution points. Dispatches and subsidiaries and local offices.

Rahsaan, Inc. Squid cloud blinding and bewildering. Escape, flight, a thing that bladders with air, propelled and propelling by virtue of its hollowing, its interval. Solvency, insolvency.

What he builds. Fingers that run and crowd and cluster, fingers that grow themselves into candelabra, into fans, into webs. Mahogany wood, structural steel, rocket titanium.

What he builds. Throat. A tower through which an elevator rises giddy in its ascent, through which an elevator drops vertiginous to the lowest subfloor. Gears and cables humming and whirring, odor of power, every friction smoothed with oil. Top of the Empire State or the Prudential, the view over the city. A clearing in the air, down below and far off the murmurous traffic, the crowds and the streets. In an almost-silence the infiltrating vibration, the echoing yen, the need to roar.

(In the movie: Godzilla playing with trains, power lines crackling around his spiky head, airplanes weaving and diving. The frantic crowds trapped in the carriages, their terrified cries. From the frantic monster, a sound like a stalled locomotive inside an express tunnel, a sound like an air-raid siren strapped to an atom bomb, a sound like a Japanese technician shouting into a length of bamboo an incomprehensible voice that might sound like the fury of a god.)

What he builds. Wind. Mountain of air, caves of its body, at the summit the whirlwind. Wind over the swaying bridge, the catwalks and girders, march of the piers. The river below running heavy and swift, tangles of branches and flowing hair of weeds.

Liquidity, liquidation. On the highest verge where the cables hum and quiver in the wind, the monster also sways. He gazes over the dark water.

1976, Ratso's, a club on Lincoln Avenue. He'd suffered a stroke a few months before, but Rahsaan was back again working, touring. Audience: the applause sounding like rain on the window, sounding like green leaves in the wind. Sounding like skin talking about skin.

And the thing we were waiting for—the Rahsaan-machine, Kirkatron, the mystic organ grinder (lost on the way to Cleveland, the carnival in Cadiz, in the dark night the wild calliope seemed the only living thing in that town ...)—it had to be impossible, it needed the right and the left. Rahsaan a little unsteady walking through the audience to the stage, touching people's shoulders, absorbing greetings, wishes. The flute sung through Minnie Ripperton's "Loving You" and then the breath spitting and snorted and hummed and rumbled through that love futile and necessary, the song turned over then to the tenor like a hard-boned wing taking it up, chorused a while with the stritch a gigantic soprano, long body without a bow, crocodile with speed, and the tenor coming back alone a different creature, a different song, "Theme for the Eulimpians," those gods in the ears of all of us, and the tenor now the master register, keys of a monster organ, fleet as a clarinet and heavy as a bari, stops skated across, stops plunged full tilt, circle and cycle of Rahsaan's breath and the hot mob of the notes pushed, pushed, approaching collision and smash-up, paths tracking out in all directions and then swept again into the whirlwind, everything being eaten up and in an instant almost nothing left, Rahsaan's groan over a stuffed-huge repletion where the phrases and runs at the same time never stopped, columned up and spilling in frantic cascade, an extravagant cataract that seemed stilled even as it was crossed by mutating intervals like jumping looping ropes, elastic stochastics, doors of his face, lamps of his mouth, shagged and shaken skins of a dark matter.

Don Moye/Lester Bowie   *Photo by Fred Burkhart*

batterie

1970: *Lost Notebook, Elvin Jones*

The drums—I loved their powers of battery. Direct attack. Pounding the enemy. Strafe and bomb and rapid fire. Or subtle: the glancing blow, the single swift shot out of nowhere. And most of all, the capacity of surprise— listening to music, I often didn't notice the drums at all, my attention focused on the lead, the solo, the main line, but then a space would open between the verses or among the chord changes, a fill or a rumble suddenly revealing the universe of the song to be a shifting thing, holes in it because it was stitched together in and out of time. A heavy-breaking roll across the chorus of a Phil Spector production, Crystals or Ronettes; The Rolling Stones' "Satisfaction," Charlie Watts stomping hard through the suspended "I can't get no . . . "; The Doors' "The End" punched through with John Densmore's hissing cymbal spurs and abrupt stumbled hammerings. Amidst the exaltation of lyric and melody, the extra part of thrill—the song seemed forever but the drums told me the song would have to come to its finish, inside the battery of rhythm a recess of elegy, a bending of the synchronous glories of harmony toward a death, drums the pounding of nails into the coffin, drums the handle and blade of the weapon called music, arc of reach and hit and smash for which I felt a confused gratitude, a desire to wield the weapon myself and at the same time to suffer its blows. The wound-up arms, the nodding head, the jumping knees, the slewed feet. The drummer the machine, the timekeeper, and the hard laborer all at once, but the drums too the part of commentary and irony—immediate yet distant, drunken yet sober: in the pulsation a point drives off from itself, not quite gobbled up·in ecstatic fusion or constelled in grand possession, and in the slip between, on the stick, the wham, the bam, you're banged, shot, boomed, everything is happening, grass springs from pavement cracks and trees drape across the skin of the wind, the leaves are tousled and danced, thunder rolls and rain falls on the roof of the world.

An assemblage of circles, rounds, containers. Powers struck out of hollows, out of emptiness, time out of space. And everything depending on skin, on surface, on what offers to be touched. Whoever strikes a drum has to strike it once again—the vessel holds nothing but the insistence of a repetition, a return. There and there and there; take that, that, that. The fingers buzz and tingle, the air hums, the hands leap away from their own motion. Children drum their chests for the sheer pleasure of a percussion that rumbles under the skin and vibrates the internal organs; we go to arena rock shows and symphony performances to feel the physical volume of music like a throbbing blow inside our bodies; people equip their rooms and their automobiles with megabass speakers that pummel the air as if music is no more than a scaffolding to be worked over by rhythm. Space stripped naked and raw, the infant kicking legs, hands flailing around. A whole lotta shakin' goin' on.

Drums: skin stretched across a frame, the body's plenitude scooped out, its innards, its organs gone, nothing remaining but a sounding void. By virtue of that spacing, powers of coding and measure, friction, twist, and iteration. The modern drum kit is an ambitious, excessive gathering of equipment. Bass, snare, tom-toms, high-hat, cymbals—from the twenties onward, the separate instruments brought into a system that presupposed a virtuoso athleticism, a bold ambidexterity, a controlled abandon. Among the multiple traps and pedals, what one person could get up among all of it and not be overwhelmed, what one person could really use it, move it all into play? About the drums there's still an aura of sideshow, carnival, novelty act, of the incredible and the impossible: the one-man band, the strongman and the juggler, the hyperacrobatic tapdancer, Fred Astaire hoofing the ceiling. Drummer: indispensable, the one who makes the people dance. And when the band gives the drummer some, the one who dances, too, climbing over and around and between the beat all the while in the making, the equipment rocking, the sticks and rims and skins as if on the brink of flying apart, the drummer ready to go down with the ship yet swarming to the topmost mast to wave a banner signaling disaster or glory.

Documents and images, mere scratches, remnants, fragments from which one builds and constructs, threads and weaves, but feels at the same time how much is selection, a roughshod editing—the rhythm of memory is a matter of forgetting as much as remembering. The desire for coherence demands that we restore, repair, manage a shape, a theme, even though we fear the work is a ragged stitching, a cobbled-up job. Perhaps it's a matter of primary traumatism: from the very beginning we've been hit, stunned, battered; and, bestruck, bewildered, we hasten to assure ourselves we're all in one piece though such a condition has never really existed. I'm hearing now a Wayne Shorter composition from the sixties on which Elvin Jones might have played, a song called "Lost." It's a lush, floating melody, at the same time insinuating, casually sinister, the gothic Shorter as in his "Danse Cadaverous." It's music you'd hear straying in the woods, apprehensive of a too bright or too dark world pressing you with chances indefinite and infinite, an unexpected where at every turn among the spilling light and running shadows you're exposed to surprise, where the *be* of bewildered betokens that you've lost the power of knowing your track, inflected as it is by a step that dogs you, that loses your footing.

From a lost notebook: a memory trace of inked lines knotted and swirled, the pour of late afternoon sun through the muslin-draped windows of the ground level room in the North Park Hotel, site of Joe Segal's Jazz Showcase in those days. It was a 1920s building set in a triangle along Clark Street near Armitage, still an elegant place with Art Deco touches on the lintels and sills, a doorman stationed at the entrance, a view across to Lincoln Park and the Chicago Academy of Sciences. Five o'clock Sunday, the all-ages show, and we must have been dazzled by the sun in the walk through the park, sitting as we did, all three of us in the first row of chairs no more than a few feet from the drums. We were dazzled too by what seemed to us the luxury of the place, a cool, cavelike refuge where at the same time the golden June light was captured, firing the draperies and the white tablecloths into bright panels, flickering blanks. Viv and Rachel and I had drinks without being asked for ID, brimming glasses of red wine swirled with dark sparks.

Trying to remember that afternoon, I wonder whether the entry in the notebook was after all the best expression of it—a messy versing across a few pages, weak, tentative, yet really the closer track, not a construction but only a notation of having gone lost, a hatching on the portal of a labyrinth. Elvin Jones—a plain name, a black name, the spelling of Elvin with an E linked in my mind to the Atlantic album *My Favorite Things* where I first read it while listening to the song, under the trance of Coltrane's soprano and the long modal glide of McCoy Tyner's piano, not noticing until almost the end a sound like a whisper and an explosion, the whooshing murmur of the snare, the time washing, splashing across the cymbals. It was a subtle aural tickling: looped, scribbled, hard to trace, the stuttered rumbling and the glancing blow of it also an itching inside the air, a fine scraping at the bottom of my listening where the sonics of the instruments suddenly came into sharper relief, the lush pipe of Coltrane's saxophone edging to needle and blade, Tyner's floating chords swaying over themselves like bells in the wind, Steve Davis's bass throbbing a deeper heartbeat.

In Rimbaud's system of vowels, E corresponded to the color white. White: the unconditioned, the pure, the blank upon which all things are inscribed. When I was a child, we often played in the lot along Archer Avenue, a broad vacant triangle formed by the confluence of three streets, a place which, wild as it seemed to us, we named the Prairie. Among thistles and goldenrod and whisklike iridescent grasses were the ruins of old buildings, bare grids of foundations and in one spot an extended stretch of a shop's floor, black and white ceramic tile in a diamond checkerboard pattern with shags of weeds running its courses. It was our favorite location for smashing bottles, the adamant surface of the tile offering a sharp, concentrated impact, a sound both gratifyingly vehement and hollow like an exclamation drawn from the slick and the hard of matter. The spray of the exploded glass, silvered-clear or water-green or amber-brown, scattered across the four quarters, its splashed or lopsided or near instantaneous dispersal like the blown seeds of a shaken dandelion taking to the air. We found in the Prairie any number of things to toss and belabor and wreck, in one phase *pulverization* becoming an obsession, a ritual pronouncing of the word marking our turn from the pleasures of broad, violent strokes to a fanatic hammering and grinding down of bottle shards, bricks, and whatever else came to hand into the closest possible approximation of absolute dust, dull or glittering or powdery, that we pounded out with rough oblong stones. Later, we discovered the dumped heaps of blue-black steel cutouts, paper-thin and shaped like the letter E, parts for electrical equipment of some kind. When you picked one up, the razor-sharp edges, tinged with rust, could slice easily through your skin, and in the touch of the burnished metal I recalled parental warnings about tetanus, imagining it lodged like venom in those orthogonal fangs. Along with their use as fast-whipped weapons, the supreme pleasure of the *E*'s, as we called them, was their easy lofting into flight. They seemed almost weightless and with the correct grip, a gentle enclosing arrangement of the fingers along with a forceful thrust of the wrist, they launched effortlessly from the hand. At a distant but swift-tracking tangent to the truck and auto traffic passing us on all sides, the *E*'s brokenly wheeled and soared across the Prairie in whizzing trajectories, by turns being transformed into *M*'s and *W*'s, the raw force of our attack on the world sublimated to a scripting across the air.

El in—in the name I'd read the jazz iconography of the mean, the bad, the evil—the brooding Miles Davis, the ex-convict Gene Ammons, the hardass Sonny Stitt. Evil meant being black, being aggressive, powerful, uncompromising. I'd heard it in the way he played on "Summertime," Coltrane's tempo whipped with hard sticks, with overbounding run, roll, crash, and rumble, all the language of the drums transposed in a demiurgic battery of forces and matters I could scarcely follow but felt anyway I needed only to absorb. In the basement room under my parents' apartment, the air around the Silvertone speakers seemed to vine and blossom with snarled algebras. *Bad, e il*: Elvin Jones a man who could get away with things—wrecking Coltrane's car and walking away unscathed and laughing, taking a prison term in Lexington for junk without losing his job in the Quartet, banging off stage and kicking the shit out of his set when he reached his limit with Coltrane's taking on second drummer Rashied Ali. And in the music, too, I heard him getting away, the hard bash, the violence of his attack on the drums so intense he could be heard blocks from whatever club the Quartet was playing. He told an interviewer every night was life and death, they were playing on the verge, yes, literally, of being struck down, beyond exhaustion, beyond rest, getting away with it, those shows lasting four, five hours, the audiences going crazy, people frantically drumming along on their wine glasses, their tables, chairs, their feet jumping all over the floor; and getting away from the Quartet, finally, enough of Coltrane's demand for drums, drums, more drums, as though Jones gave him what he could never get enough of, the getaway of a glory toppling over itself, hard-shaken flowers tilted off in a dazzle of blows, receptacles bulged and spilling, membranes stretched to an ultimate curvature, their outsides turning inward.

Two years since Coltrane passed, the bright sun through the window curtains of the North Park Hotel. Trousers riding over alligator shoes, a white polo or maybe that day a richly patterned dashiki. Among the drums his dark face was furrowed in work, a steady sweat. His body seemed long, in a posture of chasing or being chased, the loosely gathered intensity of a cheetah or a greyhound lifting off its own track, limbs poised airborne, ready for motion and ready for motion and then ready once again, the stroke of the instant forever lost to the eye, you flinched or you blinked—what was going to happen, what had happened?—too soon, too late, all was the fake, the feint, the plunge, Elvin Jones precisely *on* the drums.

At the same time, so much involving the cymbals. An extremely light touch, the whirring sticks all over the place, a ubiquitous splashing, crashing. Not the climactic, spectacular, brass-ringing smashup of a Roy Haynes or a Keith Moon but a canny lateralization forever moving off to the side, or sounding on all sides, or posing the question: what are sides, what is form? It's breaking from all over, spun circle whose center is nowhere and circumference everywhere. The attack as if reversed, the cymbals up front carrying the time while the heavier equipment follows but so fast forward and so behind, so before and after, the track is forever almost getting lost.

Wilbur Little: tall, bearded, a leaf-green vest, the double bass held with delicacy, a giant lyre in his arms. Joe Farrell, white-shirted, bluff and nervous and flushed, throughout the set applying colored liqueurs or salves to his lips, trouble with his embouchure. Little swaying like a tree in a stiff wind, later himself the tree, exposure coiled into home, shelter, cave on a lofty promontory.

Farrell gushing fat and lean, bolding a trail and then running back on it, scraping it, roughing it, kicking across its traces.

Little singing out of a blown grove, Farrell looking for an eponymous pharaoh, loosening the tenor's ligature, tightening it again, dabbing potions to his lips.

Snares stuttering, tom-toms in a grumble, bass pedals hard-jabbing.

Little hoisting a trapezoidal sail in green breeze.

Farrell pacing the ten feet of stand, looking down at the floor, meditating resurrections.

Jones: tacking in a hard wind. Jones: attack itself being attacked.

You'd think someone might die in there.

We were far too close—the drums seemed to be pounding our heads. Think of a sheet of beaten tin: the blows of the hammer that distort and bend the metal into shapes and patterns, the flat surface articulated into divergent planes and surfaces. Think of that sheet attached to nothing, and possessed of an indefinite extent. It takes hit after hit, meanwhile humming and gonging, sweeping unsteadily through the air, almost curling back through itself like a Möbius strip.

Body flowered out into skin blooms, hard cartilage of ribs and rims, tremble of shimmering hissing mouths. The drums—an externalization of the components of the ear; the ear, too, an open flower. Canal and vestibule, the offering of a surface hidden yet exposed in the angle of the tympanum, not a container but a sounding plane lending itself to vibrations, reverberations, repercussions.

Duk Koo Kim, the Korean boxer who died of a brain concussion in the notorious match with Boom Boom Mancini, trained by beating a tire two hundred strokes with a sledgehammer.

Inside the hot of the gym, the traffic-horns outside on the street insistent as gulls, as rain.

With every blow, the air sang.

Sometimes in the Archer Prairie, we played a game called the punching machine. It wasn't much of a game, more a matter of who was to be victim that day and, for whatever reason, subjected to the treatment. A loose gauntlet wasn't so tough, but the tighter grouping, the circle, was serious business. Face to face, the guys going at you fed off one another. There was no exit until you dropped in surrender to the ground and begged for mercy, or you did the near impossible: beat your way out. In the middle of that battery, you were being bombed, you almost were the bomb. A strangely exhilarating ground zero, still point under a flurry of blows, a slow explosion where you expected an impact that was pure and direct but instead suffered uncertain, ragged intervals of suspense. Each time as the instant between seemed to extend itself, tempting you to make a break for it, the next stroke landed. Others might follow in rapid series or a lone roundhouse might be winding up to stagger you from out of nowhere. You covered your head, you leaned over to protect your stomach and your nuts, you crouched inside a stretch of time suspended, intensified (a robin was singing in a tree, a truck passing, a few younger kids calling in high voices down the street). You were like a troll, like a ball: old thing, naked thing, crawling next to the ground. You knew the simplicity and the dumb justice of being target.

But under that battery—it was playful and cruel, and somehow what you wanted, too—you sporadically rose up, leaving yourself unprotected, your arms sprouting punches like hard fruit on trees, your arms boning punches like spurs on embryo wings. You essayed your escape by virtue of what seemed an exact timing, a just-right moment, yet you were a mixed creature, and on your way out through the wall of shoes and legs and swooping arms, if you even made it that far, you lingered an instant under a rain of blows mingled with your own outlashings, battered between taking it and dishing it out.

Wilbur Little was running down a wave of shots, stammers, dives.

Laid out for so long it seemed he was finished, Farrell stock still with his eyes closed.

Elvin Jones: the drums backing into themselves, getting away from themselves, the distribution through a triplet wheeling, a laminar spillage, the room battered with undersounds of digging, excavating, as though the drum set was being torn down and rebuilt from a scatter of parts, heavy chrome knobs and piles of skins and rims. Whatever locks inside a frame beats against the borders; soon there's a cloud where you can't see what's going on; pressure builds and it takes on another life, it quickens, the container wants to leak, run, burst. And as it's happening there's a mix-up, you only know what's happened afterward, and that by way of resoundings, distant relays.

What do I remember besides lines on a lost page, Elvin Jones beating the daylights out of me, black stars and silver asterisks, a sun-spiked bedazzlement—he threw the first punch, the others, all.

Or the ending of "Spiritual" from the 1961 Village Vanguard recordings, after the dirgelike vamp and its release have run through one last time, Coltrane and Dolphy winding down but the whole thing sounding like it's starting again, the drums once more rolling out, the wash of the cymbals, it's beyond measuring, it could go forever, rain striking the rooftops and the disheveled leaves of trees, rain pounding the earth and carving streaming paths, rain tickling the skin, caressing the ear, tracing the soft ramparts of its exposure.

1968: Beatitudes

Down at the workbench after supper, a household repair or an improvement project in hand and a can of Schlitz on the floor next to him: my father, pounding. After supper, doing my homework, reading a book or listening to music, I would hear it first as a sound I might safely disregard, background noise that didn't signify. For a moment the floors upstairs took the vibration, the ductwork faintly echoed, and some object took a hit. A wayward nail in need of a stroke to drive it in good, or, clamped in the vise's jaws, a recalcitrant block of wood being set right with a single sharp tap. Then, I hoped, it was over, my dad taking a swig of the Schlitz, lighting up a Muriel Corona, quietly pondering all the work he'd done down there, the basement finished in varnished knotty pine and terrazzo-patterned tile, his own bar with a bank of whiskies and mixers, a leather dice cup and decks of cards, a Miller High Life sign with foaming water-fall and a revolving blue globe around which the gold Schlitz logo belted the equator of a glowing world. But usually the single stroke called forth another, as though the hammer once started had to go in search of more. A short lapse, during which whatever I was doing was surrounded by a slow, languorous silence, a deliciously pure and meditative air—and the pounding resumed. Sometimes it moved swiftly to full-force percussion, the house seeming to shake to the rafters, my mother sighing, "Oh, boy," and setting aside her newspaper. Often enough, though, the pounding would only gradually reach the point of emphatic signal, the tapping for a while tentative, sporadic, testing its mettle, my dad or his hammer not quite committed yet, perhaps giving us or himself a respite.

When the definite signal came—the pounding was seriously proceeding, blow following blow, and wasn't going to stop anytime soon, and if no one responded by going to see if my dad wanted help, the next moment would most likely bring an escalation to a sharp clanging on the water lines, as if the house indeed were facing a structural crisis, something about to give or burst—I was generally the one who went down, my mother staying out of it unless called specifically by name. There might be a cloud of smoke still floating from a cigar he'd let go out in the ashtray, and he might be finishing the last of the can of Schlitz, probably his limit for the evening. A diminutive piece of metal or wood, part of a chair or lamp or doorjamb, was usually the item at issue, squared off in the vise or lodged on the floor under his foot. The work was nothing, not even work, really, compared to his exertions on the job, but he sat on the stool sweating profusely, the dark skin of his face shining, deeply tanned from being outdoors, darkened too from his job as a welder, as if the years of gripping rods among arcs and flames had permanently imbued him with a furnace heat. That heat was pouring off him, making me nervous as I felt the pressure building. There was this damned thing—as he put it—that I would have to hold absolutely tight until he finished marking or sawing or drilling it. Sweat would run off his face, drip on the bench, the floor, stain like a hot rain the piece we were working on. I would strive to focus, imagining my grip a hard steel claw, and often all went smoothly—the thing fell together, everything shipshape, *beautiful*, he'd say, with a sudden happiness touching his face. On other occasions, my attention wavering, I'd soon be thinking of whatever I'd been called away from upstairs, and in no time, we'd be in trouble, the job gone awry through my dad's fault or mine or simply the jinx that inveigled itself into the wood, the drill, the rasping saw. My dad, so hopeful at first, would finish by muttering about doing it better himself, and I would finish by saying I was sorry though I wanted to tell him to just do it that way next time. At that point, he'd usually quit for the night, both of us cleaning up and then going back upstairs, leaving it for another day.

I was afraid of my father, and in retrospect the workshop trials seem painfully Oedipal, both of us sweating over who hammered and who held the board. Yet beyond the family romance, there was in my fear an awe, a fascination—he wasn't a tall man but he was strong and well-muscled from his work, about him that aura of heat and fire that, when I was eight or nine, made me now and then imagine that he wasn't only my father but an infernal being. The CCD nun said the devil could take any form, be anyone, and it seemed to me my dad might well be one of his avatars. Dark, hirsute, his blue eyes always bright with some latest feeling, some idea, gift, or grievance, he saturated the air around him with his energy, it poured off just like his sweat. He worked in a deep stone quarry in Hodgkins, repairing the twenty-ton Euclid trucks, lumbering monsters the size of tanks, or the dust-pitted tower-assemblies of the ready-mix plant. Sometimes in winter he was all day in the site known as the Hole, the lowest, darkest point of excavation, when the big shovels broke down. He drove a fast black Ford, formerly a State Police cruiser, out Archer to Lawndale Road and old Route 66, under which the quarry had been burrowed so that it dropped off on both sides of the highway. He brought home fossils studded in coarse rocks and Dolese and Shephard Company matchbooks, themselves a dark-orange color like fire. He brought home red sticks of dynamite with the blasting caps removed and stacked them in a box under the workbench.

When at the sound of the hammering I came down to the basement, he wasn't sly, angry, or mean. He'd show me what he was trying to fix, and he'd ask, "Can you help me out with this?" He was grappling with a damned thing but he was humble before it, humble even before my mother and me. With a vitality in him he could scarcely contain, he was forever cursing or blessing. All his life, according to the doctor, he'd had rapid-heartbeat syndrome, and in later years he often couldn't sleep, he said, hearing it beating like mad in his ear. The damned thing was jazzed up, it wouldn't rest.

Thus I lived the paradox of fearing but loving the devil—and indeed he was devilish otherwise, at family parties the master cardsharp in games of poker, pinochle, sixty-six, against all odds taking another hit, raking in the pots, pissing off the brothers-in-law, giving his winnings to the kids. Playful devilry, telling my aunts how pretty they were, kissing them too long, pulling a gag where a match under the table was to make a hair stand up from a puddle of water by virtue of the heat and, with a big hand, his flattened palm the size of a saucer, slapping down hard and affording the latest believer in his science a faceful of water. Stanley, like the name on the tools; Stan the trickster, the graceful dancer while the other working men were already tired; Stan the live wire whirling the ladies around the floor at weddings, the frenzied Lil' Wally polkas stomped through with the wooden boards shaking, the long whoop and the *hey, hey* when the drums hit hard and the trumpets and clarinets and saxes broke into a joyous dash. A flushed and merry face, sometimes lighted in the glow of the cigar's red ember, sometimes in brooding repose, stories of the broken windows when he came home from school, his time at the Catholic orphanage in Niles, the beatings he took.

On occasion, the evening hammering did get a rest. We'd have an early visit from our neighbor Ralph, announced by a shave-and-a haircut-two-bits knocking on our back door, a smart pair of raps giving extra emphasis to the two-bits. My parents, about ready to sit down to supper after they both had worked all day, tried not to show their dismay. For an instant, the knocking seemed to echo through the kitchen, the living room, the whole house, as though it were possible we weren't really there and no one would have to answer. But a second knock would have been too much to bear, the accusatory sound of a failure of hospitality, and so the door was always opened.

Ralph was a tall man with pale Irish skin, hair already silver, packs of Salems in both his workshirt pockets and littered across the seats in the baby-blue Mustang he drove and probably had a hand in making at the Chicago Heights Ford plant. My dad called him a big talker and it was true. I sat listening while they drank shots of Canadian Club and Ralph held forth in a booming voice about business and politics and the auto-worker's union for at least an hour. My mother would bustle around the waiting supper, and eventually it would be time for Ralph to leave and my best friend Dave, who hung around waiting for him, to go home with his father. Finally sitting down to eat, my dad expansive tonight, eyes shining, afterward ready for the newspaper and television rather than work in the basement, we'd hear the door slamming next door, often Ralph's voice booming after Dave, sometimes Dave answering back almost as loud.

Several years back, Dave's mom had fallen ill. Clara was once a digni-fied woman who worked a punch press at American Can Company and came home in the evening neatly dressed, baked pies and had coffee with my mother. Now there were long stays in Elgin State Hospital, electro-shock treatments, a sad rocking and tearing at her hair all day long in an utter terror I later learned was paranoid schizophrenia. She smoked constantly, chewed down her fingernails, seemed to cower under an im-pending blow coming at her out of the air, from outside on the street, maybe from within her own household, nobody knew. Over time, the old Georgian-style house had fallen into serious disrepair, Ralph giving up on it. Often a pair of ladies from down the block, babushkas tight around their heads and their gestures like they were wringing laundry, would stand in front and stare at the sight of such shameful neglect. The neigh-borhood was mostly inhabited by factory workers, first-time homeowners devoted to the quality of their property, a word spoken with a defiant em-phasis as if only recently learned. The lawns were constantly tended, the windows always being washed, the sidewalks and curbs swept and hosed and scraped clean in the winter. The house had been built before World War II, before the newcomers in beige brick bungalows took over, and the consensus among all the neighbors except us was that it was falling apart and should be torn down.

Since the wooden stairs were missing several treads, I didn't often use the front door when I called Dave. It was easier to walk around the side and shout up to his third-story window, in season bombing it with the hard small apples that fell from an old tree that spread over the back yard. Once in a while I had the satisfaction of lobbing one inside, hearing its thumping bounce against the wall or the floor, Dave's head appearing right after. The back entrance, which few of the neighbors ever saw, was almost impossible because the stairs were worse than in front and Tessie, the dachshund, had her outings there. The neighbors might have said the dog was lazy like Ralph, too lazy even to go down to the yard. The yard, though, was such a thicket—high grass and matted leaves and an untended garden where the rhubarb still came up every year—that Tessie might well have given up on it. Once in a while she did venture out there, her little body almost hidden, tunneling through a lush world where anything that wanted to grow had its chance. Dave's dad rolled out the rotary mower maybe twice in the course of a summer, catcher not included, and precipitated seed-clouds of every kind of weed over the Cyclone-fenced yards of obsessively maintained Merion Blue and Creeping Bent. On a summer Saturday morning, the roar of the motor and the churning beating of the blades spurred a general indignation up and down the block, though nobody dared say a word to Ralph. When the mower died out periodically, he stood a while among the heavy, fragrant clippings, smoking a Salem and contemplating the state of his property.

Dave: my best friend, my blood brother—the origin myth of our bond was that, soon after my family moved in next door, Dave about four, me about two, he'd spotted me out on the lawn inside my playpen and come over to promptly knock it down and tumble me on to the grass. Dave: anywhere you saw him—easily throwing around a ball, or leaning for an hour on the window in front of Anna's corner store, or waltzing comic books and model kits out of Walgreen's without the slightest sign of nerves—he had a way of moving you were forced to recognize as better than you were ever likely to manage. He came at the world with a sort of open, swinging momentum, full on, but at the same time had a delicate sense of when to turn aside, to stay at one remove. It made him a good thief and an indomitable fighter. And he fought regularly, fiercely, often in a just cause, things somebody said about his mother, his parents' funky haunted house, at other times purely for the dirty joy of it. Dirty: against all the informal codes of honor, there was nothing he wouldn't do. He used his feet, kicked high and wild even though it was supposed to be unmanly, for girls. He'd grab your family jewels, he'd hawk in your eye, he'd torment your ear—he had a ready knowledge of the tender, vulnerable zones. He was skilled at prelude and ritual, too—the insults and threats, the singsong spells that sent things back a hundredfold, chains of words thick with their own sound, spittled and filthy as his combat, slurred and eruptive as if on Chicago's Southwest Side he'd tapped a vein of the Whitechapel Road. A ragging from Dave permanently changed, no matter how much you resisted the memory, your image of your mother. Deployed like the repellent powers of a lithe leper, such words kept him untouchable, undefeated.

Loitering in front of his house, Dave challenged all passersby, engaged all critics. Even the adults had words from him, their poses of disapproval or superiority deflated by a comment on their looks, a spur-of-the-moment tag that seemed to stick perfectly. Those nearer his own age had their faces washed in dirt, the ground watered with their tears. He had devised a special torture for the hard cases. With his hands locking your arms, his knees on your legs, you were helplessly pinned. From his mouth issued the threat of abomination—the spit-rope lovingly suspended over your face until you begged for release, repeated after him whatever words he judged you should say or unsay.

I knew Dave's disciplines well; I'd suffered them all, had been the laboratory, the willing or unwilling subject he'd used to perfect them. Those nights when he stopped for a shot, Ralph talked as much as he wanted, but Dave often enough got in trouble for just a few words—mostly saying no when it was time to leave, or calling Ralph the "old man" rather than the required "sir." Sometimes walking out after supper I'd hear them inside the house, look up at the window and see Ralph's knee flying up, Dave's body jerked across the living room. It could go on for an hour, Dave refusing to back down. I knew he'd be crying freely, taking his punishment. When Dave wept, his tears weren't held back at all, they just flowed, staining his cheeks, making his nose run like he had a cold. He didn't compress his eyes, squeeze them shut and bawl. They stayed open, a maddening brown color, opaquely defiant. And he never did shut up, eat his words, until he or his dad was exhausted.

When the next day or the day after or whenever it was Dave came and grabbed me around the neck, moved to put me in a headlock or throw me on the ground, I fought back hard, knowing I was likely to be hurt if I didn't. My parents on occasion said I should find a quieter friend, but never insisted. Every Friday after he came from work, Ralph treated Dave and me at Lou-Cel's Restaurant on Archer, where we had ice cream sundaes and Ralph smoked over his coffee and cherry pie. I remember the sour smell of his unwashed clothes, the rough hand with which he tousled our hair, the raspy voice with which he addressed us as gentlemen.

Fighting with Dave, in that thick battery of blows, losing my feet, rolled on the sidewalk, tumbled into the grass, then back up to take it like a man, it was never clear when it was enough, when too much. Because you were his friend you forgave him ahead of time if you got hurt. That usually didn't happen since Dave had long experience of riding the verge where pain bordered injury. Working on you, he mixed it up good, the whole array of moves that pounded your body like a drum, treated your face like a joke, all your dignity so much exposed skin, but not going too far, falling back and stepping aside at just the right time, ready to allow you a shot at him if you were up to it, ready to paint you as the assailant if anyone came along and objected to his beating up on a younger kid.

Battery: to fight meant we were done fighting, that out ahead of everything that might divide us we were already in the clear, blood brothers. When we cut our skin with a knife in that childish ritual and clamped our arms tight, I believed I felt our pulses beat, not together, but a step apart, out of rhythm like the breathlessness I could hear between us as we spun around in a hard grappling, our hearts knocking like stones against our ribs.

Sticks flying, beating the hell out of people, that night in August 1968, the Chicago police stampeding into Lincoln Park near the zoo, and later a battered remnant of a crowd along Wells Street, stones and bricks flying at the shopfront windows, smashing out the plate glass of the boutiques, on the ground long pieces like blue daggers and baby swords, the sound of their running footfalls on the pavement giving the crowd a feeling of power and at the same time a panicky desire to break up and disperse. The double impulse turned their motion into a reeling dance, to wreck and then run, but still looking back at the damage, the pursuers, as if to urge them to read what it meant beyond revenge and destruction, as if to say, forgive this because it is beating wings, only a desperate battery breaking out, hope of a different world.

By the end of 1968, Dave and I hardly saw each other anymore. He'd quit high school his freshman year, lied about his age and taken a job in a factory on Archer. In a couple of years he'd be drafted. Ralph would die of a heart attack and Clara would be sent permanently to the hospital, the house sold off by an older son and daughter-in-law.

In 1995, the night after my dad was gone, eighty years of his heart beating fast, outside my window in Baltimore the October wind whipped hard all through the night, for hours a violent banging and rattling on my window as though the sashes had come loose in the frame.

I didn't need to get up and see what it was. I wasn't frightened, and I didn't care to prove one way or another where the sound came from.

I lay there in the dark of the bed, listening.

1982: Famoudou Don Moye

Knocks, taps, the rapping at the chamber door—in Jackie McLean's 1963 composition "Ghost Town," the slow haunted march of the song treads a ground of dark excavations, the horns spurring hard over extended gaps, sunken hollows in time. In the drum solo, a young Tony Williams hammers with a patient, devious insistence, sticks clattering amidst creaks and bucklings, a muttering of bones and a skeleton's fall down the stairs under the high-hat's hissing kiss, the hushed whisk of the brushes, the cushioned blows of the mallets over the tom-toms, a sense in the attack of having moved to playing *inside* the drums, an intensified zone of reverberation.

The Dogon *nummo*, primordial lizards of indeterminate sex, do not possess an external ear, and so in order to listen they cup their hands to the bare orifices on their heads. When the drummers strike the skin, they are also touching those hands. The hands touch back.

Rapping at the door, Poe's Raven seesaws its wings, and, baffled of entrance, snaps its beak. In the poem the lines are like a tensing rope, a whip, the binding or the shrugging of chains, a hammer's stroke.

Nevermore. Worrying the stones of a prison, breaking in, breaking out, getting away, beaten, beating, black wings crashed through the door, the window, the skylight. 1982, the Art Ensemble of Chicago in a concert at Northwestern, Pick-Steiger Hall, Famoudou Don Moye with the drum set surrounded by a battery of African and Caribbean instruments, of tympani and gongs, of earth drums and pan drums and conch shells. In his white lab coat, Lester Bowie rocked back and forth, rambling around

Moye's outfit, the trumpet pointed down at the ground, the trumpet sweeping up from it, pulling from the air a solo that was one clear-calling voice and then a second voice growling, smearing, obscenely whispering, a dialogue not finding a progress or a fulcrum but instead absorbing the grain of yet more voices, across the gradient of the horn's running leaps a tottering. Like a mob of eager children grappling at legs, the guest raising one step away from them, one more, one more, but now he belongs to them and when he shakes them off they ride his feet on low swings. Tumbling him to the ground, they're all over him, uncle brought to saying uncle. Bowie: flash of the bell, a sardonic fanfare, the trumpet brightly staggering.

In a tasseled leather vest, his shoulders broad and muscular, poised over the drums with his head erect, seemingly unconcerned, almost disdainful, Moye wasn't looking in Bowie's direction but nonetheless alert, intrepid, antelope-striped in gray and ocher and scarlet face-paint, lion-whiskered with painted diagonals along his cheeks, his eyes inside that mask possessed of such power that even at a distance I gazed at him and immediately turned aside, strangely disconcerted. It was foolish, I thought—after all, this was just a show, Moye only a musician—but it was a gaze that struck me hard because it struck me not at all. A noble face, yes, a broad forehead, high cheekbones, a tapering line to a strong chin, a perfectly shaped goatee, and far from appearing theatrical, over the top, the face-painting heightened the dignity of his bearing. Attraction and repulsion affect one with a sort of violence; this was a different power, Moye himself not its subject or object but whatever it was beyond him that he appeared to be listening for with a tranquil vigilance. I imagined an anchorite in the desert attending to the first knocking at the heart of his god; I imagined a battery of winds on a mountain swaying the branches of a naked tree, a lone ear there listening. Moye: a neutral gaze, an impassioned gaze, an impartiality and tension in the deployment of body, limbs, and hands as if the drummer too must be struck, skinned, bear the blows of percussion and repercussion, their vectors marked by the lines and patterns illuminating his face.

What might it mean to attack, to strike the very air? I hear it in the sonic weight of the symphony orchestra, or the thrust of a big band like Ellington's or Basie's, or in the amplified blast of rock. Among the single instruments of the jazz armory, only the drum kit, that maverick plural, has such sheer aural capacity, such potential volume that in one regard its history can be seen as a series of experiments in bringing the drums under control, finding a way to use what seems to lend itself infinitely to abuse—the noisy, overly enthusiastic drummer, drowning out the horns, the overly busy drummer, getting in their way, the drum solo much loved by audiences always on the verge of becoming a wild beating and thrashing, a child having a tantrum with a wooden stick. The Three Stooges butting heads and Wile E. Coyote going smash, a mechanical battery of shots and rolls and bombs, vainglorious storms and thunders, the drummer a sorcerer's apprentice outrun by a welter of spirits unexpectedly aroused. To strike the very air—perhaps a desire to hammer and pound into fixity, to beat the living hell out of it because a space, a gap, persists, rises again, comes back for more. Every blow edged with its arc, the wheels and fans and blades of the flying sticks, the pumped turbulence of the arms, the knees, and the legs, the sweat standing in droplets on the skin of the face and the stunned thrumming of the skins. And a concomitant desire not merely to fix but to hammer and pound into shattering and fission, the ultimate drums no more drums but the blurred imprint of matter itself being relentlessly pursued, run down, surprised. To bang it so bad it all falls away, the power solvent and batteried so you never know what hot wire shot you.

Moye, mounted among the kit, or Moye like a clockwinder walking among the array of percussion, setting it all rocking, coming back to it, it coming back to him, meanwhile the ear waiting to catch the supreme pleasure of hearing everything happening at once—to play all the drums, approach the total of rhythm, searching and researching among the infinite combinations of paths and drawing forth the grain of a singular vibration. The wild jumped degrees of the one being brought into combination with another, answering the other, the songing, the voice, and then the all working like mad, perfectly, the drums in flawless battery, the sliding pivot where the eros of jazz reaches climax at its steepest pitch, an outpaced delight like being inside the heart of a big band blasting on stage: the Basie orchestra pounding full force at the Aragon Ballroom, the Shriners Ball, 1976, a tall leggy dancer with a huge tiara who leaped through a hoop of fire, Rufus Jones a white shock of tossing hair with his set elevated on a platform behind the horns like a second orchestra, the drummer playing to beat the band and the band beating back.

To strike the very air—in the battery of Moye's attack it was as if the purchase, the traction of attention, the almost imperceptible pause that allows the drums to be heard as drums, were baffled. You couldn't approvingly nod your head, appreciating the way the work on the snare, say, fit together with the addressing of the cymbals, and how the rolling rumbling over the toms then was picked up and moved all around with the bass drum thumping and kicking it into gear and the high-hat maybe giving it an extra push. Fine as that would be, it seemed instead the rhythm had started somewhere far beyond you or somewhere before or after, the beat-hold of that inviting pause retracted, the self-consciousness of drums, of the drummer climbing a glittering circus apparatus to deploy his bag of tricks, becoming instead something on the order of flinging into the air blocks, boulders, loads of rhythm in which the borders of each were absolutely tight, a controlled slide, a suspended fall where the power that prevented them from touching, interfering, smashing together was at the same time the power that kept them aloft, a dark gravity driving apart rather than pulling together, a rhythm that was not something you could follow or even something you could rock and roll inside of as it overwhelmed you but something that abandoned you bestruck and bedeviled.

Moye: a gesture toward another you're expecting, a pause that should save you but gets hammered down. Spirits are running all over it: the drums, plural, that racing in a flying bridge, that shadowing through a flickering *X*.

And the ghosts, the ancestors, their wings a bone batter under Moye's hands, touching back the carnal grace of his fingers gloved in time.

2002: Murmurous

Drums: the monster that made jazz by gathering up a spill of sounding organs, shining barrels, empty heads. The drums—flamboyant multiple, the many-mawed gut, whirlwind factory of tappings and hammerings and echoes. Think of horns with a banjo, a string bass, a single drum. Think of the single drum blossoming into snare and bass and cymbal, the traps. That mushrooming holds the promise of the all of rhythm, of the flowering of the winds and brass which, too, would approach that all. The driving train, the irresistible headstrong battery of Ellington, Basie, Earl Hines, orchestras that struck the air into dance, the drums their engine. Swift mimicry: if the drums could do more than one thing simultaneously and do it loud and hard, so could the clarinets and trumpets and saxophones, bunched in sections that roared rhythm, the glory of the soloist stepping out like the leap of the beat across the traps, the sound of the horn taking on weight, jumping back from itself, crossing itself left and right over bridges, hammering and being hammered in turn, beating out, beating back, in between the dancers whipped and harried like humming tops, across the floor their bodies buffeted and blown by the orchestra's force.

Rhythm, repetition, the wave that strikes again, again, each time different, each time the same, and in that intermittence the enveloping heat breaks into a cold sweat, the all getting away with you, a winging Satan carrying you off on a sprung track of energy and flying you over the world, outside-floating in a terrifying indifference where you're at any moment liable to be cast off and thrown upon the rocks, crushed and torn and splattered, or yourself to become rock, log, stump. Beaten insensible, thing, less than thing—like Beckett's *Unnamable* where being omelettes to a ropy dough, mixed and braided, across its turning worm a murmuring battery of words. To escape, to ward off blows, protective magic that works by taking upon itself the beat, the hit. "Evil," Henri Michaux writes: "the rhythm of others." Yet to be struck is to live, to be sounded, echoed, to be claimed by the time and world from which you were born, borne.

As much as our hearts, our breaths, all the processes of our organism are possessed of rhythms that belong to us, those rhythms are not only our own. They're susceptible to the world and its weathers that make the pulse race or calm—bracing mountain air, warm winds of a southern island, the bright sun of morning or the stillness of a crescent-moon night. And they're susceptible to the rhythms of others, emotional weathers of love and welcome, enmity and challenge. We don't set the clock of ourselves and allot the measure of its every movement but are set speeding ahead or slowed down by what touches us from outside. Rhythm is always coming from somewhere else, seducing, distracting, invading, and transporting. Over the years, our bodies and faces are marked by it, figures of time stretched and drummed on our skins.

In a photo from the fifties: Blaise Cendrars's face, a long-ashed cigarette hanging from his lip, the skin etched and furrowed as though he's taken a hard beating—the arm lost in World War I, the deaths among friends and family, the years of wandering and poverty—but he's survived, he's smiling, wickedly joyful, the lines in the face as singularly and passionately complicated as the polymorphic prose of the last volume of his autobiography, *Le Ciel,* where over hundreds of pages the words beat their wings, dreaming of bodies taking flight.

A warm foggy night in Baltimore, New Year's Eve, 2002, the streets quiet and along the old waterfront walks of sailors and Freedmen the rowhouses lighted with parties. Inside, the beating of human voices. Midnight approaching, they grow louder and louder, not to drown each other out, not for one voice to claim the floor, but in a crescendo like the cries of flocking birds, each caught up by the other in a contagious shifting rhythm without discernible source or end.

Baltimore: a beaten-down city, the shipping and manufacturing once its economic lifeblood long in decline. Poverty and addiction, a crumbling infrastructure, miles of parks and rowhouse hills cordoned off by a Beltway ring beyond which suburbs extend all the way to Washington, D.C. Bulletmore, Murderland, some call it: it's by some accounts the most violent city in America. A city beating on itself, hit off the bottle or pipe or needle, smash on the rival or girlfriend or boyfriend, battery of the fists, the box cutter, the semiautomatic popping rounds. The city where Poe took his last beating, caught up in an election-day sweep of vagrants or a gin-driven toxic disaster, a week later dying in the city for a time his home, the place he wrote "Berenice" and "Ligeia" and saw the first publication of "MS Found in a Bottle." The city where slaves ran for freedom to Fell's Point, neighborhood of ships and docks and jobs, and, like Frederick Douglass, sometimes made it, but often didn't, and where even the free were liable to capture and reenslavement, their chained footsteps beating down Market Street and Argyle Alley as they were led to the ships bound for New Orleans.

At midnight I watch the fireworks over the Inner Harbor, plush explosions in streamered systems of silver and gold, hot bursts soaring high and blossoming with arms and tentacles, sky-orchids swiftly decaying with convulsive flickerings over the dark water. Before each burst, a cannon-like percussion bumps and tears through the damp air, along the nearby streets car alarms are triggered, along the streets and piers people shout. Extra police have been deployed throughout the city to handle celebratory gunfire, and I'm praying the homicide count hasn't gone any higher in the last minutes of the year, but in the battery of thunders and bright lights I'm for an instant forgetting everything, the fireworks riding way up in the air, falling down again, in between the detonations a sort of crack in time, the old ghosts driven out in a pounding of bright surprise, burned off in a sparking filament of the new.

Later, as the night moves toward a rainy dawn, I'll spend an hour listening to Ed Blackwell's drums on a record with Don Cherry. The freedom lessons of Kenny Clarke and Max Roach along with the jumps and marches and quadrilles of old New Orleans—Blackwell's attack so steady and so complexly poised it seems the drums can go on forever, drawing on an infinite reserve. They scarcely sound like drums anymore, the beats pressing upward rather than being laid down, once roused the powers under his hands touching back, a prickly friction, a contact dark and murmurous.

Fred Anderson   *Photo by Fred Burkhart*

the velvet lounge

When you push your hand against the rail, the bar tilts, as if over the years it's been leaned across so often it's on the verge of giving way. My wife and I order drinks and sit for a while. We talk to the bartender, remembering the last time we were here, who was playing that night. The fluorescent haze a washed-out blue over the cash register, the ranks of vodkas and whiskies, our faces caught in the mirror behind like we've come here to meet ourselves.

Chicago, The Velvet Lounge. The address is 2128½ South Indiana Avenue, the half registering that the bar is an abbreviated space, offering the bare necessities of pay phone, cigarette machine, and jukebox. But like a stray exponent it surprises you. In the back, the narrow corridor of the workingman's tavern takes a swing and suddenly you're in a large bright room with a soundstage, high iron-trussed ceilings, oversized posters of Johnny Griffin, Bud Powell, and Miles Davis. An improvised concert hall, the chairs and tables and vinyl booths packed tight in an arrangement that must have been mapped to the very inch. All around, a medallioned wallpaper in seventies style, under the track lighting its pattern of squares loosened, disarmed, a blurring and doubling along its grid like the tracings of a pen over the boxes of a crossword.

In the seats near the stage there are five, maybe ten people waiting to hear the music, about a usual crowd for a Wednesday night in the middle of August. The instruments wait on the stand, Ari Brown's saxophones tubing bronze and silver under the stage lights, a Roland keyboard and a folding chair nearby, and toward the back Avreeayl Ra's drums and Malachi Favors's upright bass. The group will be starting late, no hurry, a sense here of the familiar, the intimate, as though we're not really in a club, we're just visiting Fred Anderson's place—he's the owner and impresario, operating since the late seventies. He collects the cover (five dollars) after we've had a drink or two; he promises us it'll be a good night, powerful musicians are coming around. Fred's in his late sixties but seems younger, his skin almost unlined, his eyes behind his glasses steady, vigilant, but mild too, a self-contained air about him, some quality of devotion in the slight hunch of his shoulders, the way he walks straight at you across the room. Though it's said the Velvet Lounge is named to reflect the smooth ride of his big tenor saxophone sound (echoes of Lester Young, Gene Ammons), velvet might better apply not to what he does on the horn—if it's smooth as velvet, it's a velvet that's regularly torn to shreds, late Coltrane– and Ornette Coleman–style, like a topsail ripping in a gale—but to Fred himself, his gentleness. When I ask how things are going, he answers as he usually does, in a quiet voice: "We're doing all right. Just trying to keep the music alive."

2128½ South Indiana: just off Twenty-second Street, also known as Cermak Road, an out-of-the-way corner, although this stretch a couple of miles south of the Loop was once the edge of Bronzeville, up until the 1960s Chicago's version of Harlem. After thirty years of urban renewal and real-estate development, only a few of the older buildings remain, the Velvet Lounge with its glass-block window and steel accordion gate the last in a chopped-off row of three-story brick shop fronts—there's also a currency exchange, a store with mysterious curtained windows, and a fish and chicken carryout. At night the block is so quiet and empty you can usually park in front, under the shadows of the young trees the city planted in a landscaping project.

Yet in other ways it's a busy corner, at the confluence of major urban arteries where traffic is moving day and night, two blocks away Twenty-second feeding into Lake Shore Drive and nearby McCormick Place with its new convention center, a few blocks in the other direction connecting to Interstate 94, the Dan Ryan Elevated stop, the Metra train station and the red-fronted streets of Chinatown. At any moment a dozen taxis are cruising by, buses and trucks gaining speed on the six-lane road, the twenty-four-hour burger and coffee place doing a brisk trade. Two blocks to the east is a 1920s building, filigreed gates and tall ornate windows, until recently home of R. H. Donnelly Company, for many years the publisher of the Chicago telephone directories, fat books thicker than family Bibles, and home of the Lakeside Press, a series concentrating on American history, pioneer narratives, and memoirs of the early West.

Long before I was born my mother worked there, riding two buses every day, Archer to Cermak, Cermak to Prairie. It was in the late thirties and she was about sixteen years old. A clean airy room with light-filled windows, girls, women only, just like the parochial schools. Everybody dressed modestly but well. Her job was to feed sections of *Life* magazine to a conveyor belt. Between each motion there was less than a minute and you had to be on the ball, the glossy pages held ready in your lap and then passing from your hands as though you were in the same gesture grasping and letting go of the finer things advertised there. Jokes, too, about the life of Riley, about living it up, about throwing your life away. The job paid well and it was a turning point for her. Though she enjoyed learning and considered becoming a teacher, she quit school, and like most of the people in the neighborhood over the years she stayed in the factory, doing assembly, piecework, inspection. For a while, my mother was employed at Cook's, maker of World's Finest Chocolate, the long foil-wrapped bars used for church and scout fundraisers. She sometimes brought home the rejects, chipped or misshapen bars with the sweet flavor of happy failure.

Work—as a child I had an almost mystical sense of its importance. It was the place my parents went each day, it was the touchstone of each evening: supper, dishes, early to bed because tomorrow was work. And feeding pages, bundling wires, punching metal, whatever it was, you did your utmost, everything counted. The chores at home, too, participated in a larger scheme. The hungry wand of the Hoover canister-vacuum I was assigned to wield on Saturday mornings was of a piece with the trucks hauling their loads on Archer Avenue, the freight trains sounding on the Belt Line tracks, the cargo planes taking off from the blue-lanterned runways of Midway Airport. Despite the occasional slip, when I let the vacuum roar into itself like a blocked tailpipe, or let it verge on gobbling objects off the shelves I was supposed to dust by hand, I understood that work made for order, pattern, the greater harmony of people and things.

The imperative of order: though we know its dangers, it's a given of modern culture, of what we call civilization. Yet order is a fragile thing. I think of my parents' neighborhood, poor families, immigrant families, always the pressure, the struggle simply to maintain: to keep the boys out of trouble—drinking, stealing, running in gangs—and to keep the girls out of trouble too, everybody coming of age young, already working at fourteen, fifteen years old, the temptations of the city bound to claim a share. And beyond that, a certain pull, a power, in the city itself, the great and deliberate patterning of Chicago you traveled going to work, going downtown, flat unbroken miles of gridded streets and everywhere the crossings of railroads, the piers of viaducts, the humps of movable bridges over the north and south branches of the river, the Loop skyscrapers and the broad parks and boulevards and bordering it all the exhilarating expanse of the lake, glassy leagues extending to a dark indefinite horizon, in those days the sky over it scanned by the powerful violet beam of the Palmolive Tower, a forty-thousand candlepower beacon said to be visible two hundred miles to the north where freighters plied the waters of upper Lake Michigan. The euphoria of the city's body—its line and its stretch and its shining downtown shores—could seduce you from the familiar safety of your neighborhood, expose you to dazzling bright lights and dark unknown alleys. Along the broad patterning of the orderly grid an unsettling pressure, a resistance to or a looping feedback of order itself, a drawing near of exorbitant chances, an edging off the map where you heard stomping and howling and you touched a desire to jump the whole thing, like overturning a checkerboard. A desire to loosen your city-skin, to whirl into a space just beyond it where the pattern you'd make, a jumble of abandoned positions, of broken-off moves, would perhaps be only another part of what you felt you were escaping but that wouldn't matter or that would be most pleasurable of all, your becoming surface-effect or epiphenomenon of the city that surpassed you. Drunk, your head soaked and your clothes wet under the drifting plume of Buckingham Fountain on a hot August night, the water and the air shot through with colored beams, the fountain a limestone castle under siege or already conquered by luminous spirits. Later, along the avenue of elms in Grant Park, lovers on the damp grass. Farther off somewhere a bold hoot, a shattered bottle. Sirens on Roosevelt Road. Crossing the pedestrian bridge, your shadow's lurch bordered with an orange haze of sodium-vapor light, and under that halo, the streets carrying you, you felt you could walk the city till dawn.

We're drawn to the Velvet Lounge tonight by virtue of that pull of disorder and order, that freewheeling pressure. Jazz: what might fascinate about the music is how it rides over edges, how it touches in between. Temptation and excess, the late-night playgrounds of urban life, the devil's music with its sensuality and ecstasy—that's what we want. Yet it's not just swooning sounds we're after, background music for a personal movie, but music born of labor, rigor, real work. Chicago, city of the fire, risen from its ashes, and the music at the Velvet Lounge can be like a house on fire, the phrase getting right that sense of a structure holding yet at the same time being overwhelmed, on the verge of tottering, dissolving in an elemental rush, the powers of making veering off into an unmaking as though there's a line where order provokes disorder, or where disorder in some phase makes an order only to exceed it and to break it up again.

My mother once said that the men of her generation worked hard, they played hard, they died too young. She might have been talking about Chicago, the way the city doesn't stop, the way it burns and consumes itself—not in the vibrant insomniac manner of a Manhattan but instead like a twenty-four-hour factory, three shifts, the machines working always, smoke and sparks and clatter, shouts and metal thunder sounding along the floor, human bodies driven like robots and taking by contagion powers of tooling and process and machine. Something terrible precipitated in those dark satanic mills yet something liberating too, the worker possessing or possessed by the machine, the tool in his hand a lever that could usefully direct the forces of production or could sabotage and dismantle, jazz up the works, make the gears screech and the pulleys scream, the belts lurch off their tracks, the steam blow shrilly out the valves.

It's like that whenever Fred Anderson comes on stage at the Velvet Lounge. The tenor clutched in his hands, his head bent, his shoulders narrowed as though the instrument would take hold of his body, would play him. But he never quite lets it, though he's been so molded over the years that in the exacting exercise of fingers and mouth and wind the city might be making him in its own image even as the horn-work shears hard across all that's been laid down, derails it with a relentless, near-mechanical intensity, a lyrical wrenching. As though in a factory the machines themselves would compose a long rattling song out of pity for the lives given over to them. Or as if the factory would contrive to make sounds that echoed the human voices calling and shouting and singing back the cranks and roars and groans and peals of the machinery, the system of production under which they worked hard, played hard, died too young.

1976: The Bird House

In Chicago the trees are lush, spreading, moving in breezes and touched by occasional rains. In this cool spell of late summer, the city tastes of the north—Wisconsin, Michigan, the lakes. The maples and cottonwoods have an aura of water, the air a glacial tang of dunes, of hard polished stones on the beach, of dark blue waves rocking up against limestone shelves. I've walked around the North Side, traveled on the El, wandered the South Loop. I've been struck by how Chicago is again on the make, to recall Nelson Algren's phrase, the lofts and condos and new construction expanding everywhere, a rejuvenated tax base pumping into surprisingly clean streets, freshly landscaped boulevards with grand planters packed with flowers and shrubs, busy work crews pressure-washing the State Street sidewalks late at night after the stores have closed.

Yes, they call it the city that works—but what is the work, where does the money come from? I suppose it's obvious: trade, exchange, communication, the options and futures and contracts and services effected each day behind the windows of the Loop towers, linked out to the suburban centers which are themselves becoming little cities, and all of it of course speeded and intensified and made more profitable by the powers of the Internet. And the rest—the crossings and stagings of railroads and neighborhoods, of buses and museums, of police cruisers and storm sewers, of El tracks and shopping strips—in one respect or another serves the larger imperative of conveyance, transfer, everything borne across and away. Chicago is not so much what it contains but what it does, how it bridges and carries, the city a metaphor of metaphor. Though the same might be said of New York or London, those great city-systems retain a substantial core, a long-settled concentration of power and wealth. In Chicago there's the Lake Shore and the Gold Coast, sure, but there's a sense of the wealth floating still, the money being grabbed here and there and everywhere while it keeps making the rounds under this broad expanse of vapor-trailed sky, a theater of routings and deliveries and expedited orders, a big blue sky for planes.

The city that works—the motto embraced by Chicago in recent years catches me on its off-edge, suggesting as it does that it's the city that counts rather than the people who make it. The power nexus of its infrastructure, the order, the pattern, seems to operate in an almost monstrous way, drawing lives into it, using them up, or appearing to be used yet ultimately only feeding itself. The city that works—but move on past the lakefront, past the new wealth in Bucktown and Wicker Park, stay on west, or stay on south or even north, and there it is: the same old tenement

Chicago, slum Chicago, gang Chicago, Lou Rawls's city without a heart. Living on the East Coast now, I often hear how wonderful it is—the lake, the trees, the architecture, the music and art; it's so clean, it's so happening, almost as good as New York but lots cheaper. Yet I can't help wondering whether the new face put on by the city is no more than a mask for an ever-hungry spirit—one that devours human lives, chews them up and spits them out, a raw animus of capital still wedded to the old soul-killing demons of phobia and hate.

A true history of the Velvet Lounge, 2218½ South Indiana, as I remember it. In 1976, Fred Anderson opened a loft club on Lincoln Avenue on the North Side. It was a narrow long storefront, ivory curtains in the window, located down the block from the Hild Library and the Davis movie theater, not far from the Ravenswood Elevated station at Western. A mostly German neighborhood, a pleasant street with an easygoing European feeling, the Brauhaus restaurant, Meyer's Deli, the Hansa Clipper Lounge. In the library (today, home of the Old Town School of Folk Music), I discovered books by Trakl and Guimaraes-Rosa and Cendrars; I spent hours there browsing the shelves where in late afternoon the casement windows filled with sun and the leaves of a tall maple brushed against the glass, light and shadows across the rows of titles like the burn of treasure in a dark wood. The opening of Anderson's club—called the Bird House, in honor of Charlie Parker—was a happy event. The venue wasn't a bar but an open space for listening, a music gallery, a big empty room with folding chairs and couches along the walls. Walking out on Lincoln after hearing Fred Anderson with trumpeter Billy Brimfield, or after a Sunday duo concert with Joseph Jarman and Oliver Lake, it seemed Chicago was coming alive in a way I hadn't felt since the sixties. "Great Black Music"—the motto of the South Side AACM collective— was reaching across the city and finding an audience. The Bird House: it sounded like freedom, it sounded like a home.

The Bird House lasted less than a year. Legally, it was a matter of zoning, a rule about off-street parking for businesses providing live entertainment. It was a transparently biased decision on the city's part, based on what shouldn't have been surprising but still was—essentially, some influential people in a white neighborhood objecting to black people in their midst, as though the Bird House represented a dangerous inroad, a creeping plague. A disappointment, a scandal, an ugly business—and not long after, Fred Anderson took over the Velvet Lounge (already possessed of that name, if I'm not mistaken). 2218½ South Indiana: a location where nobody could object, a block from the Ickes Homes public housing and a once-bustling commercial corner, but now an intersection where things seemed to be forever passing by, a vast service entrance for McCormick Place and Burnham Park, too far to walk from the Loop, not close to any other music clubs. A dead spot, really, so you get the uncomfortable feeling that Fred Anderson's twenty-five-year run at the Velvet Lounge has been not so much a triumph—though the audiences and recognition are now coming around—as a stubbornly extended last stand.

"Just trying to keep the music alive"—the word music is touched very lightly as he speaks it, like something sacred, like something very fragile and very strong.

1989: The Verge

Bob Anderson—he was a keyboard player, a songwriter as well, and though his surname was the same as Fred's, in many respects there couldn't have been two people more different: Fred from Louisiana, one of the black elders, the early driving forces, of the AACM (Association for the Advancement of Creative Musicians), since the sixties an artistic matrix for the Chicago jazz avant-garde; Bob a North Sider, an intense blond-haired Scandinavian-American rocker, a loner who wrote music that was a world unto itself, too difficult or too idiosyncratic for most of his peers. While everyone admired what he did, his bands were always falling apart, and he was forever searching for another bass player, another drummer, another lead guitarist.

We met at Central YMCA, an alternative high school for the rebellious and troubled that was located on La Salle Street not far from the Board of Trade, an incongruous setting but convenient for students who came from all around the city. We were friends for years, although during the eighties I moved out of Chicago and lost touch with him for a good while. I assumed he was continuing on with what he'd always done: music, day and night, and by the time I came back in 1988, nearly twenty years of it supported by a phone-sales job he worked on the afternoon shift, very occasional gigs, and most recently an informal school in his Lincoln Avenue studio/apartment, voice and keyboard and guitar, handling ten or twenty students a week.

As a child he'd been a piano prodigy, in the course of the sixties he turned to rock, playing professionally in bands while he was a teenager and developing a hard-driving style that was mostly British in its inspiration—Procol Harum and Keith Emerson, King Crimson and Cream. The years passed and he stayed with it even as different trends emerged— punk, Bowie, new wave, heavy metal—working at his writing and becoming a powerful singer as well as a pretty competent guitar player, all of which supported what he was for a long time building, laboring over, and perfecting: his cycles of songs, probably two hundred or so altogether, and his goal of recording a set of them properly, flawlessly, sending off an irresistible demo and being offered a major-label contract.

We became friends mainly through jazz—he knew the music, his father had taken him to Duke Ellington concerts when he was young, Ramsey Lewis was a member of the Unitarian church his family attended in Oak Park, he was well aware that his rock music models drew on people like Ray Charles and Jimmy Smith and John Coltrane, and he had his own history of inspirations from Oscar Peterson and McCoy Tyner (he wore out *Something Warm* and *Inception*). A virtuoso player, an omnivorous listener, Bob let his music get seeded by many things: whatever excited him, whatever had an edge of passion or excess, whatever he respected as composition or as song—especially song. There was always a new song, or two or three new songs written in the course of an insomniac night; there were new versions of his old songs, the tempo or the arrangement improved; there was the quest for the right accompanist for the song to sound precisely as he wanted it. Sometimes when we were sitting in a restaurant—he liked the Melrose near Belmont and Broadway, a window seat in a booth to watch the world go by—he exhausted me because he so seldom stopped talking, gesticulating, his food going cold, his eyes blinking nervously, insisting on approval, agreement, but one day I realized that even here he was singing, his energies caught up in song like a bird on a tree that can't stop itself, its body aches with music and it's swinging on a branch so hard it's almost falling off, a world coursing through it. His dream was to do in two or three minutes of song an amazing number of things: melodic hooks, touching to the quick primal emotions of love and hate, the bedrock of the popular; at the same time a superstructure of agitated and complex keyboard lines, modal point and counterpoint running between the Steinway grand and the Hammond B-3, and tempos, too, shifting in turn, frenetic guitar licks wiring up the arrangement as he topped it off with a gutsy, soaring vocal, the song working up to an overpowering synchrony, an explosive pressure and release that would effect something radical, unforgettable. He said he wanted to take off the listener's head, he wanted to blow people's minds and make them free, he wanted to lay them out with a surge of powers beyond the human, he wanted to give the world a pure blast of heaven and hell and everything between.

When Bob was really moved, say, by Coltrane's *Om* or a Cecil Taylor show or an AACM concert with the Art Ensemble or Richard Abrams, he'd call the music rock; for him, it had the same rhythmic intensity, the same rebel spirit, the same imperative of freedom. That was why he loved Fred's music, the Velvet Lounge about the only club he frequented; during the late seventies he often called me on Sunday afternoons to see if I wanted to hear Fred play that night. That was immediately after the Bird House period, and the Velvet Lounge had no stage, no track lighting, only the tables and chairs and the booths, a bronzed chandelier hanging at a tilt from the ceiling like the remnant of a crazy wedding party. There was still a rough crowd, the old regulars mixing uncertainly with the small group of listeners gathered around the tables in back, the place dividing sometimes into territories as if replicating the zones of the city outside the door. At a certain point Fred would just walk out from behind the bar and start blowing fast and hard—an ascending, cycling phrase interrupted by low booms, buzzing temblors, almost a panicked feeling in it, a pressure there to pull it all together and whatever the odds to make it work. Bob would be transfixed, his ambitions and agitations quieted for a while. At the height of the music one night he grabbed my arm and said, "My God. This is a paradise." Fred had achieved with the Velvet Lounge what Bob would have liked to do himself—to break out, to turn his back on the illusory promises of the marketplace, to make a space to keep the music alive, uncompromising and uncompromised.

Of course in one regard Bob had been following a similar track for years, and he did finally produce and record his demo, called *The Verge*. It was a good title, reflecting the edgy, maxed-out character of the music as well as the hope that this would be it, he was on the verge of success, the big contract. That was in 1989, not long after I'd returned to Chicago. I'd seen him a few times though not very often since I was living on the other side of town and caught up in work of my own. I knew already that things had gone badly the year before; his sister had called me one day and let me know that he'd been diagnosed with lymphoma. But he was so strong, and still so young—only thirty-six—and it appeared after a while that he'd beat it. He was singing and playing, teaching and writing, working hard. The remission didn't last, it came back, and by the summer, unbelievably, he was gone.

Afterward his friends went through different theories about how and why. It might have been the years of proximity to electronics, the wiring and power lines he was always rigging up wherever he lived, more or less sleeping with his equipment. It might have been the studio with its peeling paint and ancient space heaters, and outside the windows the constant exhaust fumes from the street he called stinkin' Lincoln. It might have been the students he kept taking on once he quit the phone job, the way he expended his energies not only teaching but becoming a friend and an inspiration, letting them play at his place on weekends, often laying back from his own music and serving as a one-man house band. It might have been a fate driven by his trafficking in extremes: the Romantic-utopian forces of his music, the near-hubris that demanded everything perfect, everything at once, everything pushed to the verge and over, Bob the narcissistic demiurge of his own wild universe.

Or it was a punishment, as one of Bob's uncles, who had always looked on him with disapproval and a kind of horror, might have suggested if he'd bothered talking to us. In 1970, Bob had been beaten by the Chicago police, for no good reason except his acting defiant, a foolish bit of theater on the street. I witnessed it, I was with him, but while the cop was throwing Bob against the hood of the squad car I was making my escape, a couple of other police in hot pursuit of me. I crawled through yards and alleys and eventually made it home, and Bob in the meantime was worked over on the corner and later at the stationhouse. They punched his head, pulled out clumps of his hair, and one cop broke his watch against Bob's face and told him to look at he what he'd done, he'd damn well be paying for a new one. They repeatedly asked him who his friend was, the asshole who ran. He wouldn't say, and they hit him again.

That same night Bob's father came to my parents' house and told us what had happened, warned us there was a warrant out for me. Carl was a tall well-spoken man with an almost scholarly air about him, something demanding, too, ascetic and driven. He was a federal official, the Equal

Opportunity Commission, I think it was. By the time he'd come to us it was past one o'clock and he was obviously extremely upset, overwrought, his eyes glittering with indignation and disbelief. He never did get to sleep that night. He had spent hours contacting everyone he knew in the world of Chicago politics, personal friends, state senators and a congressman, people he had autographed photos of at home, people he'd met through his public appearances as an American history expert. Now he was being stonewalled—they had nothing to say about what had happened to his son, they couldn't do anything for him. And so he went on for another day: we saw him again at our house when Bob was released, having been charged with assaulting a police officer (he'd brandished a plastic crucifix at the cop); we saw him again the next morning when I went downtown to give a deposition to Internal Investigations, warrant or not. By then Carl couldn't stop talking, couldn't stop thinking and thinking it through, he'd been up three days without sleep and that was the limit. He suffered a stroke, and after a couple of days, Bob and I visiting him every afternoon at Henrotin Hospital, listening to a jumble of words he spoke that made absolute sense, that made no sense at all, looking into the deep blackened orbits of his eyes and then looking away again, we learned that in the course of another sleepless night, he had died.

Someone said after the wake that Carl was a man who had believed in America, believed the system worked, and when he found that it didn't, or realized how it really worked, he couldn't absorb the shock: his own system broke down. And a family member, that same self-righteous uncle, said the whole thing was Bob's fault: his rebelliousness and his arrogance had killed his father as surely as though he'd planned it. In a sense, the years of music, the near-impossible strain of the song Bob wanted to make—a song of revolution, a song of love and hate, a song of freedom— was an answer to that accusation. He would redeem his father's loss. And the music would be proof against the system, would subvert and surpass it, would mock it as the uncompromising art of *The Verge* brought money and what it could buy in the way of time and mobility, making possible if nothing else Bob's own freedom.

The city that works—that works on you, into you, maybe with you, but equally likely against you. You not only believe in its power, you participate in it, mimic it, work yourself up and wear yourself out—but the hell if there isn't a moment when you're on top, or better, you're catching the power in its interstices, its in-betweens, you're razzing it and goosing it, jazzing it up, you're tooling down Lake Shore Drive doing seventy and jumping over to Lower Wacker at Columbus, forcing the traffic lights to green all the way to wherever it is you're going off Canal Street, your destination doesn't matter, it's the motion, the force, your growl in the throat at the thing that at the same time is making that growl in you, giving and taking your voice. "Life in the city / ain't very pretty / under the wheel . . . "; the grim lyric of Bob's song is delivered anyway with gritty exuberance, a joyful irony orchestrated through spiking trains of minor modes and deep-drilling piano riffs, as if he's exalting in his powers at the very instant the city-machine is rolling him under, or as if he's echoing the city itself, he can't help it, no one can help it, it's a work that works you over, a making that unmakes you, an ever-driving wheel that drives you everywhere out and across and under, the thing you try to catch on fire there is its in-between, raveled edging of its pattern and order, loose thread, hot wire you take up that takes you up in its turn.

Every time, as soon as we walked into the Velvet Lounge, Bob would talk to Fred for a while, shake his hand and address him as "Mister Anderson," enjoying the small joke though I'm not sure Fred was aware of their shared name or even knew Bob was a musician. I'd watch the two of them together there, feeling happy anyway that their worlds were touching, feeling grateful for their gifts, feeling the roaring lion of the city outside the door and how there was no safety anywhere from that lion and how inside here, with the music, I'd hear that roar taken up by human voices, human hands, their works of subterfuge and exorcism, of exile and failure and glory.

The Verge—I have the cassette. I listen to it now and then if I'm not afraid of the pain. Among others, I like especially the song about the wheel. It's strong work, it holds up, though only a few old friends know it anymore, keep it alive.

1999: For Paul

It's nearly ten-thirty. We've carried our drinks to one of the booths along the wall, the bartender will check on us later. In the meanwhile Ari Brown and Malachi Favors and Avreeayl Ra have quietly taken their places. A few runs, a swift drum roll. The stage lights brightening, the grid-pattern of the wallpaper flashing as though run through with silvery water. For an instant, it dazzles the eye, a torn netting swimming with ghostly dashes, crosses and lines.

Standing offstage, another player, unidentified (the bill tonight says Ari Brown Trio). He looks about fifty, fifty-five, ebony skin, a broad forehead, his hair thinning along the top with two short braids in back. He's wearing loose dress slacks, low tasseled shoes, a black and gray shirt patterned with figures like blocks or stones.

Although the group hasn't begun, he's launched an audacious statement, wild fluidity and dissonant verve, managed through some effortless synthesis of the tenor saxophone's registers like the fiery peak of an epic Rahsaan Roland Kirk solo but staying up there, how can he stay there, and he's still offstage but claiming his ground as if the group is there to play behind him, and pretty soon we're wondering what's up—is he one of Fred's or Ari's students, or a street musician wandered in for an impromptu before the show? Someone blown in from New York, a famous name we should recognize? Surely he can't maintain much longer the sort of thing he's doing on his tenor—it's an old one, burnished bell and bow, a wealth of engravings and scratches on it faded to a gold hieroglyph—yet he's not stopping, and although he doesn't have a microphone the sound is bold, loud, almost overbearing, as if to say he really has arrived however and wherever he's come from tonight.

Ari: wire-framed glasses, an oversized blue tie-dyed shirt with saffron sunbursts, a loose dignity like a professor on vacation. Without a word—no intro, no greeting, no announcements—he starts up his tenor and offers a gruff stirring-over of what's been broadcasting from Paul (that's all we'll catch, though later he'll tell us his full name "in the system," as he says, along with his African name). Volume, mass, lift: a broken chain of modal fragments like flung boulders, like tumbled rocks, an upsurge through several versions of Paul's message issuing in a harsh and stately line that leaves a space and with a subtle faltering blurs that space, roughens its edge, gives purchase, traction, welcome, Paul skidding off now on a plane already driving itself apart, the plush gutbucket of the tenor's bottom sleeving to hyperaltissimo gustings, Ari wheeling back around hoarse and declamatory, tale of a downward spin, elation of a spiraled ascent, Paul's mounting the stage now and doesn't ever stop playing, he takes the mike across from Ari, Malachi Favors lowers a boom and Avreeayl Ra suddenly ignites, sends a shiver across the tenors going straight to work, no time to waste.

The thrust of the music is so hard, so resolutely against the grain of comfort, so far from the realm of jazz with a hook, jazz with a groove, jazz counting you down through changes and melody and easily lifting you with the buoyancy of the solo, I imagine my wife instantly hating it. I too want to refuse it. Like on an airplane taking off, when, eager as I might be to make the trip, I essentially don't like the feeling of relinquishing control, losing the ground, I move restlessly, fantasizing my foot on a giant brake pedal that would bring the proceedings to a halt.

But then of course we're up, outside the window the lights of the city wheeling past and then settling back down, the plane climbing a pillow-like stair of the air, soon the seatbelt signs are off, drinks on the way, we're comfortable reading our books among the clouds and forgetting how ferocious, really, is the matter of flight, the turbines detonating truckloads of fuel, the engines pluming exhaust so it looks like the wing is on fire, and how ferocious, too, the flight of this music that doesn't level off, doesn't ease to a glide, a smooth cruise, but instead exposes its instant of creation, system skinned to its innards, the hatch door sprung on the pipes and feeders and circuits where the system holds tight and the system ravels apart, science of the contact, the spark, the flow, poetics of the disjuncture, the surprise, the naked shock where you put your hand to the work and the work puts it hand to you.

Paul: a line bears all it can take, it vanishes into air. Ari: a wind sweeps through. My eyes are closing here. My wife, about whose response to the music I'm still anxious, is sitting close to me in the booth. I smell her skin, a faint perfume. I think of leaning over to kiss her. A bottle of Guinness, I know, is on the table. At a later point I may take a drink from it. I remember the idea that space is infinite because every line you can imagine marks a space one jump beyond it, or is it the line that's infinite, lacing space? The line twists into a knot. Space would forever be filled, topping the tank, but it can't, something resists. It fractions, froths.

Paw in the labyrinth. The fevered air. Messy weather, where each one's sounding, the bore and the weight of each voice, lets itself get lost in the other. Ari brooding over it a while, the storm of the tenor laddering, swelling, and then like a tower collapsing down to baffled steps, a monumental ruin. Paul suddenly on a steep rise, broken footing, the ground slipping, a

slide that gathers it back by riding it out. The two stitching across a border where the piling, the climbing over the pile, the piling again, rise off
each other until the threads stalk together in a cloud, a ferment, a bloom
singular, irreversible, and unrepeatable as the touching together of two
flames inside a fire.

This is the joint. On every side, place. Echoes down a passage. I have
not an idea but a body, a passion. I do not want to sit here, really, eyes
mostly closed. I want to rise, dance, but all is just now finished, all is just
now commencing, Malachi traveling me with dromedary grace, these are
hills, these are skies, Avreeayl Ra brassing a kiss, Ari and Paul, Paul and
Ari, the thing is ripe with its gravity, its antigravity—hot fruit falling off
a tree, roots climbing out of the ground into a sky garden, a hard-earned
moment, lifetimes given over to it, and surely it must have to stop any
second yet it doesn't, it lasts, Paul taking off his glasses after a while and
laughing as he turns the horn aside and instantly brings it to his mouth
again, Ari swaying there, his whiskered lips pushing at the saxophone's
mouthpiece. Turning the neck he lets the reed out for a second and it
darts back in like he's kissing a cobra, across from him Paul planted on
what seem too-short legs carrying his solid trunk of body, his chest and
his diaphragm feeding the horn the air as regularly and as impersonally
as the ocean pushes a wave, as a pump fuels an engine.

Ari: swift-wrought figures of deliberation and weight, as if stoppered
under iron. The air pressure inside the horn a maximum poundage,
time-hydraulic telescoping Chicago years, the systems of Gene Ammons, Von Freeman, and Johnny Griffin, the heretical encyclopedics
of Roscoe Mitchell and Anthony Braxton. Paul: a later redaction that
might have a claim to being more accurate than its original although it
lets itself tremble and gets itself stained, releasing a stagger of overcoded
sonorities that swarm the scrambled breaking rank of the double-firing
horns—they're burning Dexter Gordon and Wardell Gray, Coltrane and
Pharaoh—where an impossible ear would discern the infinite intrication
of the tenors' separate lines, the density of their exploded fugal relay, the
ministries of their leaguing, the statistics of their mobbed plaguing.

In the close of the eyes, where I am is a corridor. In a building, the extra space whose only use is access or escape. Somewhere in the distance,
I'm hearing work underway. A hammer on an anvil, heat beating down on
it, too. The sweat just rains. The swing and fall of the hammer is steady,

unrelenting, but in each upstroke is a small quivering, feed of the blow, in each downstroke, a correspondent tremor. In between, through grip and hand and bone, sings the work.

After a while, Ari moves to the keyboard, sets his feet wide, his knees are jumping, he's almost rocking off the folding chair, the Roland has a chocky, hammering sound, it's like a deck of bright cards fanning out, the kinds and suits slotting and stacking and dominoing across the spidered pulse and low bowing of Malachi's bass, Ra's global attack, the scared-up beats, while Paul's powering still through hard-bucking phrases, reeling turnbacks, never a pause, high-pressure overtones producing an organlike tearing at the air that at the same time pulls around and catches the spill, begins once more to strain against it, to force it against its own edge.

I look over at my wife to see how she's taking it—an hour, two hours, have passed without a break—and I realize that I've had my eyes closed for a long while and that she's been the same, sitting there in a trance almost as if she's asleep. She meets my gaze but we don't say very much— words here and there we can scarcely articulate, don't want to articulate because we're floored, we're undone, the music is still going, and one or the other of us says it wouldn't be so bad to *just die right now*: hyperbole, I suppose, a naive sentiment, but inside this whirlwind where there's nothing but giving, giving, I'm gripped by an *amor fati* that surges through the music's ravished blessing, happy fool who was able to walk in off the street and be provided with so much, why shouldn't I be satisfied to lose my life, why would I want to hold on to it anymore? A shit-eating grin: I'm laughing without knowing what's happening, something erupting, I'm in love, say—the dangerous passion that throws everything away, our eyes again closing I clasp her hand as though we've already died together, the Velvet Lounge is our sun-barge, our souls' plush coffin passing between worlds making an escape without a landing, riding off some asymptote that has the shape of what's falling into place just now, song being scattered to the winds, Ari back hitting hard on the tenor and Paul with a whispering fluting that carries all the way down through the lower register, tops off again, again, I want everyone to be there, the living and the dead, I want to record this moment for posterity though its power must be precisely in its coming and its passing without any possibility of saving it, the house is on fire, the roof raising off the beams, the other night is pouring in, the night of which the city is the shadow, the night that's the reversed imprint of its networks and orders, the night that's the bright blacking-out of the work done and the lives undone, at a stroke past midnight another sun rising inside the Velvet Lounge, the old broken chandelier shining like a burning flower.

I let out a shout, I can't help it. It's the shout we used to make when we were children, walking through a viaduct or standing at a junction of the tracks on an embankment where the trains came through fast, you had to keep watch in every direction, the silver Northwestern or the Milwaukee Road in a second might be bearing down on you, you wouldn't be the first kid out there to go under the wheels. You planted your feet anyway on the treacherous X of the intersecting rails, the Loop skyline shining off in the distance, the ladders and catwalks of the signal bridge above you with all the lights showing green and down below the traffic ganging down the Expressway, a current flowing into your body that made your throat swell and your mouth open wide as if you were infinitely hungry or something was infinitely hungry for you. A sound leaped out of you that was all yours and that wasn't yours at all. You yelled for joy.

The Velvet Lounge, a quarter till two in the morning. Closing time: the night train disembarked, the bride and bridegroom gone off on their honeymoon, the launch-vehicle passing out of sight, burning off its fuel miles high in the sky above flame-scorched ground. My wife and I look at each other again. We don't say very much: words to the effect that there are no words for this, or basic words, admiring or grateful or exclamatory nonsense—wow, oh lord, goodness gracious—or some reflection on how we'd like never to leave this place. What this is should be the world.

Paul's been talking to friends in the audience, joking, laughing, sounds of delight. He extracts a single Marlboro from an otherwise empty box but doesn't light up.

"Paul: you got to take that horn out of your mouth sometime," says Avreeayl Ra, and Paul grins. "Hey. We were just getting warmed up."

We thank him for the music, he thanks us in turn. He tells us he's been playing since 1983, when he was still with the CTA. He worked an early shift and afterwards would take the horn down into the subway tunnels to practice. Sometimes he'd spend more time there than he did on the job. For hours he listened to the sounds of the trains coming through the system. He taught himself how to talk back.

Heading north that night we might be riding through one of those tunnels, maybe off the red-pillared Harrison Street station, maybe off the screeching turn where the wheels seem to verge off the track, blue sparks jumping, from Clark and Division to North and Clybourn. For years we traveled that damp infernal landscape, going to our jobs every day, often heard the musicians down there, their echoes mixing with the echoing clattering and the cool breezing of the trains. The system—the work that the millionaire Yerkes forged through money and political muscle in the early twentieth century, cobbling together a group of independent rails into the monopoly that later became the CTA Rapid Transit. It never matched the Chicago street-grid, instead following an irregular pattern— the sudden loops of the Howard through the North Side, the winding progress of the Ravenswood, the jogs of the old Jackson Park and Englewood Lines, the straight path of Lake Street unevenly paralleled by the Douglas Park slanting off south. (In later years, perhaps seeking a more satisfactory result, Yerkes would endow an astronomical observatory to study the system of the heavens.)

I imagine Paul listening for the train from the far end of a platform. Or standing near one of the sheds you see in a flash between crumbling arches underground, a chamber there with a red-glassed lantern and a pile of discarded machinery, gears and wheels. Because he's listening, what he hears is as much silence as sound. Down the tunnel, a station away, it's not just the conductor's buzzer, the rolling slap of the doors, the motors spinning again into their hum and the wheels smoothing the track, one or two rattling, the rod scraping the third rail. It's the space from which the sound is emerging, it's the time in which it's verging upon him, in that interval an echoing, a resonance—the work he's done that day (was he a conductor, a supervisor, a motorman?), the work he's doing now, the push and the drag of the approaching wheels, the air that's parting, breezing, draining off the cars of the train, Paul down inside the heart of the city, keeping it alive.

Julius Hemphill   *Photo by Michael Wilderman*

le serpent qui danse

Trees

It involves a humming throat, it involves a dance of breath, it involves spit. Drooled blowhole of fat importunate lips, sputtered cunning flutters of hungry lascivious tongue, press and wheeze of diaphragm like a bird's throbbing syrinx. At first rounded and mellow, the lyric envelope of the melody soon punctures, somewhere an octave above high C a split tone shrilling as though a mere Boehm flute cannot bear the force of the wind, the body of the instrument blown away, spirited off in a whistle piercing and distempered and intemperate. You would say the flute suffers it, if that microtonal spasming were not so sharp with the joy of override, like a tree's sudden flush of leaves silvered and battered and tossed, all its hold and measure offered up to what compels and punishes and indifferently caresses.

Rahsaan Roland Kirk's tune "Trees": a sense of his big horn-strapped body gobbling up all the air, in the puffed-out cheeks that air being tasted and chewed, the flute in turn bursting with it, a song-swollen bird landed on his fingers. In the evening park, divination of the blind musician hearing the rushing whispering run of leaves in a grove of elms, a sound like a subway train whooshing far off in a tunnel, through distant plumbing a clattering stutter and traction of wheels.

I sit on the second-floor porch on Cullom Street, my eyes full of maple trees. The hang of their branches is casual, occasional, disorganized. In my Chicago neighborhood, the maples were common, shading the front terraces, the sidewalks, the yards and the back alleys. They offered a complex shadow, often solid, heavy, and dark on a hot summer afternoon, sometimes lightened, though, with the different turns of the branches, the uneven shuttering of the leaves that were not quite star-shaped, not quite hand-shaped. You licked their pale undersides and tasted a green sugar. You remarked the minuscule dots of the red galls along their veins. You saw their flagging into burnt gold and brown-streaked crimson in the autumn.

On this tree, the one in front of the building, the leaves grow thick. Many of the smaller branches have a tubular, rubbery look, rather like wires or cables. A stringy, descending growth—not so much toward the sun but hanging willowlike as though to float upon water. A riverine tree, in need of a creek, marshland. The leaves seem to yearn toward making a wall of some kind. Say, a vine-covered rampart, itself made of green beneath these hanging gardens that insistently tremble and flicker and ride with every motion of the air. Responding too with a sound of very soft hissing—is it hissing? It's hard to decide: a car is passing, the couple on the steps across the street just said something exclamatory and insulting; now she's laughed. Is the sound the famous *sussurus*, the murmur of leaves? But it has a swishing quality. Or a sound like thousands of sheets of paper rustling.

The leaves—pointy, spiky, clumped, and perhaps too many, crowding one another. Lateral cuts below the tips, and then deeper angles farther down. Like a knife becoming a hand. And with a look too of having been chewed, bitten, the prey of leaf-cutter bugs or beetles or caterpillars. In the view of the traditional homeowner, the maple tree is often no better than a weed. Growing unevenly, messy, careless—a few of the main branches reach upward in a dignified way, but others fan out and away from the pattern and at the same time exhibit a tendency toward reaching across or down. It's unruly, pushy, heading in the wrong direction. To an orderly mind, it seems perverse that it won't simply grow straight rather than splaying itself out in this dropsical, lackadaisical way.

And the trunk, the bark. Gray, light gray, weak-looking, porous. Those vertical lines or cracks all along it, showing the tender reddish-orange color of the wood. And in this tree, a real wound. Someone was fleeing the police: the car ran up the curb, and now the maple bleeds slowly year after year where it was struck. A tree prone to trauma of many kinds, sometimes a richer foliage sprouting in the places where it has suffered injury. It's the tree that makes the helicopters, all that spinning and detritus in the street, the conscientious neighbors sweeping them up. Stripped of its translucent covering, the soft pulpy seed looks edible, a pale bean. It is almost tasteless, a trace of the color green on the tongue. In the lore of homeowners, the maple tree is a destroyer of plumbing and foundations, a vegetal termite. Often they cut it down, skeptical of all those leaves overloading and overlapping the branches as though waiting to be combed, drawn, and stroked, every fall those same leaves steeping the sidewalks and lawns in perishing reds and golds. They see the green mask of an insidious underground power that digs deep, roots into footings, runs cracks into walls.

Francis Ponge once wrote that because trees, unlike animals, are essentially immobile, they exhibit a monotonous and insistent will to expression. Stopped, arrested, imprisoned in their positions, they must branch, divide, offer in their poses what they have suffered or achieved to be read like a book. For Ponge, they are baroque and static beings, writhing, imprisoned fixtures in the bourgeois parlor of nature. Without powers of locomotion, they lack drama. They can leave no track, no trail. Yet for Martha Graham, all the powers of dance were in the spirit of the tree: the body's motions turned from the pillar of the spine, the limbs holding yet swayed like branches in the wind, all the nerves exposed to a shimmering of sound and air, all the skin naked to a touch of world.

Trees: lineages and histories, organizations and dialectics, elders rooted deep in earth, priests with their robes brushing heaven. A halt of motion, preserved and preserving, confining growth and change within a harp vertical and horizontal, holding back a potentially free play of lines and flights that would dart and delve and take off in all directions. Grass springing up everywhere, the climb of vines, the irrepressible dissemination of weeds—trees standing over against such seedy inconsequentialities, trees marking a horizon, a sky, erect and yearning upward, even the smallest sapling already self-assured in its forthright, almost human bearing. Stately and classical, a full-grown oak is something on the order of a library, shelves and leaves, lights and shadows, irresistibly indeed like a book, to be written and read.

But an oak riding a stiff October wind can appear a being expended in ecstasy, a great glory hand signaling for a halt to the same procedure by which it is letting itself be consumed as though it exists only to offer exposure to what teases and frets and rags. Or the columnar maple on my Baltimore street: in the still air of a June night it scarcely moves, its branches thick with leaf, a texture like thick curled hair. It does not offer refuge to the eye by virtue of a shapely upreaching form. It stills the gaze with intimations of obscure verdure, of interior crossworks and bosky shadows. The slightest air sets it astir, a languid dash of leaves, the swayed laterals of the underbranches, a sort of arrested shake, a slacking of attitude by which systems of things seem to lend themselves to being messed with, pleasurably raked and disarrayed, soliciting scratch and drift and friction.

St. Louis, February 1972—the horn blast of a Mississippi barge, smoke-smell lingering along brick-rubble blocks, the square teeth of old red cornices dusted with snow. Julius Hemphill in a Black Artists' Guild session: "The Hard Blues," scraping the alto saxophone through what no longer seem notes and octaves but the sweetly hoarse throatings of a mud-rooted tree coming to speech, the flutter tongues of its leaves, the honeyed cough of an air clouded green with breath, a river twisting through hills and banks, crumbles of levee earth. You hear Delta, but that root too is another tree, branched and fanned in alluvial sweep and tangle among black channels mirroring skinny jack pines and frayed shawls of Spanish moss, across the dragged glass of the water a float of languid shivering runs like gliding moccasins.

One winter day along the north branch of the Chicago River, the trees along the bank with the tips of their branches frozen into the ice but in a slow thawing lifting above the water and hanging over the middle channel of the river. Over a stretch of forty or fifty feet, a fragile system of glittering filigreed medallions, irregular objects of such rare chance they seemed impossible, unearthly, messages or mementos or ephemeral architectures of an alien visitation.

In the same session, "Dogon A.D.," the raw abrasion of Abdul Wadud's bowed cello pulling against the stops, Hemphill's alto earnest and grainy and fluid, at times seeming on the verge of a happy faltering—the song is greeting, is joy of welcoming—the runs so pressured through a leap of jubilee the phrases overload the branching spaces they articulate, loop and drop with sliding soft-shoe grace.

In the burned-down blocks and vacant lots the invasive, nonnative species, the Chinese tree of heaven in thick fabric fronds, impervious to drought, pollution, and piss, the latter something like its own cloying odor. It comes up anywhere, an impudence of rich and generous green, of cheap and easy shade. Abundant in young, a tree which often grows tall and lines the alleys and cracked streets, like funky loitering mobs the leaves muttering and brushing together under sun, like rowdy testifying congregations the leaves tonguing wild before a wind as though their sway and restless wake would conjure a city paradise. Once he started drinking, my friend didn't stop, bar to bar, bottle to bottle, arms and legs outreached flailing to haul the slack weight of his body down the middle of the street flapping and waving, wheeling into traffic as though to wrap himself around it, sometimes he'd finish the night on the Welles Park lawn laid out on the ground with his limbs treed between earth and sky.

Maybe off a truck-rutted road in Tulsa, maybe down a treeless alley street in east Baltimore—a stripped Christmas pine in a bucket of concrete, jammed on the branch stubs a two-liter Mountain Dew bottle collapsed in green folds, a pocket half-pint of Wild Irish Rose, a cluster of Shasta cans, a King Cobra forty drooping heavy and trailing a last tag of its crimson and silver label. In the raw sunlight you wish for a breeze, a low murmuring to blow over those hollows, but the music is all in the color and glare, a bright forbidding forest of swimming unblinking eyes.

"Thanks for Those Beautiful Ladies": Rahsaan bristling with the horns all around his neck, dreaming the tenor over the Coltrane solos he so loved, "Syeeda's Song Flute" or "Afro-Blue," the scalar incubations of the chords Mozart-lush but at the same time a spiraling spiked and bent with thorny shadows, a music blacking and bolding its track as if unjustly confined, carrying the surge of itself across the tree of the changes run and leafed and everywhere green, tongues brightly divided and flickering as if catching a scent of light floating on the wind.

Tales from Underwood

1975: one night coming back from a date of sorts (shamefully, I don't remember her name and don't even have any recollection of where she lived, what the house was like), it was three, four in the morning, I was driving down through the North Shore back into the city, Sheridan Road, Highland Avenue, Ridge Boulevard, and I was drunk and probably disappointed, I was doing eighty and then almost ninety in the Chevy Bel Air, I was in a cool tunnel of dark and trees with the wind blasting through the windows open all around, front and back, and it was late, there was nobody out, but I knew all it needed was one, and I was blowing through the reds and each time thinking, well, this could be it, I'm dead, they're dead, at the same time feeling a sort of blank as I hit each signal and each intersection through which I seemed to travel elevated, over a bridge, and inside the blank I was possessed with an utter belief in a luck, a power, as if the very concentration on the possibility of dying in a crash shifted it to the side where it rode among the dark of the trees, and so I shot down to the bright lights, slowing down finally at the city line, Howard Street, Clark, home.

Gaps, confusions, inside that year of floating through jobs and apartments and pursuits of a love or lover, Chicago-spell when the raw street feeling of pushy traffic and none-of-your-business and hey, it's party, party, beguiled me with a sense of possibility everywhere, and so to celebrate beforehand, never mind what would happen, whether the night really sometime would offer its flower. Under the driver's seat I stocked a fifth of El Presidente that clanked and rolled whenever I made a turn, if all else failed a ready means—a straight dose, aromatic and jalapeño-hot—to catch a taste of the general fever.

With a comrade or alone, I'd cruise all around the North Side, Division and Armitage, Clark and Lincoln and Broadway. There were scores of bars, neighborhood joints and places with live music and all the standard on-the-town destinations like Wise Fools and John Barleycorn. Yet wherever I went I'd feel uncomfortable, out of it. Who were these people? I didn't know a soul. Either I didn't live in the neighborhood and so wasn't a regular, or I was a lost cause among an affluent, animated crowd by whom I felt outclassed. Looking for women—I would feel as the night wore on that it was both the weakest and the most unacceptable goal to be pursuing.

And those times when a woman seemed friendly, maybe interested, I would fumble the chance—study too long whether the signal was real or imaginary, or suddenly realize that I had nothing at all in the way of a rap, as one's account of oneself was called in those days. Who the hell was I? I would read the personals in the *Chicago Reader*, envious and hopeless in view of the accomplishments and credentials of others: writer-athlete loves the mountains and his Lincoln Park apartment. Stockbroker by day, musician by night, seeks passionate companion . . . I was a guy who drove a delivery truck for an automobile paint distributor, hauling buckets of Bondo and exotically named color matches, Orchid Murano Pearl and Montezuma Tropic Gold, to body shops where cars were lavished with complex attentions, a fussy science involved in the repair of damage to the point where all could agree the car looked as if it had never been in an accident at all. Often I had dummy orders, items billed and not delivered and providing the shop foreman with a kickback courtesy of our salesman. Camouflaging the scheme, a portion of the order would be for real—the usual cans of enamels, boxes of respirator masks, a Devilbiss spray nozzle lodged like jewelry in a small tight box. Or I was told to deliver an invoice billing the shop for hundreds of dollars of materials that existed only on paper. If anyone questioned the procedure, the blame could be thrown on me, the driver—I'd been confused when I was loading the truck, or maybe I'd lifted the material and sold it off myself instead of delivering it to the shop. Along with the others, a mixed crew of young and old, most of whom had sworn off the dangers of taxi driving for a route job, I was expendable.

They were uncomfortable deliveries, walking through a zone of dizzying solvent fumes and following a directive that usually sent me to an empty office or to a foreman's accomplice working on a car and barely acknowledging me, gesturing toward a corner of the shop where the bogus order could be safely deposited out of the way or signing the invoice according to arrangement. On one occasion I was stopped just inside the service door by a manager type. He fit my image of the invisible body shop foreman for whom the dummy order was intended—slick graying hair, dress slacks and shirt and tie a bit rumpled as though he now and then worked a spray gun himself. "Who are you?" he asked, and I muttered the name of my company. He gave me a knowing look then, but no more, not a word. He signed the invoice with a careless scrawl, a signature that could have been written by anyone—plausible deniability, the salesmen laughingly called it.

On my way out that afternoon, I felt slightly intoxicated by the spray fumes, insidiously tainted by yet another shady deal. It was late April, and outside Suburban Dodge or Thatcher Ford or whatever the place was called, the trees along the Des Plaines River seemed impossibly green and pure, the sunlight on the new leaves richly gold. I had an urge to retrace my steps, to go back and say there had been a mistake. I would force the manager to admit the scam, push my way into the front office where I would tell all to the people on top.

But I knew it wouldn't work—I would be the accused, the one in the wrong, a mere cog in the machine presuming to question the way it functioned.

The trees leaned in the spring wind, their delicate green leaves carrying the light in what appeared to be an absolute clarity, a perfect adequation to their position in the world. Blue sky flared around the tips of the branches. Underneath was a floor of shadows, the naked ground patched and prickly with new growth. I imagined walking there with a woman, a bottle of wine swaying in a straw bag, a blanket we'd spread over the slightly dank but freshening lawn of a small clearing.

I stomped on the gas as I turned out of the dealer's lot, squealing tires and smoking rubber, half hoping I'd burn my truck down, wrap it around a tree, rocket my employer's insurance rates through the roof.

I didn't care what happened to me. I was going nowhere, or, as I sometimes felt, going backwards. Like the story where the thief attempts to elude his pursuers by hiding and letting them pass, then walking back inside his own footprints, returning in the direction he started from. In my nights after work that spring, I often found myself walking under the trees, in the woods, not sure whether I was in flight from or in search of something. I hiked along a muddy track along the north branch of the Chicago River, under the black oaks spears of green piercing the dense bedding of leaves and along the lower ground occasional catches of violet and crimson, humble early blossomings. The trail followed the dark river, at different points branching off into the thicker woods, paths following from paths. There was the familiar rank smell of the water: dirt and humus and oil. There was the sound of traffic on a nearby main street, and often the horn and clatter of a Milwaukee Road freight train on the nearby embankment. In the night woods I was usually alone, only once in a while encountering a person walking a dog, or wandering teenagers out for a bonfire and beers down along the bank. I had a sense though of obscure powers, of hovering presences. In the hazy air of the river mist, I would see a thickening, a sort of clotting. Looking at the shadowed ground beneath a jagged oak or the dim, hutlike canopy of a still bare mulberry, I would feel something like a water crossing my feet, pulling at my legs, my knees, as though in another river I waded through the years, touching the earth at the same angle as the long-vanished as well as more recent wanderers of the place—Miamis and Potawatomis, French trappers, secret lovers and lonely deviants. I made it my principle to creep over the paths in a way as nearly silent as I could manage. My goal was never to crack a branch, stub a stone, cross another's track; to make no stir so I could discover what stirred around me in the obscurity of the evening light: a motion or halt, a sway or song or a movement of flight surprised.

The woods: they were the Cook County Forest Preserves that ring
and in certain areas penetrate the outer neighborhoods of Chicago: sometimes parklike, with picnic groves and equestrian trails; sometimes neglected and rough and wild. With plenty of land along the rivers and their
tributaries and most of it prone to flooding, places like Ottawa Trails,
Chicago Portage, La Bagh, and Forest Glen. The woods—notorious, seductive, dangerous: site of dumped corpses from gangland executions or
domestic vendettas; site of homosexual assignations and blitzer drugfests,
closed at dusk with chains across the entrances and the Forest Preserve
Police making a cursory check with one sweep of their lights. Though
within city limits, there were deer among the oaks and maples, families of
possums silver under the moon, along the paths the crisscrossing tracks of
fat raccoons. One time in a hidden creek near a row of oil storage tanks I
saw a pile of junked timber and branches and heard a furtive splash. I had
stumbled across the cobbled-together rampart of a beaver dam. It took
me a long while to recognize it as a thing that had been made rather than
deposited there by accident. That evening I sat nearby for a good hour,
amazed. The dam looked like pure smash-up, a chaos of gray twisted
limbs and thorny broken spars, the deadwood dump of ice storms and
runoff. It had been created by design but the difference between design
and accident seemed to waver—it was impossible to say how much of the
material was purposefully placed, how much was already there and then
built over, how much collected there by virtue of maybe just one or two
limbs strategically positioned across the channel of the creek. Shelter and
protection were indistinguishable from spillage and wreck.

I gazed on the trees catching the last of the sun, the scant foliage of
the underwood already fallen into dark, among the coarse grasses and
thistles and vines a buzzing nursery of insects stirring in the dusk, flies
and hoppers and beetles so tiny and sometimes so closely shadowing the
vegetation they inhabited they seemed to have been born from it. Landed
on my arm, the vivid green body of the leafhopper was a mask that mim-
icked the lush growth among which it fed, a sort of ghost of the plant, the
plant in turn its haunt.

Later in the year, the woods lush and rank, I struck off from my silent
tracking along the paths. The nets and snarls of the underwood caught at
my feet and I made all kinds of noise, cracking twigs and rattling leaves.
I was acting like a big dummy, crashing through the woods like a fugitive,

a monster. I was scaring off everything, or maybe letting my position be known, plowing through ghosts while becoming like one myself. It was as if I were breaking clear though what I trod was the opposite of any clearing, instead the world below pulling at my feet.

One day in the shop, in the middle of one of their elaborate and obscene jokes, I told the salesmen: no more. By winter I was out of a job.

Out from the ensemble, stepping off the changes, capturing the melody and carrying it higher, levels and degrees that blossom, that flower, that leap into flight, bird from a tree, a sky full of wings—the jazz solo, the Hot Five tracks where Armstrong struts off gold, the Fletcher Henderson slots where Coleman Hawkins rips off ten or twenty seconds from a meticulous orchestral gearing, the multiple studio takes of Powell and Parker and Roach where the whole group attains a soloist's intensity, the long album sides of Roscoe Mitchell or Anthony Braxton where the other instruments disappear altogether and the horn's sound recklessly dilates or is by turns concealed in its underwood, rabbit on the run, started and scared up and driven to its chances along random, diverging paths. The solo: jazz offering its most convincing proofs, durable logics by which the humblest of elements are distributed into systems that thrill through the process of finding their hinging and jointure, all their elements set into motion at once, not so much the placing of tones in their mounts but the tones making places, mounting themselves, structure itself exposed and dramatized.

But sometimes sounding like it can't get off the ground. Or like it's launched all right but determined to bump and drag or maybe to discontinuously touch the surface or plane it has broken away from. Wayne Shorter's "Night Dreamer" or "Footprints": a hovering, a coolness and shade even when under full steam, the tenor insensibly tracking into a different region, the full-up runs foregone and a sort of stumble, a dragging traction, a plowing into ground but not quite mining it, a sort of going wrong as if the lines can't get up to speed or can't fix their position. Shorter's sound rich and full yet a feeling in it of being imprisoned, down under, straining to escape—"Witch Hunt" or "The Soothsayer"—a space thorned with chambers and gates, from a hermetic enclosure a cavernous quavering issuing forth, powers straining against their frame. Like certain clarinets—say, Barney Bigard or Jimmy Hamilton's—there's a liquid sense of the tubular, run of the shaft or tunnel or secret passage, of *hollows*, the lush tone as if coming from somewhere under the lowest stop, Ellington's jungles floored with ebony underwood, glissandos that in their slide wreathe and shadow and vine the ensemble. Wet soil, scoops of ponds that never quite go dry, vivid hair of wild grass tousled over intermittent flows of springs. Archie Shepp's tenor saxophone restlessly sounding down among the tarry thickets of a bottom register something like Coltrane's and much of the time staying there, working what might be the twist of a long tangled root, choked and throttled, hang of a conjuration.

Briar, thistle, and fern. Jack-in-the-pulpit, monkshood, foxglove. Shell-like outcrops of ivory fungi, amanitas on stumps. Where to hide, withdraw, build your power. Concealed in the thick underwood, Frankenstein's monster, abhorred by the cottagers who formerly blessed his generous spirit, vents his pain and studies his rage. In Clarice Lispector's novel *Agua Vi a*, the narrator is a painter brought to words by an unexpected turn of passion. Page after page, writing for her absent lover, she seems to be stalling, saying in one way and then another what it is she wants to do. There's no story, only her desire to make words become light, rhythm, space. She would like her writing to be sheer improvisation, all of her intention offered up, shaken prey in an eagle's beak, a power dispossessed, confused and fabulous and awkward like the coitus of mythical beasts. She dreams of a language sharp with particulars yet fitful and obscure, approximating ferment and fever. It is to be dense and gnarled and palely glowing like the forest's underbrush.

The Ethnic Heritage Ensemble, "Alika Rising": Joseph Bowie reaching a point in his solo where the trombone fades from blustery thrust to muttering flutter to an instant where there is nothing anymore you can call a note but only the faintest shadow of one, smeared and prickly and then needled fine as a green follicle on the stalk of a wild bramble rose. It almost bleeds into silence, muffled, tunneled, buried. It makes all the notes around it shiver and flare.

Max Ernst said his art came from the forest of his childhood, his life forever changed the day his father led him by the hand into the woods near Cologne and showed him that great exoskeletal body composed of teeming plasticities, vines and boles and leaves and branches, the wiry coursing of the dark underwood. A world bristling and itching with life—irritability, Ernst later called it, drawing upon the language of cellular biology. It was an informing principle of his work with collage: the

contact and friction of things, composition not a matter of genius giving
birth from some deep conception but instead a skimming ovum, not the
mind taking in images but vision being teased and fretted and insensibly
infiltrated. Gazing at the worn floorboards in his studio, the grain of the
wood irregular and singular, lines and blotches and knots, and feeling the
scratchy traction; rubbing, rubbing, he took the print of that bony tissue,
frottage of "The Horde" with its figures like carvings from the charred
logs of a brigand's midnight fire, "The Grey Forest" with its outcrops of
trees and birds, its ramparts exposing the secret interior of a lunar wood,
Ernst tracking the motions of a world on an underside of the world.

Ernst admired the writer August Strindberg, who believed the artist's
visions came through the graces of the wood spirit, a lovely female form
who as she turns aside reveals a skin of rough, furrowed bark. She's a
swift being who takes her lovers delicately thrashing on a bed of leaves,
among the wet shrubs a smell like absinthe bitters. In his *Inferno*, Strindberg confesses and dissimulates among the deep wood of a madness that
descries faces in planks and doors, traces features of masks and effigies,
suffers apparitions of matters that obsess and exasperate him, plots and
conspiracies and downfalls, all the grain of his fate rubbing him the
wrong way. Like the *materia* of his alchemical experiments of the 1890s
published as *Syl a Syl arum*, the material of *Inferno* is an endlessly susceptible element, wishful with blooming desires and woeful with thorny
twistings and risibly paranoid in its narrative texture—dogs furiously
bark and bar Strindberg's path, a lugubrious jackdaw squalls bad omens,
the face of the King of Denmark glares significantly inside the ashes of
the kitchen fire—and yet the hard going ultimately seems to bring Strindberg a sustaining power, down in the dumps his vision taking deeper hold,
the frantic scramble of mind woven into something full of holes but tough
and brave and bearing its cross.

Under the hands of generations of players—Kid Ory and Lawrence
Brown, Jimmy Knepper and Britt Woodman, Grachan Moncur III and
Lester Lashley—the slide of the trombone, loudest of the brasses: the
startling volume of its lustrous plaint, the gut-catch of its sound like a
bottled howl, the feeling hearing it of a weighty, elegant thing that's nonetheless on the run, pursued and pursuing, pointing toward the ceiling as
if to take its tube ladder off to the sky, whooping, swooping, swinging
back down toward the floor as if to dig in deep, as if to pull the music

out of the ground sodden and glistening and draped with muck. Sawing at the crossroads of high and low, the player measures off intervals right in front of you, the thirds and fifths and sevenths loose-clocked through their frames as if demonstrating a system of mystic waterworks, valved alembics. The broad bell like a tandem head, mouth of a gold ventriloquism offering itself to mutes, plungers, and derby hats. Crybaby yelp and caterwaul growl, rooting grunt and snort and heave: the trombone dragging its tail through the underbrush of music.

A smell of wet sawdust, of newspaper-stacked basements with leaky foundations, of the forest preserve on a soggy day in late autumn when the underbrush is littered with the leaves fallen off the trees and the ground is slippery, almost slimy, and with one careless step you can lose your footing on the banking path and find yourself, too, among the thorns and vines, on the dank floor of the wood breathing an air that might be the fog of feeding roots, nitrogen-rich and vaguely intoxicating, the whiff of a miasmal whisky. *Pulp*—I learned the word later, after I'd carried off the old magazines from a Maxwell Street stand where a man was selling them for a quarter, cheap because they were water-damaged and had no covers. *Thrilling Wonder Stories, Fantastic Adventures, Argosy All-Story*, issues from the thirties, the titles partaking of a damp smell of neglect, age, and slow decomposition, the futuristic tales contained inside colored before I even read them by the fact that they were history, held within pages as brown and crumbling as I imagined those of the Declaration of Independence or Lincoln's Gettysburg Address. The paper both clung and flaked away under my fingers. Pulp—the lowest grade, not much more than pressed sheets of waste wood: paper for the common man, for the war years. It felt like something that had been in a fire, doused with water, yet by some miracle of inertia or persistence had managed to preserve its original shape. Among the columns there were little splinters of pale wood, and along the margins dark smoky stains. The coarse paper had the texture of a rotten plank, blottered with mildew, engraved with the inscriptions of worms. Now and then I stopped my reading and gazed at the page as if I were smelling words.

Though dating back only three decades or so, the magazines were to me ancient, archaeological, raw evidence of the years through which I knew my parents had lived long before I was born—the Depression, the War. Those events they had experienced were to me as remote as the

spacemen with rockets strapped to their backs and the busty girls floating among planets depicted in rough black and white illustrations or in
hauntingly precise ink-stippled panels by Virgil Finlay, images which immediately seduced me as if in those years before my time I also must have
dreamed of days to come. Among the musty smell of transient hotels and
deep, step-down alleys, I searched for their proximity in the secondhand
shops on North Clark Street above the river. I found the ABC Magazine
Service ("Seven Floors of Books"), where the owner and his friends sat
drinking around a coal stove, and I learned the going price for such magazines was far out of the range of a thirteen-year-old and the seven floors of
books strictly reserved for regular customers. Down the street at another
shop, I searched again but saw that it was hopeless. After a long time looking, and rushed by an impatient owner suspecting I wasn't going to buy
anything at all, I settled for the closest approximation I could afford. The
book was *Tales from Underwood* by David H. Keller, MD, a name I recognized as one of the old-timers, a contributor to *Amazing* and *Weird Tales*
and author of a very scary story called "The Thing on the Doorstep." It
was like new, in dust covers, and only two dollars. It smelled clean. It had
no aura of time. Carrying the book out of the shop I wasn't disappointed,
however. I was euphoric, as if I'd happened across an unexpected charm,
the title reverberating with the whole range of sensation and idea that had
hovered around the word *pulp* and bringing to fulfillment a logic of which
I wasn't aware yet absorbed the force. Pulp: it was me, a shapeless mass,
an ignoble thing that could be pounded down or readily formed into whatever mold history and the world dictated. Pulp: it was also the power of
language, the fleshy parts tasting sweet or bitter on the tongue, the pith
and quick of words prickling the mind. *Tales from Underwood*—the tuck
of the clean pages inside, the smooth of the shiny cover pressed in my
hand, the invisible imprint I felt of the words of the title—a compact thing
satisfying because it was a first abstraction, an epigraph or motto.

Perhaps there are two main roads in jazz. One is the track of the run,
kicking into gear, kicking over the traces, flowing lines and swift restless flight. The other is a circling, sometimes tentative track working back
over itself, taking pause, probing and pondering. As if one impulse is to
move restlessly off and away, another to study settling into place. Lester
Young or Coleman Hawkins, Dizzy Gillespie or Miles Davis, Bud Powell
or Thelonious Monk. Obviously enough, however, the music travels both

roads at once. The power of great jazz seems to be in the richly specific way the artist strikes off, precisely insinuating a space between flying run and digging-down excavation, keeping the exact coordinates in suspense, to be moved away from in turn and to be discovered again somewhere else. The music's resource of abiding by flux: home away from home, a temporary, temporizing pattern like the loosely strung weave of a nomad's portable dwelling. Imagine under the roof the brightness always crossed with shadows, the stable disposition of objects and routines unsettled by seasons of wandering, the light troubled and renewed by different angles of shift and loom and foreshortening, falling into rhythms dictated by the chance passing of clouds and birds and trees, themselves making shadows. Starts of fresh distances, the jump and leap alongside you on the road as though they are carrying you along while you're forgetting what is the shadow, what is the substance, your forward track across the earth at the same time an under-trail along which the world walks you.

Music—it's said to be the most rarefied, the subtlest of creations, sound approaching something absolutely pure as if divorced from objects, from any material substratum. Distanced, impersonal, yet near and intimate, with the mystery of echo and reverberation in it. A phenomenon of air and ear made by us, though like dreams or like shadows, we partake of it not quite knowing what it is. Yet of course we do know what it is, this other body. With the liberty of shadows, with the rigor of shadows, it's you and me dancing the night away. Running all over the place, across the floor, the ceiling, the rough-plastered wall, our shadows forget and remember us. Shadowed by flickering flames, all the shapes of the wood move forward boldly, all the shapes of the wood delicately hang back. In a bonfire night, one can scarcely distinguish the upper from the understory, the crown of the forest from the underbrush. Rooftops and alleys, the iron traceries of fire escapes, everywhere the chance of a motion, flight or concealment, reconnoiter or capture, objects seeming to slip out of themselves, to slide in again. The joint is rocking, going round and round..

Shades of Chicago: wheeling around the stage and around the room, snaking through the audience, the members of the Sun Ra Arkestra marched in hieratic poses, heads and profiles and sweeping cloaks and robes turned toward you in brightly colored shadows and moonstruck silhouettes. Outside, the city ran through its courses, traffic touring the streets, people strolling late on the shaggy lawned parks, Lake Michigan rippling silver and black under a lunar brooding. I'm listening to trombonist-composer George Lewis, one of whose projects has been a series of works called *Shadowgraph*. What I'm playing now is *Voyager*, an extended composition featuring Lewis, saxophonist Roscoe Mitchell, and a software program also named Voyager. The music launches itself with bristling portamento, whirled stirrings of drifting, enigmatic signals nonetheless internally coherent and sharply delineated, as though in Plato's cave the shadows were to claim all the clarity of light though bodied still within the dark. The music seems to braid and layer and encode a bright obscurity, as though a distant nebula were emitting so much information bewildered monitors must spark and splatter and explode. The order goes out for damage control, but control itself may be damage, sustaining damage a style of control. Whatever happens, the Voyager program will process it, the parameters loose and capacious yet along the shifting stochastic tracks delimited, tightly structured. I'm reminded of the patterns of Haitian *ve e*, those graphings that compass coordinates and trajectories while restlessly adorning their confluences and their tangents, at the same time including in their design something like the instructions for their own undoing. Blossoming and thorning and wrapping, the music is a crosshatching of figures and timbres, tempi and textures, a bold gesture of power by the same token a prayerful acknowledgment of vulnerability and change. It sounds like a *prima materia* brooded long, a tough stock as intricately imprinted as the serpentine helixes twisting up a strand of DNA.

Le Serpent Qui Danse

Nets in which the elements are coursed and canalized: sails of wind, sluices of rain, biers of solar fire, doubling upthrusts of the roots that snake into earth. Under the hand, against the skin—when we climb into a tree we gain the higher view ostensibly a model for panoramic knowing, yet like the tree itself we also feel our exposure there, our hands, our knees and our feet searching for purchase. We save our asses within nestling forks, we touch or are abraded by the smooth or rough or bossy skin of the tree that rides slow underneath us with a reptilian tortoise grace. We reach for a hold mounting the antlers of a beast whose face is a mystery. Sometimes we come away with scratches and bruises, green streaks on our fingers.

Arborescence. Hierarchies, rubrics and slotted planes, roots and fruit, the binary symmetries of branches tiering toward the light. Entelechy and taxonomy, candelabra and catalogue and encyclopedia. The tree overloaded with metaphor, sustaining the press of thought because so stalled, so exposed, so available to the gaze. Offered up to thought, or maybe itself a thought that the mind cannot help but mimic. Nodding boughs, hurried flutters of benediction, elusive presences that invite and gesture and signify. Allegory and prosopopeia, dresses and cloaks bedecked and bedizened in promises of meaning; or all their raiment harried and torn in flashing divestiture, tossed among ragged garlands, tattered wreaths, frayed festoons. On a cloudy night after a rain, they confer and conspire and consider, pillared boughs juiced with green gossip, trees within the tree jostling one another in an intermittent wind. They are high and they are thick: gorse, furze, sedge—a lawn of the air where they hang out like slaphappy drunks bumbling over double-visioned fields, for all their leafy confab never *doing* anything, though in an instant of breezy distraction you might contemplate the subtle drift, theoretical and casual, of their re-ciprocal molestations. And the trees forever leaning into their own wreck as they shelter and nourish a world of things that infest and worry, the dig of borers and the saws of caterpillars, the offhand stripping of birds and squirrels and children, the avid eyes of outlaws, solitaries, and lovers seeking a tablet upon which to. engrave their names and dates. A signal indifference, grand and humble, that offers itself to ghosts singing through the wind, to souls hiding and scouting, hanging out and looking over home and country at a farther distance, to solitaries dreaming suspended among the branches, swaying hammocks outside the urgencies of work and time.

Tree: a story told twice, how it attains being and then how its being is mere frame and skeleton, a bare stick on which what climbs might be a serpent mounting second limbs, second mind, second crown bright with flaming eyes. A flaming sword strikes instantaneously into being the eight sephira of the cabalistic tree of life, which descend from Kether the Crown to Malkuth the Foundation. But the great hierarchy of emanations would cohere only for that instant and lapse again into the Ain Soph, nothing-ness, were it not that the serpent of wisdom ascends the tree and so ar-ticulates the paths, its head lodged at the topmost place where the sword's stroke first fell in a lightning flash. The serpent is connection, enchain-ment, or perhaps better, syntax. It comes up from under, omphalos, down in the hole, wreathing through the middle of the branching rays, tangling among the complexes of dyads and triads, the dialectics of receptive and active, masculine and feminine, the glide and slide of its insinuation so devious all the paths approach stumble and confusion and contagion, the under becoming the over, the subordinate the superior, the serpent ascending and descending at once in such swift oscillation the up and the down coil and knot and flare like a stick of twisted, burning wood.

On its double road, should I stay or should I go, the serpent partakes of thrust and shine and coiling and climbing, fat slow snakes tubing into branches and the flickering tongues of leaves. Moses's wood staff turned serpent, the straight of the rod shedding its envelope, taking curve and fold. The tree stories of threes and fours founder and flounder, at sixes and sevens, bending back round with tail wrapping crown. Damballah and Ayida Hwedo, twined and twinned serpents on the palm tree making love, in each quadrant the coil of one or the other body, which god is which impossible to determine. See one, you see the other, but never both at once because the one already is two.

You cannot contemplate such a tree, not only because its power blasts you nude to the bone but because tree and serpent wind together in such a way that two heads, two sets of eyes, would be necessary to see them whole, eyes that would be crossed in an *X* that would dazzle, hex, and rescue you.

The shingleback lizards of Australia have tails that look just like their heads, though with closed eyes, as if sleeping. They are rough slabs of dusty dark blue, their hides a basketweave of animal thorns. Lying in the sand, their bodies seem to hover between placid self-defense and devious provocation. As I watch them in the reptile house terrarium, one rouses, mounts up, crawls over another lizard in a manner totally oblivious, as if clambering over a rock.

Faking it out, switching front and rear, flipping upper and lower, fold and bend of a reversibility breaking toward the purely lateral. Difficult sometimes to tell forward from backward, whether the timber rattler is fleeing your steps or moving into position for an unexpected angle of attack. The rattle itself attains the dignity of a second head, a twin crown intimating hydralike powers. The Guatemalan guy down the block stencils "Toyota Celica GT" in oversized yellow letters across the top of his windshield, both awing the eye and drawing it across another path, his car looking at you as much as you are looking at it. Not one tattoo on the wrist, elegant though it might be, but two or three. And then on the other wrist, and then up the arm, at the elbow, at the shoulder. And down the leg, at the ankle. The other ankle. Narcissism? But Narcissus wanted to be one with the image he saw; instead, one wants to divide, adorn, shadow the body with a panoply of forms.

The floppy slithering of a silverfish in the bathtub: motion becoming repellent as though horror must accompany the sight of a body that refuses the tracking of the eye, the unit turning plural. Too fast or too slow, a movement excessively loose and flexible, a squiggling polymorphism, a slipshod scrambling where, disarmed and disarrayed, the directions lose their compass.

"If You're a Viper"—the pencil-mustached Cab Calloway tagging the hiss of the reefer toke that makes the head spread like cobra hood. A worm of blood hatches in the white magic of the heroin syringe, "The Serpent's Tooth," Miles Davis and Charlie Parker in a late recording session reviving the screw and pump and thrust of Bud Powell's "Dance of the Infidels." Snaky jazz, scary jazz—the quiver of sinister misteriosos going back to slow drags and second lines of funeral dirge, to "St. James Infirmary" and Ellington's Jungle Band, to the ghostly poison-tree of Billie Holiday's "Strange Fruit." Book of haunted nocturnes and suicide notes, gravestone mirrors and walking skeletons: the mortal love-chill of Parker's version of "Out of Nowhere," the door-knock lurk of Miles Davis's "Drad Dog," the hijacked jinx of Monk's "Friday the Thirteenth." On Andrew Hill's 1960s *Point of Departure*, the music is loosed to vertiginous drift and chambered insomniac dread, "Refuge" and "New Monastery" also places to which one might be compelled, schools for soul research, freedom labs. Unctions and coctions, vacuumings of astral debris and grinding of Qlipothic shells: Eric Dolphy's bass clarinet a swarming statistic alarum, Joe Henderson's tenor intrepid and suspicious, Kenny Dorham's guttering trumpet a study of skulled night, and the vine and bone of Hill's piano confessing vermicular complicities, judgments of an inquisition that finds its sentence turned back on itself.

"Le Serpent Qui Danse"—it's a Hill song from a late Sixties record, *Andrew!*, with John Gilmore on tenor, Bobby Hutcherson on vibes, Richard Davis on bass, and Joe Chambers on drums. It's been a long time since I first heard it, but I'm just as provoked, mystified, and tantalized by the way it moves. The melody could be a fragment of Thelonious Monk, stage-dancing, pile-driving, jump-Monk—I imagine "Little Rootie Tootie" with a spun-long solo approaching the instant when it sounds like it's forgotten where it came from and will never find its way around again. Out on a limb, and the limb moving under it. Yet the phrase rumbles, trinkles, ramps in such a way that you hear it coiling back and striking as it slides off from itself a track both farthest limit and nearest throbbing heart of the song, the line undulating, hitting against itself, a path made from its own breaking away. Intellectual, mental, cerebral: words sometimes used to characterize Hill's music though he came of age in the fifties on Chicago's blues-saturated South Side, accompanied Dinah Washington and recorded with hard-driving horn players like Roland Kirk and Von Freeman. "Le Serpent Qui Danse" and other songs like "Duplicity" and "Symmetry": his Blue Note work, produced after he moved to New York, is perhaps close to the rooftop edginess of Monk's science in tunes like "Epistrophy" and in those participial titles—"Rhythm-a-Ning," "Jackie-ing"—that propose the nominative luring away from substantialization. The music's thing is off its home ground and wandering island streets cloaked in arithmetics and alphabets, at every corner the chance of a transitive dwelling, the instant's shacking of shadows and light.

"Le Serpent Qui Danse"—like a fragment of Monk but under pressure, testy and tested. Almost a straightforward jamming session, the angular vamp offering a spur to inspired improvisation, but the twists and turns disconcerting, the hard-bop groove of the mid-1960s Blue Note idiom diverted through what Bobby Hutcherson recalls as something like strange rooms, places where time seems to approach a stop until from arrest and containment there's a flash-forward ignition, a luminous fire. A stretch beyond the expected span of the interval and then a hammering as though tacking up a great jagged oblong but hanging it from bottom instead of top, the thing bending and turning back toward you the shear of its border. As in Sun Ra's compositions, there's an insistent irregularity, a seeming wrong that comes right by virtue of its bold, indifferent stroke, its sideways stripping-bare of harmony. Gilmore's saxophone approaches the nervous bump and cut of the melody with a hunted, haunted sound. A day of swift clouds and sun flickering between, late for the train under limestone skyscrapers echoing with thunder, aquarium light washed over stormwater alleys, somewhere a wailing ambulance trapped in loading dock traffic, somewhere a locomotive's warning horn through a tunnel's long winding.

And Hill's solo: not an approach from the top but emerging from an indefinite middle that may seem nearly muddle (turn it way loud). Thicked among heavy lumber, the left hand and the right nearly indistinguishable. Each formulation of a forward path immediately interrupts itself—the percussive block-chording dispersing into overstuffed, spilling clusters, the breakout to frantic comping misfiring and flawing deep, that errance a hook through which a lyric snatch of laughter crashes into a whiplashing arpeggio that batters itself to pieces, those pieces quivering and brave, one and then another rising again in turn. Like Sun Ra's work: music as protection and exorcism, tones for mental therapy, programming for liberation. A sense of willful disorder, madness, a near-clinical production of anxiety and dissociation, the principle of Hill's compositions a universal rubato with nothing left untouched by it, all the comforts of where to hang back, where to attack, where to take it from the top forgone, every moment stolen from some other, every other moment giving it back. "Compulsion," from an earlier recording of the same name also with Gilmore: the restless cross-traffic of multiple drummers, African and Cuban percussion added to Joe Chambers's already explosive battery. Again the float of Hill's opening solo, not connecting riff to riff but the riff somehow hiding, lodging inside another riff equally fine-grained, the relation precise though impossible to fix. As if geared a second time from outside, forced to repeat itself within itself, those wheels within wheels wobbled by a power that could close the loop but instead knots it one more time, drawing it out to the four quarters, breaking it on its rack, and excruciating it. Compulsion: the occupied, turbulent mind of the prisoner revolving in mutinous travail, stalled limbos, a passion of heavens and hells; yet the song is constantly sprung, spaces falling out and the piano's sped ostinato tottering, the propulsive tempo compelling a broken code to read itself over again, lapse of phrase where a line escapes and leaves its flourish.

Across the trail the sidewinder does not slither but leaps and dances along the ground, skating the declivities made by its own passage, its body touching only at two points while the rest moves through air. Through every millimeter of its skin it absorbs sound, the slightest vibration. It sloughs a fine diamond skin and emerges new and gleaming.

Flux and undulance and metamorphic wisdom, but the snake is also deceiver and flatterer, dragon and Satan, wicked serpent of downfall and undoing, and so battered, slain, and driven under, mastered in a signal triumph. Apollo nails Python in a shower of bright arrows, the dark earth deity murdered by light. The hero, though, is after all Pythian Apollo, inflected by his monster, his hubris punished in turn by the quicksilver dart of Eros. He must carry a sex-snake for the underwood girl, Daphne of the matted hair and delicately fluttering garments, she whose correspondent dose of antipathy runs her into the laurel. And snake runs back to tree, the serene reach of upholding branch, the agitated quaking of the leaves, in that love out of phase the beam of Apollo's light struck blind and in implacable sibilance the oracle whispering still through rustle and slide and subterranean echo, serpent dreaming through word and strophe.

Baudelaire's "Le Serpent Qui Danse": all the things you are, your skin like silk shimmering, your hair like dark sea, your moves like jelly on a stick, like a snake convulsed at the point of a wand. The woman imposed upon by the poet's metaphors, decked out in fetishes. A power in her, though, as she rocks her lover like a boat shipping water, hissing spit in his mouth as she comes hard, leaving him spangled with stars as if in some infectious transvestitism. Not so bad to be the dancing serpent. But the serpent is also the man's desire, conjuring images of infant wobble and bumptious baby elephants, the phallus leading the dance. Autoaffection, autophagy, the poet choking his tropic snake—the serpent that dances is perversion, desire's track sliding aside or kinking back on itself. Yet the serpent seems also to be poetry, that split-tongued snaking of sound and idea, the dance as much meditation on its doubleness as devious slink of desire. A snake cannot dance, really—nonetheless the metaphor suggests what the poem, what any writing, including that writing we might call jazz, has to do with spacing and syncope and rhythm. Jazz would express desire, but is so mobilized by its forces and so wrought upon by its exposure that desire twists and turns into glorious, sensuous abstraction. An explosive and tender elaboration, something that would be not just good love but as in Charles Mingus's song title, love as a dangerous necessity. Listen to Eddie Preston's trumpet swept through the blue changes: love breaks up, distorts space; love remakes time and history. The lovers' darting tongues cross and quiver and weave and never quite bridge the distance between. That tension makes the dance of their love, its acuity and its difficult bestowal.

1976: a Sunday afternoon at a club on Wells Street, the AACM big band in rehearsal. Richard Abrams at the keyboard wandering in a far anchorite distance, the narrow turns and broad veers of the compositions driven into a plunge of music that seemed to offer itself to steeped solitude, the ensemble however collecting right out front the thorn and prick of impurest common touch among the austere opulences of Abrams's song lines—a blues-staggered rush off one of the tenors, a chattering scrabbled bravura off a neighboring trumpet, the tilting stilt of mobile, motile figures off Henry Threadgill's alto. No telling anymore what was solo, where the breaking into the clear and where the tangling underbrush. The love-calculus of jazz: to be alone and singular and one, yet to be troubled and haunted and stirred by another, the susceptible pulp of the soul flecked and printed and shadowed. All things pay the penalty of their injustice according to the ordinances of time. I let a song go out of my heart. This song is you.

And the woman sitting close to me that day—we'd found each other though we knew it would go wrong, and that was the draw of it, years of wrangle as if it were necessary to study every detail, the serpent's fang of betrayal, love's casual murders and the shivered mirrors of its contemplations—I could feel the force of her listening in the coil of her fingers through mine, pressing, clasping, drawn tight as our names engraved together in the skin of a riverbank tree, low-wage worker seeking low-wage worker for the pleasures of midnight fights and arrowed hearts and the unaccountable belief that every moment was writing a history that said *here in the place where I am always alone, I will never forget you.*

Later on, through the black painted door of the Blue Max, a gust, guest, sudden arrival. Lester Lashley the tall laughing elder, Abrams's old friend. So big and loud he positioned himself as far as possible from the band, making space among the chairs, almost taking himself out the door again. Pitted burnished gold, the buttery strut and harsh sweep of his trombone, and the ground tearing out from under it, caving, at the same time a light resurrecting itself, glowing shake and throw of the air taking seal and impression, deep tread of the irretrievable moment, glowing shake and throw of an air expelled in rapture—who was I, who was she?—and forgetting.

Roscoe Mitchell *Photo by Fred Burkhart*

dreaming of roscoe mitchell

1972: Bap-tizum

September, the Ann Arbor Blues and Jazz Festival, John Sinclair the master of ceremonies, a stage among tall pines, the lineup of music unbelievable, encyclopedic, a historical reach from John Lee Hooker and Ray Charles to the Count Basie Orchestra, the Mingus band, Yusef Lateef, the Sun Ra Arkestra. On one afternoon, Ornette Coleman dressed in black and red, the hard and sharp of the bright alto in sun speaking rigor and joy, a breeze blowing across the trees and on the body of the resined air a sound clear as light, a freedom running hard for a train, running for dear life.

And there was the Art Ensemble of Chicago, an unholy ruckus. Grating, mocking vocalese, a hullabaloo of declamations and shouts like fragments of work songs and gospel hollers and tremendous chokings and gaggings, not an intoning of history, a sober framing for meditation so much as the exposure of a crude plenum of harrying spirits, unruly forces, memories, and ancestors not mounted in their shrines but messy, bloody entities mounting whomever would venture to touch them, their hungry flocking only purged through a sonic disgorging. Except for the beating of drums, the players didn't take up their instruments, instead marching around the stage like mad clowns in an exasperated wrangle, paint and feathers and fringe, jackets and ties and wingtips, Favors and Jarman at one point singing a verse about a flower that seemed devised to tear apart all hope of beauty and symmetry.

Somebody near us on the grass was shaking his head, asking aloud why in the hell they didn't just play music. It was an understandable sentiment. For most listeners, jazz performance meant taking care of business fast, delivering the goods—the hot ensemble work, the blistering solos—and even the edge-exceeding dissonances of Sun Ra's band, even Coleman's off-minor anthems had lost no time in attaining an impressive level of instrumental virtuosity. My friend and I were drinking Rolling Rocks like water, the music so riveting we never once sat down for seven, eight hours, the bands and the crowd getting off like there was no end, this was for ever, no matter what happened before or after, Watergate, Nixon, Vietnam, time was ours, we were continuously swept up and roaring for more. It was like the place where all the trains came throbbing home, the trains all disembarked again gleaming on their runs, Capitol Limited and Zephyr and Silver Streak and City of New Orleans, an ultimate roundhouse privy to the secret codes of dispatch and tower, switches and lights and levers and controls, the Labor Day weekend dissolving the hours into an eager eternity where in the green chamber of the park the mystical body of jazz itself was in its real presence, all of it together, Basie to Mingus, Hooker to Ra to Coleman, stage and pine trees and proscenium lights the radiant innards of a gigantic console stereo system where all the greats played themselves.

The Art Ensemble's shouts and theatrics were putting static on it, rumbling the needle. The piece ended, another started, but there was little applause. A judgment, almost—it was their right to do what they wanted, but it wasn't stuff for the master takes.

A paradox of jazz: glorified as free expression, passionate, improvised, risk taking, its audiences nonetheless strictly demand a delimited, high-finish object. There's a sacred aura about the record, the tape, the CD, those spinning train wheels of glossy tracks that magically miniaturize, cool down, slot into an archive the musical event. With that jive noise, AEC was instead fucking with our time, wasting it—and of course that was precisely the intention, though it was hard to deal with. It wasn't only that history had to be changed, made, moved in another direction—most of us knew, or thought we knew, all about that. It was that history had to be blown up, time exploded, so that some new creation might, or might not, be born. How would it happen? That was the problem. The revolution would not be televised, nor would it be played on a record. The question was back at us.

A hard blast of the horns, led by the trumpet, roared into the Coltrane tribute "Ohnedaruth," Bowie's high-velocity runs at once jagged, brash, and elegiac, masterfully fleet while driving off their road and bumping through the dark, and Jarman, too, riding etheric, scaling the breakneck tempo on low-caving overtones, a message that might have said: you wanted your time, well here it is; stop this train, we're leaving. The healing power, the soaring hope—*Trane, Trane*, the cry of the diesel through the night, the late bloomer ahead of his time, the horn that thrilled a ladder to God, his track a road to freedom on a hard-labor machine, train man on the run, the five hour-long sets, the years of tours across the country and across the globe, and now the cool Michigan air was running with echoes, the boughs of the pines stirring and minutely trembling, the stage lights starring sharp like burning votives, a sweep of the festival's arm paused an instant in mortal lament, that instant railing the big train, the jazz train, running us off the track on a wild speedball like the one that had delivered up the master.

With long white robe and a knit helmet, Mitchell looked a second to Bowie's lab coat, signifying an imam-like corrective to the polymorphic Africanisms of Moye, Jarman, and Favors. Bowie: as much as he hung back and coiled and whipped and struck unexpectedly around the beat, he seemed to be always riding a forward edge, delivering a restless, explosively generous outpouring—the dream druggist, the cosmic obstetrician. Mitchell was the theorist, the master of doctrine. On "Unwanna," his own composition, his tenor phrasings across Favors's lithe, hammering lines came from behind and between, with the runs absorbing the expectation of something like Coltrane, something like Coleman—and indeed the horn was full-bodied and bristling and loading on an angular momentum. Yet as the choruses accumulated there was a continuous break in the chain, a missing link, the lost step on the staircase where you tread a void. The ear wanted to partake of a flow, wanted the train to get itself off, wanted to feel in one continuous motion the thrust of the engine and the pull of all the cars behind. But each time through, the ear was stopped, baffled. It was as though for one chorus to advance, the one before it had to be forgotten. That in turn meant that the chorus here-and-now already was breaking free not only of the chorus that preceded it but also of the one that would follow. Like a train impossibly hovering in the wake of its own motion: time at an impasse, time out of joint.

A scary roughness, that impending clanking shudder of the couplings, the spaces in between and the iron wheels turning below, that traveling place where you know you could get killed. A delight anyway in the motion, since for all its gaps, the sway of the cars almost breaking the connection, the iron ladders offering you a hold that sweeps by faster than you could ever hope to grab it, the train keeps going, carrying on, carrying itself off. But in that intransitive junction where the streamline of Mitchell's tenor promised the ear a ride but abandoned it in the offing—you heard a silence there, behind, between, maybe fearful, maybe awesome, maybe simply incomprehensible. Time broken, and in that break another time, a time of creation, of birth, that you couldn't, however, put a hand on. You could only listen to its echo.

I dream one night of an extradimensional object laced through with streamers and holes, floating over the loaded deck of the stereo system like a time-inscription of all the tracks it's ever played and replayed—until I realize such would be a dream of dream itself, and so I must awake.

Bap-tizum. I ponder the irreverent title given to the recording of the Ann Arbor concert released the following year, perhaps a word dreamed up afterward since it designates none of the songs performed that day. If baptism is the ritual of naming, *bap-tizum* names it again—bops and rocks the order of its world.

Yet the word, too, says: there was a birth, and again there is a birth. It commemorates an advent, makes present a past, makes past a present, in the here-and-now the gift of the chrism flowing, splashed, dripping with time.

Sometimes in suit and tie, sometimes in dark turtleneck and denim jacket, sometimes in a white robelike coat, he by turns suggests uptown elegance, streetwise radicalism, or holy-book rigor, but never quite settles into character. It may be a matter of indifference—amid the Art Ensemble of Chicago's freewheeling theater of America and Africa, he's the utility man, wearing whatever, his focus strictly on the work, the music. While Joseph Jarman, Malachi Favors Maghostut, and Famoudou Don Moye trance through ritual intensities in tribal paint and Lester Bowie in white lab coat ponders that wild bloodwork, Roscoe Mitchell seems to float like a wandering ancestor, participating without exactly belonging. Yet in the AEC's hybrid *commedia*, perhaps the trickster isn't the one who catches the eye but the one who slides off from the gaze, forever switching tracks, hovering somewhere between.

The between—the instant when we prick up our ears because, through whatever rhythmic or harmonic signal that's alerting us, we know something's coming, imminent, on the verge of a breakout. There's a slight hurrying of the drummer's tempo, there's a propulsive chording on the piano, there's an upriding, double-stopped cry on the tenor saxophone, and we know we're about to get hit good. If the word jazz really does mean sex, we're lubed and we're hot for it. The main thrill: like one hell of a foreplay lovenest, each detail seems painstakingly structured to support a point of excess, a near overwhelming of that structure, and, as much as the listeners, the players participate in the paradox of making it and being made by it. What are we waiting for? The air ripped and luscious as silk, the ear with a heart beating fast inside, skins touching together with a shock and a yielding, an indelible perfume of time. The first deep stab of a Coltrane solo, Elvin Jones running all over it while Tyner and Garrison comp with aerial calm; Miles Davis and Wayne Shorter in swooned surprise, trumpet and tenor luring each other (try "Iris," on *Sorcerer*), Hancock, Carter, and Williams rustling in parallel *frottage*.

AEC: they concentrated the jazz-quantum of suspense and let it run riot and blossom in unexpected places, let it run to terminus and wreck, silence and echoes, swarming fermatas. You sexy thing: trumpet, woodwinds, upright bass, and percussion; yes, a conventional lineup (though in free-jazz idiom forgoing the piano), but the instruments didn't keep in their stalls, the Ensemble notorious for the proliferating sound apparatus with which the players surrounded themselves as though to assemble a mad bricoleur's orchestra incorporating bicycle horns, African percussion, "little instruments" (a particular interest: the sounding of everyday objects—cups, tins, bells, scrap metal), and a proliferation as well of scandalous practices among the families of brasses, woodwinds, strings, and percussion. Jarman's or Mitchell's saxophone chants, threads a parcel of song, or all the horns vamp a while, and without a warning something happens, you check the speed on the record, the display on the CD player, the window to see what's going on, and before you have a chance it's leaped, there was a sputtering alto glissando, a jerked bass line spanking off the tempo, a punctiform muddy honk or a triumphant trumpet fanfare, or an embattled rattle over bells and chimes, but it's already retreated, perhaps coiling for another strike, perhaps fading, drifting, wandering off. Or all the sounds seem to be warnings; the alarms are everywhere ringing, you're suspended in suspense, from every direction hammered and slammed. Or just as disconcerting, there's a patch of silence that continues for too long, it won't let up—quiet, too quiet, and the pressure is tremendous, though a cry or whoop or sob might by now be emerging at the threshold of audibility, faintly scratching at the doors of the ear. In other pieces (check the live "Dautalty," from early 1972) they strip to a lean quintet that from the basic kit of horns, bass, and drums produces sounds of an all-out emergency, the ensemble wound up like a fast, crash-bound train upping its speed even as its brakes grip hard the long slide of its wheels.

Often with rich orchestrations, soloist showcase pieces, the lead voice in many compositions Lester Bowie's subversive though lush and full-bodied trumpet, gloriously drunk with what might be called voice itself—he speaks music's own speaking, interprets interpretation—the AEC's work could also be an elegant ride. But they relinquished the plush saddle, the teasing nightclub smoke, the bosses nodding their money over who would be next young lion of the trumpet or the saxophone. AEC—the group's name came about by chance, as story has it, their tag in France simply "Art Ensemble" and a promoter adding "Chicago" on a concert poster. It was a strange echo: atomic energy, federal commissions, the University of Chicago with Fermi's first controlled fission reaction in 1945, when Roscoe Mitchell was probably just starting grade school on the South Side. Along with its renowned department of sociology, which sometimes used the nearby working-poor neighborhoods for studies of criminals, Negroes, and immigrants, the U of C was steeped in an atmosphere of arcane knowledge and advanced studies: Sumerian religion, existential psychoanalysis, nuclear physics. In earlier years, when I'd dreamed of studying there, I imagined red-enameled university basements equipped with powerful cyclotrons trembling the floors, tunnels, buzzing with the rushing looped express trains of subatomic particles, their invisible almost-bombs subtly exploding inside immaculate shadowless chambers while white-smocked scientists recorded the distributions of infinitesimal series and dissonances, microcosmic geneses and apocalypses and disasters. In later years, I learned that during 1965, in a South Side school a mile or so from the university, pianist-composer Richard Abrams initiated the Experimental Band, the basis of the AACM black artist's collective from which the AEC crystallized. Away from the nightclub scene, it was a setting where musicians explored new directions in performance and composition, their work informed too by Abrams's encouragement of far-ranging researches into the humanities and the arts and the sciences, everything from African philosophy to Cubist painting to quantum mechanics.

Behind, between—no leaders, no followers, all leaders, all followers. A rare and fragile anarchy: the voices insistently individual expressions yet still within the fold of a collective endeavor, that collectivity, in turn, incessantly probed, stretched, and transformed. As though the cyclotron were to lose its chamber and its roof, be open to the sky and the elements, the world mix up with the very experiment determined to uncover its secrets. Passing through the arched tunnels of the magnets, the shotgun trains of the particles gather an immense velocity. They bump against, over, around time. Lattices and filigrees, clusters, plasmas, and strings, ephemeral time-jewels blurring and flashing with multiple, disparate tracks. AEC: time on their hands, all over them like pollen. AEC: steeped in time, time travelers out of the jazz mainline, not just ahead but behind and between, in the flux and reflux pushing with or being pushed against, pulling or being pulled, they stop there a while for you waiting.

Behind and between—however shifting and elusive, Mitchell might have been the AEC's provisional center of gravity, the Tao-like hub from which the spokes of the wheels spun and ran, sped along or scraped over or jumped their road. A floating exponent, a moving pivot that traced the centrifugal swirl. Yet listening to the recordings, I sometimes can't tell whether it's really him I'm hearing—it could be Jarman, who also plays alto and tenor, whose sound and attack at times are very close. The heroic individualism of jazz, inspiring as it might be, seems beside the point. Indeed, I hear the latter phrase differently—beside the point means moving off from it, the stylus inscribing the aural signature "Roscoe Mitchell" displaced to uncertainty and indecision: I could just as well say it's Bowie, Favors, or Moye who's the hub. The AEC's image in my mind after many years is still one of a darkened stage, an intimidating array of instruments, in different zones of the performance space elaborate batteries of winds and percussion and strings. In the beginning dark, each of the players is deeply occupied with his own research. Jarman stalking around his shells and rattles and horns. Moye touching, stroking, testing his equipage, every sort of drum, racks of bamboo and shining gongs. Mitchell scarcely visible among racks of bells and a stand of woodwinds like the parts of a disassembled pipe organ. Bowie meditating sitting on a chair, Favors assaying the resonance of a lone string—you waited in suspense for the music to begin, having paid for your ticket and found your seat, but it seemed anything could happen. It might be only a single player permutating a scrap of melody, a serial echoing, an involuted mood, for twenty minutes or longer. It might be sudden duets, trios, or with a bold flourish the group jumping in full tilt right from the start. And always the possibility in the air that they might decide not to play at all (which did occur at least once, when at a concert in New Orleans Bowie stood and directed the audience to listen with them to the spirits of the ancestors, maintaining the silence for half an hour). AEC: an enigmatic mechanism that worked precisely by not seeming to exactly work together, the unfolding of the group's music apparently casual, extemporaneous, disorganized, drawn forth according to some inordinate principle: ensemble rather than band, quintet, or orchestra; associated with, between, and among one another by virtue of their separate tracks touching, binding for a time, and again parting.

I think of the mimetism of insects and birds, of humans daubed and masked, dance and ritual and the dreamtime. I think of the contagious streamings and the infectious effervescences of sacrifice and magic. I think of the condensations and displacements of the dream thick and braided, fine spun and thin-stretched as lace, the track of the wish with its long and trembling and broken trains. If jazz is music of desire, it's perhaps also music of the dream. Not dreamy music, but as long tradition attests, train music. The dream a thing composed of trains—loaded and overloaded with freights bursting from boxcar doors, a mob of passengers blocking the aisles and cleaning out the beers and snacks in the club car, the train so packed it sways over its rails, the sleepers creaking, groaning, the momentum headlong and runaway, the wheels throw off dark sparks, lights and shadows fly swift in a whirl of stations and semaphores and switches and timetables, Freud traveling from Vienna to Rome, Breton from Paris to Zurich, Armstrong from New Orleans to Chicago, and the train sweeps up like a cloak its tunnel and its bridge, the cast of its lone eye light, the echoing fade of its horn, the boulders of the mountain pass, the waters of the river, the suburban yards and red brick warehouses and the cracked pavement parking lots and the silence that spreads behind, between, the lovers in the berths, fevered riders under blankets, at the X of the crossing riding an instant off its rails, arriving and departing, before and after itself, it rains time, we feel it coming, we feel it gone, when? when? right here, right now, the train running through the great black music of the night.

1982: Ex Tempore

It had been a solo performance, mounted on the stand a great, lowing woodwind, some rare monster akin to the bassoon. Like an astronomer beside an exhibition telescope, Mitchell seemed dwarfed yet exalted by the outsize apparatus, its curator and its engineer. Across its upper range he tracked a sharp-pitched, insistent cry, at the horn's bottom a series of flutters gruffly erupting in response as if unwontedly perturbed. The large-bore instrument with its heavy pads made for a slight lag in transmission, a delicate fumbling in the otherwise aggressively agonistic exchange from which there gradually emerged a deep, shuddering overtone impossibly edged with an altissimo shimmer, as though the air itself were collapsing inward. Distracted from the sparring figures, the punch-drunk, looping progress of the composition, I felt the pull of a contrary motion, an exuberant drag cutting across the grain of the music's brilliant dispatch. In the train of that interference an almost imperceptible backwash, a blurring as of something rushing by at terrific speed.

Eternity is in love with the productions of time—later, thinking about the concert, still hearing the clinging overtone dashed across the gruff rumble of the music like a spider running its silk, I remembered William Blake's infernal proverb. Its meaning, though, was equivocal as ever. In one respect it sounded like straightforward idealism, with eternity in the slot for God or a realm of Forms above and beyond mere temporality and phenomenality. Yet, characteristic of Blake's unorthodoxy, eternity's love wasn't necessarily a detached benevolence; being in love could just as well mean that eternity was seduced, provoked, in a passion. Eternity wasn't master of the game, as first appeared, but was helplessly embroiled. Indeed, if eternity were in love, it might be forever lost and wandering among time's productions.

The Ravenswood El train passes above me near Damen Avenue, throwing shadows in flickering ladders on the ground beneath the tracks. The wheels rumble and clatter, a wind gusts, in a back yard a tall catalpa stirs, its fibrous, heart-shaped leaves trembling. Late August, and the seven-year cicadas are singing in the trees. In the wake of the train, there's a bare trace of sound, an uncertain ticking that seems very far away. It increases through such minute gradations I can't discern any change until suddenly a cicada's racket fills all the air, as though it must be immediately near, maybe in the catalpa, the song attaining a strident, buzzing apogee, a sound like a live wire down from a line sputtering and crackling. Just as imperceptibly, the shrilling vibrato subsides in a dry muttering, clicking down to quiescence. And as though a tap has been shut off, it abruptly stops.

It was like music, but I had not really listened to a song. I had, rather, construed song—a rising to a climax, and then a fade, a conclusion—when I didn't even have the time to measure it. It was too fast; I was collared, arrested; like the Ancient Mariner's auditor, I could not choose but hear. And in that moment after the El passed, I felt time too had come to a stop. My ears were importuned by the weird clamor of the cicada, and the look of the street and the buildings settled into a different focus, clarifying but also softening, the green of the lawns and the gray of the pavement and the brick of the walls struck with a fresh illumination, something tender and fleeting in it. I might have been touched by the eternity of which Blake spoke, its fortunate fall among the productions of time.

Walking back to my apartment, I heard the cicadas down every street. I supposed they were calling one to another, a courting signal, but I couldn't discern any pattern—one seemed to start before another finished, others sang at the same time together, yet others halted midway through and went quiet. It seemed as much a general sounding of desire as purposeful communication, and in some way a voicing of the trees that hid and harbored them, a raw vegetal lyric composed of the lush fragrances and seedy branches of late summer. Simply though elusively itself, this too was a production of time. Yet there was no need to impute eternity to it; the wonder of those cicada songs was their ephemerality, their confusion, their mystery. They didn't need anything to be in love with them, they were carried away by their own nuptial serenades. Soon enough they would fall to the ground, their dark blue, almost purple bodies to be swept away from the walks by the brooms of homeowners and custodians or blown along the streets by the winds off the lake.

The cicada's music—was it a song before I heard it, so that my construction wasn't a rationalization but a recognition of something I didn't, however, know before? It was unexpected, like hearing an echo with no idea of its provenance, like discovering a letter that falls out of an old book, the signature of a long-ago reader in a flourish across the bottom of a page. Must there be eternity, because without it time would dissolve, would be a featureless uniform flow or a series of isolated instants each of which would have no memory or link to the other and thus would leave not a trace? Perhaps being in love with the productions of time, eternity would both hold its distance from time and be liable to time's intrigues. It would be a roiled, impassioned love, the two never quite in phase, always one drawing away the hand just as the other bends over to kiss it.

In the attack and pitch of Mitchell's giant baroque horn, as in the stretch of Blake's sentence, I divined a scraping or rubbing, an irritant crossing of planes like the friction that makes song from the cicada's whirring wings. As the performance approached its close, long rests, tracts of silence, irregularly interrupted the truculent call and response. It was a confusing signal, sounding each time as though the piece were finished, and after a while the audience stirred in their chairs, becoming uncomfortable. Beyond complaint and mollification, the upper-range phrasings indefinitely pursuing and pursued in a circuitous courting with the low-riding guttural honks, the silence seemed to broach another issue, a stubbornly opaque matter that was forever being adjudicated, never coming to a decision. I could be amused, nearly laughing aloud at the horn's risible tracking of ducklike muttering complaint, top bothering bottom, bottom mothering top, rocked in a cradle of irony. But I could feel, too, with the blank pressure of air in my ears, my own audition abruptly exposed. .

The ear: open to the air, to vibration, to world, within its secretive chamber the steep angle of the tympanum offering a maximum receptive surface. And the ear, more than the eye, making the heart beat with the measure of time—the organ of apprehension rather than of comprehension, the hole in the head without protection, without a door to close, time given by what the ear hears nearby and far away, the ear dividing off the before and the after, and in between them a momentous trembling. The melody that haunts the ear, that hunts it down, that sometimes lodges itself and insists, repeats, and, forgetting about memory, takes on a life of its own, is the song that catches the frequency of that trembling.

Eternity is in love with the productions of time—Blake's sentence rides like a mighty train, the first word its iambic engine, the cars of the anapests following behind, but against that locomotion the terminal feet pushing back, the train's progress suspended there between, in love.

The Examples

On the cover of his *Nonaah* record, he sits with one foot up on a spool table, the sole of his boot dominating the foreground of Roberto Massoti's photograph as if to defy the conventions of portraiture. It looks like army surplus, the boot of a worker or a militant, up in your face. His arms are loosely crossed, the saxophone strap angling like a thin bandoleer over his chest and one jacket pocket. The flap of the other pocket is undone, displaying a heart-shaped object difficult to identify. It might be a case for glasses, a wallet for reeds, a packet of something to smoke. In the background there's a grillwork of pipes in staggered courses like bricks, a wall with paint delicately scaling, here and there peeling to a layer beneath, and on either side a door with inset panels making another gridlike pattern. It's Chuck Nessa's recording studio or a practice space somewhere in Chicago, but the room seems abandoned and decrepit, the surfaces minutely scarred and pitted, the raw structures incubating decomposition. The two doors are mysteriously close together, as if one simply offers immediate egress through the other, like stage doors, and the function of the pipes is unaccountable, the works of a fountain without a source. Mitchell is leaning back in an attitude of listening, maybe hearing the tape of *Nonaah* for the first time, the expression of his face complex and equivocal, a very slight drift or squint in one eye like the trace of a gaze or a style of attention, difficult although imperative to maintain. A face that appears abstracted, powerfully focused, yet washed over, touched by, liable or susceptible to his own listening—disinterested, dispassionate, the composer's stance, but also exercised, traversed, caught up or engaged, as though absorbing the furrowing of the music's track through the air.

I can't catch up with him because he's before me, he's after me. Sometimes I quail, shiver, in dread of those crooked paths so resolutely singular they teach me the productions of time can't be possessed, reproduced, or retained. In the very instant I'm experiencing the live performance or listening to a recording, they're lost already or still coming, looming up in the past, fading into the future. A convulsion, a thrilling vibration, it feels like church, it feels like a magnificent channeling of world, it is the world, the sublime here so overwhelming it reaches a plateau, very high or very deep or tilted in some extradimensional way, where there is no sublime anymore, only a tract of nudity, sex and death; yes, jazz, the ritual, the offering stripped to the air, intimate with the bodies of the day and the night, shaken out among the elements.

As though time keeps measuring itself and stumbling over that measure, and such stumbling is the broken track of something other—call it eternity, or whatever—that doesn't so much participate in time as precipitate with it.

Love of the air for the fog, the fog for the air.

In a recent online interview, Mitchell is asked what he's been working on and replies that he has so many ideas he feels his head is exploding. (Laughs).

My uncle tells stories about old days on the Southwest Side, the neighborhood around Midway Airport when there were still open fields among the city blocks. When the Belt Line freights parked along the tracks near Fifty-fifth Street, enterprising neighbors would pull up with trucks, break in and unload everything they could take. At the Catholic church, just across from the runways, there was a popular priest, known for doing Mass in half an hour and for the swift administration of communion. The blessings came in an incomprehensible jumbled rush. The hosts jumped from his hands like scared birds.

I was about fourteen when, near the corner of Wabash and Van Buren, I saw a bearded man wearing a cloak looking up at the El train passing over the tracks. He appeared to be studying the shadows and the light, listening to the irregular clatter of the wheels over the rails, the echo down the canyonlike street as the train made the turn. I followed the track of his eye, his ear. I thought then I wanted only one thing in the world: to be somebody like him.

The El trains are composed of cars each of which has its own electric motor, powered by the voltage from the third rail. There is no locomotive, no leader; any car can run on its own.

Tart and acerbic as Coleman, stringy as Stitt, swiftly sketching a succession of tilted syntheses, scuffed topographies, working maps of the alto tradition: the looped strokes of Johnny Hodges, the wired filigrees of Benny Carter, the dashed slants of Jackie McLean, the perfect prescriptive scrawl of Eric Dolphy. And the almost faltering of it, too, a strange wavering subject to echoes, the keening pitch of Mitchell's saxophone on a ride that writes the alto's signature in the air as though it all belongs to him, as though it all belongs to no one, the lean frame of his body hanging from, depending on the instrument, at the same time stepping to the lean and the dance of it. Even with Mitchell right in front of me on stage I'm forgetting what I'm hearing, I'm in deep, suffering damage, inside a dark unknowing where the saxophone's *up* and *down* are utterly confounded under a swept veil of time where I undergo accusation and judgment, sentences I can't read though they read me off, in a long tunnel I'm trained by voices like those of the dream, voices outside time or themselves a concentration or saturation of it, time's lovers or beloveds or both. Or the inside silence out of which every melody is apportioned in time, the suspended instant, the silence just in front of the onrush of the train—here I must stumble, fall, because music is not about time, nor about anything but itself—

But the ear: like the eye, it wants to have, to hold, to know.

In the solo works, Mitchell's explorations strip naked the saxophone. Not only are the usual instrumental contexts, the support of bass and drums, the interweave of other horns, taken away, but the horn's body itself is denuded and exposed. The 1978 composition for alto saxophone, "Series II Examples": the horn's sanguine plenitude is beggared, its silver and gold teeth knocked out, its house keys lost, the saxophone offered in rags and tatters—keening, vulnerable overtones sawed across by guttural harmonics, distresses of looping whistles and squeaks, one interference pattern convulsed by another, stacked fractuosities. The horn not anymore a speaking mouth but only a raw auscultation. It shells wide. You hear the sound of its inside turned out, skinned by every air. You hear a listening no longer yours, but that of another ear, listening through you.

The pitch of Mitchell's attack: a sense of *piping*, strange as the word sounds, the tone starting off way up, a tight coupling of air. It speaks a detachment, a distance, a holding back. I hear Johnny Hodges playing a ballad—that manner of waiting, delaying, a poise and address that make time move while being moved by it. And like Hodges, too, in the attack there's a softness and a pliability: fragile, tender, the specific engineering of the alto's love song leap that slides up with clarinet grace and bears down with a tenor's gravity, the stroke of that love an exquisite teasing friction. On an earlier "Ohnedaruth," after Coltrane-style free blowing from Jarman and Bowie, there's the same ritardando, against the tempo's push a suddenly open spacing, a diverging loop, a maximum exposure of line like Oliver Nelson's solo on "Stolen Moments," and sometimes across the purity of Mitchell's tone a very faint scratching or graining as if in all the fullness of sound there must also be fade and decay, a raking of time, of age.

But a skeptic might say the saxophone is not being played right. It's like the fantasy of the amateur, the basement experimenter, who, untrained and negligent of all technique, nonetheless plunges ahead and finds something being created by sheer luck. Such birth is a delight, a gift, although because it's unrepeatable it's immediately tinged with regret and melancholy. To track deliberately such crooked roads without improvement as Mitchell's requires a research into shadows, a dream-science. "Series II Examples": after several minutes a full-bodied saxophone tone emerges. It seems not to be a single note; it weighs a chord. Folded into it are countless adjacencies, misfires, sidetracks. It bulges with unknowns, boxcars on a mystery train. Already it's spilling, taking losses. Already it's shadowed with the branches of the embankment trees, the grid of the Cyclone fence, the dark hide of the tunnel, the gliding fretworks of the iron bridge.

"Series II Examples": fury and babble, throating and roar, lush multiphonics, riffled tone-sheaves, a momentary defeat of the time dictated by the saxophone's stepped design, the diachrony of octaves and registers. A running out of the arpeggio, a chasing down of the run. Time blurs, fuzzes, and dreams, as the saxophone is revealed as no longer bucket or container but as a knife full of holes, a punctured blade. The seventeen-minute cut feathers its edge across the air, dissolving as it goes. Its seeming irresolution holds a refractory force. It declines to develop—indeed, the least move toward a musical rhetoric of parts and whole would kill it. Its ending: a conclusive surprise. It closes off, having never caught up with itself.

Mitchell speaks of a compositional concept he calls "stabilized tension." The dream runs along the edge of time, the LP revolves edgewise on the turntable and as you lean over it you see a distorted image of a finger, a hand, a face. The stylus has a blunt snake's-head look, rides the grooves like a lazy locomotive, its track coming to meet it in a seductive ribboning glimmer. A spiraling edge, a slow oblique corkscrewing, the trains of electrons routed through circuits to the mouthing ears of the speakers, the blank band where the music stops. For a while, you hear the shadow of it still.

There's a sound in the small hours that wakes me from my slinging through the air, in response to an enemy's challenge, a long kidney-shaped mahogany table, an object I heave like an ungainly boomerang. It breaks apart midswing, and I bat down one section of it with the other. On a couch, a trumpet is waiting to be played, when I find the time.

1994: a composition for solo alto, performed live at the Hot House: "Near and Far." With circular breathing, Mitchell sustains long, looped processions of notes that for fourteen minutes don't once offer a pause.

An inexorable driving wheel, a mobile equilibrium perfectly geared, perfectly balanced—but in time and by design it must wobble and drift.

It is a wheel on a train that never arrives. The train hurtles through the stations, the crowds stand and watch it pass, the express blowing by. Occasionally it slows, as if to make a stop, and the people eagerly press toward it. But just as it seems about to halt, it accelerates and continues onward. The same thing occurs again, again, and after a time it's all but forgotten that the train is a thing that has any connection to stations and stops. Its passage is viewed like that of a distant planet or constellation; clocks and watches are set by its motions.

Then, one day a long time after, the train is rolling into sight. The same blast of the whistle, the same unsteady flickering of the headlight, the same obscure freight of promise and delay. Its approach is scarcely remarked, but impossibly, uncannily, like a train in a dream, this time it really is stopping. As it approaches the station the wheels ride solid and heavy on the rails, the lettering on the cars appears vivid and bright with meaning, the clangor of the bells loads the air with a new urgency.

In the interval, time hovers. A distant vibration shudders through the whole system of trains and signals and rails and stations that has come to be called the world.

In the damp oiled air: a singing as though motion itself has just been born.

A dream: to have no fear of time. Out of sheer pleasure in your freedom, you would run fast and run hard, almost catching up your own footsteps. Out of sheer pleasure you would let time pass, ride, or you'd turn easily and ride against it. In enough stillness, you would feel where it breaks.

Mitchell on soprano saxophone in 1997 performing Joseph Jarman's "Ericka." Coming from a place very close, so close it could be inside my body, my brain, and the ear has to be still, concentrate, absorb a quantum of silence to hear the sound clearly. Nonetheless, it remains indistinct, wavering, hovering off from its own edge. I want to call it a murmur, a burring, a blurring. I essay it on my own lips, a humming throating breath, but I blubber over it or I break it off, I can't approximate it. On the bare threshold of audibility, tentative and delicate, a seeming weakness in it as though it would after all withdraw, retreat, though now it's started it appears there's no turning back, it's become possessed of definition, gravity, increase. At the same time, it continues to sound with a memory of its near fading, a ring, an aura, a halo persisting around it, the ear pricked by a reverberation coming from somewhere very far away, so far it could be outside, miles off in the city, the world.

You might imagine that world into which it disperses, the rooms of your neighbor's house, the sidewalks and yards, the streets and the expressways, the bridges and the power lines, the stretch of highways and rails and rivers and seas, the trains of clouds running their shadows over the land, the earth axled among the stations of the moon, the sun, and the planets.

Eternity, naked in the arms of time, or time, partying through a long night with eternity.

An advent, being born.

And the example—looked at closely enough, it begins to undermine or exceed the principle it's meant to demonstrate. A particular escaping its general.

Louis Armstrong said: the music is what happens between the notes.

In *The Thief's Journal*, Jean Genet writes of his love for an older tough who had taken him in and treated him as an equal. As much as he knows he's loved in turn, however, Genet leaves him behind in Brussels, travels on to pursue another destiny. On the Paris express he gazes out on the trees and fields of the Flemish countryside and thinks about that love, how it's so strong that, if the railway bridge which the train is crossing were to blow up, that love would repair it, and indeed has already repaired it, in the very moment he's making that crossing.

1994: Very Large Skips

L'esprit de systeme—it makes Chicago a modern city. Unlike New York, London, older places, a city made not so much by accumulation, a tangle and weave of historical growth, as by the aggressive stamping of a grandiose pattern on Illinois mud and river and marsh. A city presumptuous, encyclopedic, and autodidactic: like a shelf of books by Herbert Spencer, the nineteenth-century intellectual jack-of-all-trades in whose work one finds every aspect of life and history and politics relentlessly slotted under headings and subheadings, phases and sequences. Laid out against the horizon by the outworks of railroads that made it all happen, Chicago might be Spencer's dream, a late-Victorian panopticon of orderly parks and boulevards and streets, a place there for everything and everything in its place. The marshes were filled in by its own waste products, the downtown lakefront built on its junk and construction debris. Along the branches of the river that course through it, shipping was made to pass by means of movable bridges, the roadway tilting temporarily toward the sky and afterwards gearing snugly back into place. With its monumental lakeview skyline, it offers a sublime by manufacture and design; with its engineering, a pooling and canalization effected by a huge working-over of raw material—embankments, viaducts, pumps and sewers and drains; that eighth wonder of the world called the Sanitary and Ship Canal, product of a deep cut in the earth that forced the river to run backwards, clearing its mouth at the lake and sending the city's excreta to points far south, downstate. The Columbian Exposition, White City; the American Rome or the Paris of the Prairies; a city for Goethe, for Freud: where all had been mere waste, there would be *bildung*, cultivation, and mastery. Coming back from Europe or the Southwest, I can't get over how big it suddenly appears, the broad streets and the buildings oversized, jumbo, as though a carpenter set out to design his own house and, with labor cheap and materials at a discount, determined to double the proportions of everything.

The paradox of Chicago: metropolis of the early West, don't fence me in, but a city made of nothing but fences, itself a great exfoliation of lines and routes and barriers. The very scale and scope of it perhaps self-defeating; all of Spencer was deflated by a few short passages in Durkheim that spoke of the force of the collective as opposed to an elaborate epistemological machinery of statics and dynamics, that simple concept serving to explain a vast range of social phenomena. Yet Spencer has long been relegated to library discards, while Chicago lives on. Because of its grand scale, it has the capacity to allow its own destruction, to cast off its parts seemingly without damage to the whole. Hundreds, thousands of buildings, whole neighborhoods, have been torn down in the course of the past century. Built upon the marshy ground of portages and passages, the city has spread and grown tall. Still, the long stretch of its utilitarian grid overreaches and trembles toward its undoing: disorderly reversals, retrogrades, backslides. Corruption, gangs, neighborhoods like armed camps. Building up, tearing down, it rides on a sometimes frayed, sometimes glittering border of ruin and glory.

The confining rack of the city grid has its blossoms and weeds, like the grass that sprouts between sidewalk cracks, the frondlike trees of heaven that sway tropically from crumbling pavement and broken masonry. On a hot August night, a drunken wind through your windows, a rolling and cavorting motion through the air upon which vague, fugal entities ride, miasmal marsh-ghosts and water-fairies that with a faint smell of mud and oil pour through a hole punched into space through which you feel the time where you're held captive, tossing on your bed and dreaming the trite and secret motto of Chicago: to live is to work, to work is to live.

In a city which, for all its diversity, still seems so oddly German—not really like Germany but a dream of it, an orderly dream of rows and columns and squares, of ample volumes and generous measures—I find in a bookshop a translation of Schlegel's *Fragments*, where I read that what matters isn't so much the comprehensiveness of a system as our feeling for what is outside it, our human passion for something beyond the human. For Schlegel, such passion is coupled with an ironic clarity that grants the justice of what cannot be grasped, comprehended, or ordered, that unknown which is eternal agitation, swarming chaos.

Chicago: a system that would comprehend and contain all differences, manage each and every one of the productions of time, yet an irreducible friction, perhaps an effect of system itself, distempers its grand orders and harmonies. Growing out of the tree-lined streets of the South Side, bordered by the Illinois Central tracks and the clattering Jackson Park El trains: AEC. Jazz positionality, the bebop-quintet schema of backup and sideman and lead, was tested, pressured, and exploded, as if among all those routes and tracks crossing their lines there must be a loose thread, not just a way out but a way altogether outside, not just a run at freedom but a freeing of world. Accomplished though they were, the music wasn't a matter of players in an all-star setting where each would have a chance to shine in turn. It was a matter of embracing the very factor a proper jazz combo usually excluded in the distribution of musical work and the management of time: stops and starts, clinkers and flubs; the too-loud, the too-soft, the too-dirty, the wrong. Noise.

Some years back, Jacques Attali argued that in the history of Western music noise defines everything that doesn't fit, those elements marginalized as static, nonsense, interruptions of the proper and the normal. A distinction of music from noise has traditionally served the powers that be, harmonized a dominant political order. Yet despite its service to power, music also has something inherently subversive and baffling about it. It is like yet unlike language (at least in the conventional sense), is inherently unstable insofar as music doesn't necessarily refer to an object, locate a signifier in relation to a signified. Music is signifying itself, signification at its furthest remove from designating objects. This divorce from reference means that music has the possibility of doing no service, no work. Western musical forms operate though stable melodic and harmonic laws. The key signature sets the rules within which any given music may wander as it may but will always return to the tonic, the refrain, the chorus. Order may be briefly unsettled, may drift toward dissonance and noise, but only to be reaffirmed and plumped down again into itself. Noise, however, disturbs this order in a manner that defeats such a comfortable return. Invested with noise, music is no longer comforting, is no longer orderly, no longer stages a disturbing yearning or fear that ultimately finds its rest, its peace. Music becomes wildness, upset, an accelerating inward turning or a wobbling spinning outward, past control. Or it becomes austere, distanced within its own realm of structures and techniques, perversely indifferent to making things whole. Tones and tonal production, for example, can refuse the correct and the well-tempered, the distinct identity of the scalar note. Slurs, bends, split tones, microtones, overtones—those sounds that make music grainy and rough, that don't calm or reassure or follow a track of sentiment and containment but scratch, tease, and diverge from themselves, starting up into raw points, jagged planes, broken series, harmony no longer a concord in time but a parting and division that makes time beat, skip and stagger.

1969: breaking out, taking back time (*Watch out for that time flak*, William Burroughs had urged all resisters in his *No a Express* of a few years before. *Ride music beam back to base*), sounding those intervals where systems and orders tottered and stumbled, where a track of freedom took its road as becoming, as creation, as surprise. Malachi Favors recounts that the AEC started as the Roscoe Mitchell Art Ensemble, but Mitchell didn't want to be leader nor did anyone else. A collective, then, without hierarchy; a creature, maybe a monster, without a head; yet in such anarchy a power stronger than itself, as Mitchell describes it, perhaps a counter to the powers and principalities of the city, perhaps itself tapping those powers, looping, short-circuiting, and crossing their wires. Compositions from the early years like Joseph Jarman's "Non-Cognitive Aspects of the City," Mitchell's "The Ninth Room," and a host of later

works—unlike the welling uprising of New York free jazz, the music out
of Chicago often was fugitive and devious, itself systematic in its breakout from system. Albert Ayler, Pharaoh Sanders, Charles Gayle, David
S. Ware; they shouted a glorious noise, often enough heard in Jarman's
and Mitchell's saxophone work. But in something like "The Ninth Room"
there's a different sort of vision. You're inhabiting an airy, more than ample
musical space, plenty of compass for solo intensities in turn, yet the way the
players lay back and jump in, the way they both wait on and don't wait on
the time, effects an incremental, serpentine block on forward progress, a
redistribution of such intensities through a series of restless twistings and
windings that don't roar up into sonic climaxes but trail through strange,
elliptical backtracks and jumped, untimely advances, the instruments tracing through nocturnal arabesques as ordered and as random as a dream.
It might be a small-hours dream that startles you into a wakeful listening:
furtive, enigmatic noises overheard somewhere close by or in the distance,
behind the wall of your room, behind the wall of night. At your window
something knocking; you're uncertain whether it's inside or outside your
dream, in or out of this world. The 1971 AEC composition, "Lebert Alay"
is an elegy, a revision, a sort of manifesto, its title aphasically reconstitut-
ing the name of the free-jazz pioneer mysteriously drowned in the East
River in 1968. The piece reprograms of the furious lyric surge of Ayler's
tenor through a drifting reverie of time-dissolves and protracted silences,
the horns essaying tentative, searching runs among a swamped labyrinth of
thumps, whistles, and shrillings. There is an uncanny sense of suspended
history, a time ended and a time beginning in some telescoped apocalypse,
a judgment sounding through the vividly fading traces of Ayler's fiery vision as though meditating long enough on freedom one must hear its cry
begin to echo, to resonate, to ring, its vibration provoking an oscillation, a
flickering, orders and systems and worlds turning themselves on and off.

Mitchell speaks of *very large skips*, those intervals steep with surprise
where the creations of music and the world's creation seem to bell and
resound and inflect one another across divergent tracks. Spaces and times
you're in and out of. Dispositions, tendencies, angles and drifts—should
this territory be called world? Music; world: the very grain of where we
are, that which nourishes us but is impossible to own.

In writing about Roscoe Mitchell perhaps I should simply write
about the world. Lake Michigan: the black stone smell, the clumping

of wet sand, its color almost brown, almost clay-orange. A night of winds, the lake waters driven, rising over the barriers, flooding the drive near North Avenue Beach. Out in the dark over the lake a distant beacon, among the turbulent waves its illumination sometimes steady, sometimes obscured by fog, sometimes pressed back upon itself like a blown flower.

1994: a chilly October evening, my son and I taking our walk despite the turn in the weather. It's one of those times when the lake, usually more or less a big lapping pool, approximates the power of the sea. Across the drive all the city looms behind us, lights already burning in the windows of the high-rises that wall along the park, beyond that wall the storefront thoroughfares and the bare-tree streets, our own apartment somewhere waiting like an open crate into which we'll later be shipped on the giant stopped train of the city's night.

The waves are rolling under the wind and moon, rising two, three feet, cresting and foaming, gaining ground on the beach where the water strands in deep puddles. I tell Malcolm to stay out of those, but he's not interested, already he's gathering the stones for skipping, those perfect stones so abundant along this glacier-carved lake, smooth ovals tan or gray or black, their small weight on your palm like dream money.

An art to the skipping, on which he's worked for several years. One finger curves around the curve of the stone, the hand whips it on a level with the water's surface, gravity pulling it down just a bit, momentum bringing it up a little, the stone getting lost a second, discovering itself again, a pleasing *fort-da,* but across the water it's the event, the stone's swift irregular imprint, that he's following. He's determined to break his last record: ten, even fifteen skips it might have been, though the count seems to be forgotten each time.

The thrust of the waves offers a stiff resistance, the stones veering off at crazy angles or failing utterly, deep-sixed. But there's plenty of time and plenty of stones, hundreds, thousands of them here at our feet. The northern air is bracing, fresh, wonderfully clean. After a while he's made the corrections for wind and rough water and the things are spinning and shooting over the top of wave after wave, he's breaking all records, the stones leaping across the water like waves themselves, sometimes flying way out into the churning dark and with a last lift jumping their track, overleaping their own wave-pattern, at the sight of which my son exuberantly laughs, splashing anyway in the water, and wondering how such rare miracles should be counted, calls them too *very large skips.*

2002: *Just Like Gold*

Holy Saturday night, in Chicago with a quartet, a birthday tribute to AACM comrade Fred Anderson, the drummer driving hard, the lustrous mercurial bravura of Roscoe Mitchell's alto arcing through slides and smears, stacked multiphonics and delicately whirring drones, the line of the improvisation so rapidly accelerating it seems forever to be leaping and overshooting its track, so abruptly retrograding it seems to be dragging gloriously through its wreckage, and at one point Anderson's tenor chasing it down until with a harsh extended stutter the two seem to catch together a far-off echo of what might be Gene Ammons and Sonny Stitt trading choruses on "Blues Up and Down"; at another, in disregard of the instrument's scalar increments, Mitchell deploying a meticulously convulsive fingering, not so much playing the horn as spelling over its air, a scratchy microtonal graffiti as though the alto is being signed by its double, a second power inscribing the uncertain outline of a shadow toward which it irresistibly moves or by which it's being restlessly pursued.

I almost can't bear it. I'd like to escape from the club, stand among the streetlights and taxis on Balbo and listen from a distance, yet I'm stopped, arrested, outside the broad windows of the Hot House the El trains folding through the Wabash turn alongside the sodium-vapor lamps raying a color like burnished gold, in the near distance the Sears Tower blackly shining with its double antennas forked into the sky, the couple next to me in the booth stirring uncomfortably at my restless rocking of the seat. Time is accelerating, rushing by, or just as likely frozen in its tracks, itself being pursued, harried, run to earth, an excavation where I'm indeed caving, my vision blurring, fading, so long have I gazed at Mitchell, his gray, close-cropped head, his thin dignified face scored with two deep lines along the cheeks, his slender body bending slightly like a reed, a sly-fox look I think I see as he opens his eyes and then lets them close again.

Facing the stage lights, in a dark blue suit with the saxophone strap at his neck like a matching tie, he holds on the alto loosely, his long-boned fingers tracking the keys in what seems an extra space, the horn engaged rather than gripped, and at the same time his cheeks puffing and between his lips the steel mouthpiece nearly vanishing as if the reed would be engulfed, swallowed, fox eating a bird that sings down the throat, a tongue in that plumage. The saxophone won't play a lowdown mellow blues, fine as that might be, won't ingeniously embroider a set of chord changes, wonderful as that might be; it's racked and screaming, it's sardonic or elegiac or tearing over the surface of its own lyric traction, fluttering and buzzing and skirling like mad bagpipes, sometimes long pitches sustained in humming musettelike vibrato or in heavy, booming double stops, sometimes pitches by design misfiring, detrained, out of joint. Tonight Mitchell's art seems at a juncture where his compositional concepts cross explosively with his soloist's passion for spontaneous creation, perhaps inspired by the showcase setting of the quartet, perhaps by the occasion of Anderson's birthday, perhaps simply because this is what he does, a music of rigorous invention at the same time so dazzlingly eccentric and exorbitant I despair of writing another word about it, only feeling an impolitic desire to shout, to roll on the floor—it's midnight, the horns are shining gold, pouring out time into the naked lilies of our ears, it's Easter—not because I'm being affirmed, the music giving me what I want, but because it's messing me up, it's taking me apart, it's a plaguing where I'm stalled and tranced in a rawly prepositional element, a wild territory of suspended objects, crisscrossed paths, vanishing trails.

Like him I am consumed—later, imposing themselves on a swiftly fading memory of the performance, images and cadences from Rimbaud's poems insistently come to my mind. After many years I hear again the intimate pressure of his generosity and his hunger; I quicken again to the great leaps he makes across time and space; I believe once more in the alchemy of vowels, the colors of words. In the music's wake, I feel a hunger, a greed, as I did when first encountering those poems, so entranced by their art, so exhilarated by it, that I thought all I ever desired was his. I had been tremendously grateful and tremendously jealous. Not an uncommon response, to wish to stay in those books, to live there forever, fierce invalid in possession of tropic gold, wounded soul enamored of the sun-running sea. *This inspiration pro es that I ha e dreamed*: the words at the beginning of *A Season in Hell*, in particular, had stuck with me, implicit in the phrase a passionate rejection of the bourgeois world, an audacious claim to a vision beyond it, a bold research into unknown powers of language and dream. For me it was to be a credo that invited a good share of confusion and failure, and as much as I wanted to be him, and as much as I followed a well-worn path of idol-worship and emulation, among my dreams I often forgot that it was *charité*—generosity, disinterestedness—which had been Rimbaud's key.

Let us be as avaricious as the sea—wanting, wanting: of the music, too, I would like to live again each note and phrase, each motion and detail, would like to gobble it up, engorge it, have it on tape, on CD, on digital video, taking property in an ephemeral passage of time and sound and gesture whose essence must be its supreme indifference to being held, its singular ungraspability. Like an ocean swell it washes over me, and in its element it is I who am possessed and shaken. And as much as I would in turn like it to engorge and engulf me, dispossession yet another form of property, my own being owned, I'm thrown back on my own devices, landed somewhere else, here.

Charity is that key. In the fading resonance of the music's train, among the traces of Rimbaud's language, I begin to remember something of the dream of generosity, the generosity of the dream.

Smokestack lightning, Howlin' Wolf sang, *shining just like gold*. I later read that smokestack lightning was moonshine, but on first hearing the lyric sung in Chester Burnett's hard gravel voice I imagined the glowing steel of a fresh Santa Fe locomotive riding out of Chicago in the gray light of early morning, a first ray of sun striking the hard metal, a swift flash like a gift of good omen across the chilly air.

Once at a festival in Wicker Park, as Roscoe Mitchell was playing a solo piece, the sun caught the alto's bell in the same way I'd years before imagined, at that very moment an El train rumbling by on the Milwaukee Avenue line sounding its horn, and the sweet and tough music of the saxophone running up with it, against it, between it.

Walking the other day through a light November rain in Baltimore, I reached a corner on Ann Street, and in a hurry, I suppose, or for a reason I don't recall, crossed to the other side. The trees had all turned, the lindens mild golds, the maples flaring through rose and crimson and incarnadine, mostly young trees, not at all tall, maybe ten or twenty years old, nobody bothering about sweeping and raking the leaves, negligently letting their colors stay on the ground where, once the wind or the rain moved them on, their faint imprints would make ghostly cutouts on the pavement.

And yes, in front of the neighbor's old Federal, dead in my tracks, the small maple flush with reds stopped me, arrested me like a signal flashing time, time, half of its leaves still clinging to the branches, washed with rain and streaked with running colors, the other half strewn thick across the steps, the sidewalk, the hood and the roof of the car parked there.

It made me happy—that corny word that smacks of smile-faces and product delivery seemed the only word for it, the sight of the tree gloriously shedding its leaves, the touch of house and street and the rainy day stained with time, and I went home and dreamed over the word, *happy*, hap meaning luck, hap meaning timing, time, as Thomas Hardy's poem reminds us in ironic and somber tones, as Mitchell's music dreams us the lights and shadows of a train passing us even as we're riders on it, curving through a long tunnel and then coming out on a high bridge that sways under us and exposes us to a river wind that shears across our road, we feel the shaking, the vibration under our wheels, and we pass before we know it a place we travelers have never seen before, another earth like our own, bearing valleys and trees and birds and cities and peoples, though when we do the only word we have for its advent is one we already know, is dream, or world.

Malachi Favors Maghostut   *Photo by Fred Burkhart*

intuitive research beings

Sparrows

The legends are various, but I imagine the famous yardbird from which Charlie Parker's nickname derived might have been a mockingbird like the one I hear sometimes among the rooftops and courtyards in my neighborhood. It is a bird almost choked with song, pouring, spilling, brimming over, the turns so swift it seems the music must hurt, the explosion of mimicry caught inside and catching up so many songs it dizzies time and sequence, one song forever interrupted trembling into another, their tracks sliding forward and back like a slide whistle blown with such force that, unable to bear the pressure, the sound goes raw and shrill and impure in what might be a voicing of metamorphosis itself.

"It's like birds do," Eric Dolphy once said when questioned about what critics described as intonation problems in his woodwind playing. The solo on "Fire Waltz" with Booker Little, or with Coltrane on "Spiritual": skidding rigor of the bass clarinet that seems slightly off pitch, the sound a lush hollowing but every instant it should cradle you instead rocks you off balance. The phrases replicate Parker's wired intensity but Dolphy's attack gooses into siren whoops and stuttered gutturals, as though music must provoke the very air of which it claims a portion, or must let the air itself speak whatever forces bride it. Like birds do: trembling forth song in a way that says how a body possesses power and how a body too feels other powers pressing, prepossessing.

To bear, be bared, to such insufflations.

Bird: from *brid*, Old English, of unknown origin.

Pan chasing the nymphs: they flee in every direction, he breasts the wake of their diverging courses, a bewildered sweaty swim. Their panic is such that it infects him as well, he strikes off paths that confusedly loop and knot, figures of his curly pelt, figures of his lost thought, a wind running him away and running him back. In one tale, the nymph Echo, having refused the advances of the god, is torn to pieces by Pan's herdsmen, her body scattered among the woods. A being of parts, particles, in flight forever, forever spun back in the rustle of leaves and the flickerings of sunlight. In lonely vigil, the arrest of the night, the grove, himself, Pan follows a thought that drives in all directions, like startled birds collecting in the same movement by which they disperse. He twists into a loop, a knot, the gold strand of Echo's hair. In another tale he pursues the nymph Syrinx. In panicked flight she strikes off among waters and grasses, in panicked flight runs her body to its change. Syrinx: his reed, his pipe. In the desire still for knowing her, he reads tracked earth, the stagger into grace, into dance.

In an old photo, Dolphy with his head of curls, his beard, his slender legs crossed, a streamer of smoke ascending from a meditative pipe. On the Village Vanguard recordings, Coltrane's soprano struck into flight, and Dolphy following in harsh verticality but boning down to a jumped tonal doublet, stuck flutter that masses and growls and keens across its interval like an arrow of iron shot into a magnetic field that quivers and spins it through the compass, its path whipped off to nebular blur, in the wake of Coltrane's bright-woven rush the bass clarinet hoarsely ringing its darker alarm.

The syrinx: a double strap, a V of muscle, analogous to the human larynx but positioned in the bird's chest cavity near the opening of the bronchial tubes. Tracking of nerve impulses in the syrinx has shown that in certain birds the song is mostly generated on the left side, in others on the right, while in others, often in complex echoings and doublings, the song involves both. Research though is divided on the question of precisely how song is produced. Perhaps it is by air whistling through a narrow orifice. Perhaps it is by vibrations in the syrinx, which higher up issue forth as chirrups and warbles and trills.

Tracking the structures and variants of the bird nester myth among Native American cultures, Claude Levi-Strauss showed in great detail how birds are operators, mediators, place markers among levels and degrees of thinking the world. And it is the little birds, as they are called, the robin and sparrow and the tiny wren, that create the arrow-chains, narrative ladders that bridge earth and heaven and bring to the people fire, tools, rain. Important as birds may be in making culture, Levi-Strauss doubts that what we know as music derived from the imitation of their songs. Like language and myth, music is exclusively human. Yet he admits that such songs may constitute a sort of language for birds. If such is the case, could one language contact and inflect the other? Practicing the saxophone in the park, the musician after a while becomes aware of subtle movements among the trees, stirrings among the leaves and fast shadows dashed across the ground. The higher register seems to provoke shrills and whistles, or sometimes companionable calls, shapely sonic homologues. The lower reaches of the horn echo into an abrupt silence as if the birds have stopped, and are listening.

Rahsaan Roland Kirk: the blind saxophonist who dreamed his compositions, who often played two or three horns at once, emulating what he loved in the music of Ellington and Basie, the sheer volume of the horn section's sound; and through his impulse of song, crossing up dualities, the partitions of left and right, of showman and artist, of original and simulacrum. Rahsaan who broke out of the hard-bop suit-and-tie world, tooting flutes in his nose and whooping emergency on a circus-clown's siren, a big Eshu's fool's cap drooping high off his head. The tenor under one hand and the stritch or manzello under the other, cheeks puffing big and the music like a heavy double locomotive blowing over the junction where the tracks converge along the same *X* by which they diverge again; circular breathing, coming back on his trail, the trail coming back on him. The style gloriously his own but at the same time running through the powers of forebears to whom he offered tribute and memoriam: Sidney Bechet and Lester Young, Fats Waller and Don Byas, Charlie Parker and Coltrane. He called one of his bands the Vibration Society as if to make clear he was but a medium wheeling in a trance.

Strapped into his instruments, saxes stuffed in his mouth, flutes in his nose, and his words preaching whatever he liked, hawking and crowing as if he'd founded his own church of Rahsaan and was making the thing up as he went along, his voice often hectoring and indignant—*America this country, this tree, this tree*—sometimes wicked and merry—*if you want to know what it is to be free you got to spend all day in bed with me.* Mask of his oversized oblong shades and the shock of his broad frog-like face looking like he'd emerged from a place deep inside the world. After the childhood accident, a man who never looked at himself in a mirror but perhaps gazed into something like the mirror's backing, the black *tain* trembling through all apparition, like the minute internal quavering you hear at times in his horn (the song might be "Many Blessings" or "Thanks for the Beautiful Ladies"), the force of the tenor's attack so concentrated the notes seem to flicker in and out of existence at a tremendous speed, the sound ghosting over its traces.

"Serenade to a Cuckoo": the song from which Ian Anderson of the English band Jethro Tull took off on his own bird-flight, Rahsaan in turn being channeled by a rock minstrel, mimic of his moaning and talking and spit-sputtering through the delicate tube of the Boehm flute, the pushy lilt of the melody partaking of the merrily driving gears of clocks, the flapping shutter where a witless wooden copy-bird struts the hours of the day and the night, Rahsaan overblowing and triple-tonguing and darting all round the time, making the bird brain. Cuckoo: bird of spring that brings life to the bare tree; bird of plain song as opposed to the extravagances of the nightingale; one of childhood's words for the eccentric and incomprehensible, a finger winding up the ear, Goofy knocked out cold with birds twittering around his goose-egged head. To serenade the cuckoo—a diabolical conceit, since the cuckoo is the false one, the cheating bird, usurper of nests, of family and lineage. But to serenade also means to cast a pacific spell. To serenade the cuckoo is to thread a charm made up from disturbance, displacement, and change, to attract back into one's compass that which on first impulse was repulsed as the wrong.

In the right spirit, one hand knows not what the other is doing.

In a text called *Dust for Sparrows*, Remy de Gourmont proposed that intelligence must have its origin in imitation, as shown by children at play who, under a sort of vibratory compulsion, whistle in glib mimicry of the birds they hear in the yard. The Salvadoran men walking down my street often whistle in a strange, shrill piping, composed less of distinct tones than of an uneven tonal pressure, like a broken comb passing over the air. I go to the window to see what it is they're signaling, curious what will follow when the whistler catches up to the one walking farther ahead, who perhaps has whistled in turn. But nothing happens, and they don't even look at each other. Their whistling seems not a signal but a sort of acknowledgment. To acknowledge—not necessarily to know, to speak and exchange words, but to know in terms of gesture, a fleeting contact, a stream of feeling.

When he was twelve or thirteen years old, my son used to perch in the window and watch, too. I warned him to be careful—he might be sending a signal he didn't understand, a message that might be misinterpreted. Often I found him there whistling anyway, no telling whether to himself or to somebody else.

If a sparrow come before my Window I take part in its existence and pick about the Gravel: for John Keats, negative capability was about philosophical uncertainty, a suspension of thought, a stop on the path rather than a forging onward to definitions and conclusions. The sparrow of Keats's letter by the same token suggests a positive susceptibility to immersion and mimicry, the humble track of the bird and the dialectical hovering of romantic irony vibrating together, Keats the master of trance dreaming the nightingale in the wood, chanting Psyche into the weave of his brain, his song marking the impossibility of anything like mythic participation even as, subtly panicked, almost losing its way, a darkling thought stays on its run.

I first think of a passivity, an ebbing of self into another existence, but perhaps it more accurately is a leap, an abrupt dispossession like that of a bird being taken by the air even as it is the bird that does the taking off. Thought, suddenly outside itself, doesn't understand anymore to whom it would belong.

As a small child, I saw birds as a vaguely troubled portion of an intimate though generalized world whose grand division was between things stationary and things in motion. Long days in spring and summer I was a creature living on the ground, spending hours loading and dumping sand from the suspended shovel of a toy crane rather like the type used in the grab-bag games at highway rest stops. I gazed with satisfaction at the clean mound of matter my father had installed under the shade of a tree near the back of our yard. It was a substance both solid and infinitely at my disposal. When I released the crank mechanism the shovel dropped among its chains and stuck its zigzag mouth into the softness of the sand. I cranked again, watching it slowly ascend, the load sometimes trickling out the sides, at others maintaining itself gratifyingly intact, locked in with scarcely a loss. Often in awkwardness or anxiety my grip slackened and the shovel released in midcourse, the sand suddenly precious as gold as it scattered across the air. The ultimate pleasure was the instant when, racked to the topmost point, the machine delivered up its contents at my command. If the day was still, the shiny tin jaws yawned and for a fraction of a second the sand hovered in a dissolving particulate cloud. I witnessed matter held fast and contained at the same time that it was being divested of its body, raining down gently sluiced into the hillock I occasionally furrowed with two long diagonals to catch the spill dead center. Through various turns of delight and perplexity I often made the same kind of motion across my face, brushing off the stray grains and rubbing my itching eyes. In a monotone I hummed what might have been the law of inertia set to music. I had proved that all things return to themselves.

On breezy days, however, my work becoming prey to the wind, I witnessed the excruciating indifference with which things at rest suffered the depredations of motion. The shovel became a sieve through which the sand flowed in a coarse winnowing as though space would reclaim all substance for itself, though it was scarcely a matter of gaining ground but rather a careless sifting into a running void. I should have known it was doomed to be lost but always believed it might keep itself together the next time around. I cranked up and cranked down. The tin mouth of the shovel clattered. Nothing held. I sneezed, and on occasion heard a high-pitched sound that seemed to be coming not from me but from somewhere else, a keening lament of matter itself.

Motion—I didn't like it much, unless it was my own or like my own. I approved the ants traveling across the blades of grass and tunneling into the ground, the secretive black beetles in moist loose dirt, the minuscule leafhoppers whose range seemed restricted to a world no larger than the span of my hands. Crossing a field of tall weeds, however, where summer grasshoppers leaped into flight, their barred wings scissoring and flashing, I was inspired with terror. And birds—like all of the higher phyla they represented the possibility of inimical wills: growling dogs and hissing cats that had to be carefully mollified, the older boy next door whose coming home from school in the afternoon would complicate my existence, my father and mother under whose protective shadow I still longed to crawl but whose rule demanded that I stand and face the light.

Among the higher branches of the trees, across the brightness of the sky, along the ground in their high-speed business of feeding, fighting, taking flight in a panic at the merest stir as though the motion that animated them also was the source of a chronic fear: birds. They fluttered their wings with a sound of something digging and delving into the normally placid element of the air. Fraught with a disturbing force and purposefulness, they were intent on missions, smart and devious and rigorously provident. Creatures with nests, woven nets and bowls with the look of natural accidents but in reality houses for eggs, babies, families. I recoiled at the sight of the candylike blue eggs of the robins on the ground, the near-transparent fluid of the yolk oozing from the dented shell. I ab-

horred the discovery of dead nestlings in the grass, raw featherless things
that looked as if they should have never been born.

In my family's culture of work, my mother's care for birds was an ex-
travagance. Feeding others, taking on the extra—it was wasteful, distracting, frivolous. But despite the grumbling from my father, she scattered
breadcrumbs on the patio, after a time purchased the special food, clear
plastic bags packed tight with millet and sunflower seeds, the grain rich
and glistening like another species of sand. She happily topped off the
feeder, always spilling out a little on the ground. She learned after a while
how to protect the food from roving squirrels, at the same time making
provision for them in another part of the yard. She admired Saint Francis
of Assisi, the brown-robed man of the garden with birds at his shoulders,
a man once rich now poor but with his hands outstretched to succor the
weak and humble. She dreamed of attracting warblers and titmice, rare
breeds, but was content with those of our city neighborhood, robins and
grackles and starlings and the ubiquitous sparrows.

They fought and scrambled and dove, forever seeking advantage, war-
ring with one another, ganging up on other birds or on their own weaker
brothers, it didn't matter. She loved the sparrows, it seemed, most of all.
She exclaimed over their energy and endurance, scolded their violence
and cruelty. She didn't expect anyone to share her enthusiasm but couldn't
help expressing her pleasure at what she saw outside the window. Slowly
I was drawn into the realm of those dramas that had nothing to do with
us, really, but seemed so much more interesting than our own. One day I
climbed on a chair alongside her and tried to stay as still as she did, all her
attention on the day's offering of color and light, sun and shadows washing
over the glass. Among the birds in our yard, the sparrows were the most
populous but were at the bottom of the heap, constantly chased off by the
others, though immediately coming back for more. Clustered around the
feeder, most of the time they looked as if they traveled on their bellies,
without feet. The tiny flat head with the robber's mask black around the
eyes. The gray-white underside, pretty but soft, vulnerable. The oversized
triangular beak. The insistent chirping, nothing like song but almost automatic, rather like the note of anxiety in its purest form, though madly irrepressible, forever game. Brown and white and sometimes almost black,
dotted, speckled, patched and mottled, they might have been cobbled
together from dust and dirt and mud, swarmed up from a spontaneous

generation. Their movements were frantic, life at such a rate it seemed it didn't really adhere to their own bodies but was a force pushing and pulling them in all directions, every instant consumed with the urgency of a dodge, a move, a hurried darting. Looking out the window I glimpsed a motley harmony composed of disjunction and strife.

I could smell my mother's scent—it was just soap, clean, and a faint sweat from her work in the kitchen. The greedy battling sparrows drew from her a sigh, a laugh.

"Now you stop all that," she said. "Bad birds."

But her words loved that it was impossible for them to stop, and in that moment I was overcome by a sense that there could be a shelter that wasn't so much a secret keep as the expanse of a shade open to air and trees and sky. It was like being awakened on a summer morning with my mother over my bed saying "rise and shine," and realizing I had long been awake, since the first touch of light listening to the creaky-wheel sound of a robin outside my window, the noise of the milling sparrows, in silence and then sound, more sound, like the day was cracking open, hatching, bright light and already shadows, my brain humming, stung with it, as though for the first time in my life I was having a thought and at the same time aware of how thought was always moving outside, beyond me.

Malachi (In Memoriam, 2004)

The upright bass: fat comma and black dot, stand-and-deliver of a body big as yourself, slashed with double carnival mouths and scrolled with a flamboyant curl. Drag of friction, nailheads of stiff equilibria, the slugging of low frequencies, each bumping the next, until, like spinning coins on a table, there's blur, hum, the heat of amplitude. The air shakes out as daggered cloud, as a trailing of drops and holes and caves, of beadings and outcrops and bosses. Dark bottom, foundation and fundament, yet it moves, stirs, among the shine of horns and brisk trade of the drums the clutch and pluck and claw of it as though it's forever in danger of falling behind, already started too late, outpaced by swift coursers. Or it's the ear that must take longer to hear time become audible in a staggered crossing of left and right, of steps and beats, a sheaf of digitations. Roughly caressed, it may be I or it that's hollow carapace, viscera exposed, naked gut-strings, pulse in the neck and the heart in commerce with slower organs, secretive and ruminative, coding blood. The passions of soloing horns and the troublings of the drums recede, and I fall in with how it stumps, slogs, reads off a muddy graph.

Malachi Favors Maghostut: he's about seventy, the oldest member of the Art Ensemble of Chicago, though only by a few years. Regarding his age, he's said he started out 43,000 years ago, a being dedicated to music by God and Allah. In the Art Ensemble performances, his face is illuminated with brilliant hieratic colors. A third eye, drawn in red, gazes from a jet black forehead in a 1981 concert. It's a disconcerting image that makes you unsure where to look, the pattern coruscating, the face at the same time itself like a stone or jewel, planes and facets of a diamond or a pyramid. He leans into the bass as he plays, at the same time seeming possessed of a stillness pillarlike, treelike. I hear the power and measure and weight of Oscar Pettiford, the fire and rigor of Mingus, the fleet, restless gravity of Henry Grimes. The bass wells deep and vibrant and rich with harmonics, and like a big-band player, Favors rides an expansive sense of time and interval. Maghostut—the word is of African origin and means "I'm your host." In the stretch and the bow and the immaculate hammering of Favors's strings, it's a hospitality without fuss, without show, though the house of the music is not only thrown wide open but charged, adorned, beckoning.

"Malachi"—there are at least two versions of the song, a composition by Roscoe Mitchell dedicated to his longtime colleague. In the tradition of "Like Sonny," Coltrane's take on a characteristic Rollins mood, Mitchell's regally simple melody might have drawn from Favors's work its sense of spaciousness, of generous capacity. With its lively sense of procession, its thrust of a headlong majesty, it's a melody that could soundtrack a promenade of elephants or kings, the medium-tempo walk stepping into its dance with a dignified turn, a calm exaltation and incipient joy. In one respect, "Malachi" encompasses the swinging, Africa-march side of the AEC's oeuvre, heard in songs like "Odwalla" and "Dreaming of the Master," and pays tribute to Favors's many years of work in that group. The short, twice-sounded phrase loops a slide off its main stem like a jumped double-stop and in that slide—such a small thing, almost casual, accidental—gives traction, path, fold. On the 1996 recording, Mitchell's robust tenor blows through, redacting horn histories, layers of Coltrane and Griffin, Von Freeman and John Gilmore, flooring a shadow library that stirs its pages, turns on its lights, begins to read itself. Downtown

Chicago: the elevated trains loop their returns, jolting over sparks. At the curved corners the tracks divide—Lake Street, Ravenswood, Englewood. The tenor indexes a book of night, through the song's middle section a long, ragged tear. The trains start into new distances with a shudder of wheels. Malachi: mark, slide, finger on the place.

"Malachi," one more time: Lester Bowie's trumpet loitering through bravura stalls and extemporizations, dirty chop-licking, joking dirging over dooms, Famoudou Don Moye gonging an alarm—the earlier version, recorded by the Art Ensemble in 1995, strips down the melody as if to steal up on it, to molest it, to expose it as fugitive and hounded. Mitchell's saxophone creeps in pianissimo, untongued, barely touching the notes, testing, lightly drumming. The tones swell, divide, and spoil—a tatter, a silk ragging along the inside of Bowie's swept cloak, the two horns after a while flashing together an iridescent streak, a sleeving of echoes where at times it's almost impossible to distinguish trumpet from saxophone. My listening becomes so enmeshed in the textures that it comes as a shock when, in the last minute of the performance, the group plays the melody all the way through twice, very fast. I'm struck in its wake as if I've suffered an arrow's blow, a stroke so precipitate I scarcely understand what it is. Like something stolen out from under you, the thief already fled back along his path, you never saw him. Like a gift without any evidence of the giver except across your hand a throw of abandoned shadow.

In the Old Testament the prophet Malachi exhorts the people to a generous and uncalculating sacrifice. Jehovah's refining fire will burn bright—one cannot so easily satisfy, pay off one's debt by way of ritual. Never enough, ritual is to be always challenged, always renewed. The grudging offering, the halfhearted oblation, must be transformed to silver and gold, the new flame a bright joyful leaping like the young calves in the spring.

Poland, May 1999. An exhausting circle of family reunions, coffee in glasses, food from hidden cupboards, cigarettes and celebrations and tears. We take our American dollars and stuff them into a cousin's bag of groceries without her knowing because she won't accept the money any other way. They would have given us everything. Krakow to Rzesow to Krosno and beyond, and now the car slowing down almost to a stop as though I have no control over it on the highway in Małopolska, Little Poland, driving from Sczawnica to Zakopane, green mountain valleys surrounding us and farther south the snowy dark-blue peaks of the Tatras.

Along the stretch outside Nowy Targ a great chaotic mass of sticks at the top of an electrical pole, rough black thatch against blue sky, spilling out of itself over the power lines. A stork's nest. We gaze and gaze as though to learn it by memory, so exhilarated I feel under my hands the rental Mitsubishi is about to fly, its wheels off the verge of the road.

Because he kept for himself alone the science of the woods and the gifts of divination, his house was caved in by Eshu the trickster, its stones thrown down. Now he has only one arm, one leg; he limps, he hobbles, he hops. And because he was ungenerous in making sacrifice to the god Ifa, he has lost most of his voice and now can only produce a high-pitched squeak.

Bright bird shining with gloss of green leaves, winged with the chances of shadows and swaying candelabra of branches, dusted with medicines drawn from the forest, rich with oils and balms of healing.

The orisha Osanyi. The bird that keeps your head, your cool. A bird weighted with judgment, justice, righteous powers which it borrows from the elders, the grandmothers who watch the signs, gossip over who is walking right and who is turning wrong, who shrinking too small and who puffing too big.

The birds not only participate in sky, in weather, in sun and seasons and dew and night, in squabbles and scrambles of love and strife; they respond to the slightest motion, the merest stir or whisper startling them into flight. The child waving his hands like wings, running into their crowd and forcing them up. The flock rising, the pigeons beating through the air. They seem all one yet each follows a separate track. As they rise and flutter and swerve, their bodies flash as though they are putting on a show, their fluttering rush out of reach, a fanning of light and color and of air whirring through their feathers, and the child knows a thought that comes and passes again by way of touching what is outside of itself. Not treasure thought, hoard thought, but thought on the run, like birds rising and scattering across the air, like *ashe* in the flash of wings, like the *ororo* bird of solar gold.

"The Flow of Things": Roscoe Mitchell's saxophone solo is a thought that dances, that comes from walking, moving, a skip, another skip, a continuous leap like the lines of Shelley's "To a Skylark" in restless slide, toppling-over elevation, stanzas to the left and to the right, the bird's song a tearing and stitching keen across the air, a mad swerving composed of utter clarity. The toddler's drawing inscribes the flight-rhythm of birds in a sketchbook, the conventionalized zigzag of wings in simple forceful lines that lift the crayon from the page, slash back across it, surprising in their power over space and irresistibly calling the hand to do it again. In the course of an hour, page after page of the sketchbook is used up, sometimes a near-blank struck with a lone trailing scrawl, sometimes the paper flocked to the borders, everywhere birds.

On the sidewalk below my window, the sparrows scare at the approach of something I can't see, perhaps a mere shadow, perhaps, for all I know, the shadows of themselves as they dart and search along the ground. In a swift instant they disappear, scatter in all directions. They leave in their wake the insistent, irregular sound of their chirping, a sort of nicking at the air, the ear. Never stopping in one place for long, perhaps never attaining a position from which to claim it, the sparrow scarcely possesses a song. What I hear is like a squeegee drawn across a wet window, a window that might be made of a glass that melts like water, a surface giving up resistance and softly shattering, collapsing. Among the music of the robins and starlings and mockingbirds, that pebbly dissolving sound infiltrates everywhere, swept up and down the streets and yards where the sparrows make shift through brown peregrinations, lifted and dropped and thrown through the air in negligent dispersals.

Lucky and blessed, Hesiod says, are those who observe *dike*, who are seasonable in their actions and who are knowing in birds. Auguries, presages, harbingers and heralds, birds are intimate with the motions of sky and earth and with the passions and changes of human affairs. The cuckoo's cry signifies the arrival of spring and, as it sings among the branches, it is a feathered leaf that participates in the tree's new greening. The flock of blackbirds witnesses the jealous husband seeking a tree from which to hang his innocent wife, and at the last moment they speak through their song and stay his hand. A little bird tells you the secret right or wrong of some tangled matter of neighbors on the block or colleagues at work. We watch fascinated or perplexed those we call strange birds, people who defy common sense and accountability, people who seem to live in a different world. In the passion of angry indignation, without our even thinking about it, the fuck-you bird rises on the end of our arms as though to call forth the powers of justice on our side.

Birds, with all their Romantic and sentimental associations, may be suddenly monstrous, inimical to humanity, aggressive, aggrieved, no longer solo singers to be apostrophized in the garden but creatures flocking and swarming in great crowds along the rooftops and the power lines. Alfred Hitchcock's *The Birds*—thirty years later the film maintains the power to disturb, to spur anxiety and nightmare. Attempting to account for such power one may be led in many directions, psychoanalytic, phenomenological, historical, and political, perhaps drawn into a panicked thinking like one of the characters in the story, sensing the gravity of some overwhelming overdetermination, perhaps feeling the stir and unrest of thought traversing itself. Flocking, swarming, crowding—the sound of birds in the film exceeds their individual songs and becomes a generalized friction, a grating and scraping across the air, roiling of a seemingly perpetual motion. Sinister though they are, Hitchcock's gothic birds may be not so far removed from the subversive birds of Aristophanes' comedy, which mock and dissolve into laughter the pretensions of men and gods and propose another, freer world; or the birds of Italo Calvino's stories, evolutionary sports who disorder creation with chance, possibility, the beauty of the unexpected—those scriptings of uncertainty and alterity, Uh and Or; and Mr. Palomar's parallactic starlings composed and discomposed over the skies of Rome.

Freud spoke of the conservatism of the instincts, of the death-drive and its predilection for stasis, quiescence, inertia. The organism would even convulse and explode itself as the price of attaining rest. But the birds are already driving, drilling, flocking, and the knowledge they propose, the research they effect, is one that discovers there is no stopping, one is driven again up and across and around, one is woven out of being here and then being there, though being never *is*, never belongs to one but is forgetting and learning itself again, forever in tuition.

Lucky and blessed—that which moves is also that which knows. The bird is wing, flash, dart. The bird is caw, chirp, chitter, whistle, twitter, hoot, tweet, coo, squawk. Being turns back from predications to takings off and partakings of and with, knowing not a matter of subjects and objects, of ideas and representations, but of a riding space, a riding sound, bold exclamation of the interval.

Bold Souls

Washington D.C., July 1997. In concert with the Equal Interest Trio, Joseph Jarman in loose white cotton, his head shaved smooth, his eyes calm, magnified big and shining behind gold-rimmed glasses. Myra Melford slanting the keys, underneath the piano her bare feet dancing on the floor. Like an elegant gambler, Leroy Jenkins playing with utter concentration, the track of his violin spun through a roulette whose numbers run together in a system that partakes of absolute order and absolute chance.

Jarman: on the tenor a broad, fluffy sound, but perdurable, too, something like very late Coltrane, "Lord, Help Me to Be," a harsh pour of blustery arpeggios, overtone wails and shrill pipings. The logic of it seems to be one of carrying, like numbers in arithmetic, but forgoing the tally, the places instead piling up, the music after a while hovering as though the very intention to play, the forward passion that delivers phrases, sound, and song, is in abeyance, and we're hearing only the traces of its being washed away.

At least ten years since his leaving the Art Ensemble of Chicago, that group so often caught up in a general flux of shouts, skins, bells, chimes, whistles, and gongs as though on a spirit-hunt or themselves becoming gradually possessed, and emerging from such invocation of ritual—really like a ritual of ritual, ritual to the next power—a virtuosic Jarman or Bowie or Mitchell solo stepping over what might be the footprints of the ancestors or might not, might instead be the track of the altogether forgotten and unknown and so the surprise of a future, the sliding lope of Favors's bass or the systemic ruckus of Moye's drums pulling away on another line, another beat, one of the brother horns suddenly squawking or squalling or taking a lyric plunge; or floating free and alone Jarman's tenor turning back on its track and stopping its run, its rich, hoarse spill, and instead letting the sound echo into silence; and in that silence the autoparenthesis of some merest stir, some least feather by which motion starts, leaves off, trails a path.

Equal Interest Trio: Melford and Jenkins and Jarman working a border between an overspilling instrumental virtuosity and broken-wheel structures whose gaps would almost enfold, contain it. As if one would with great precision agitate a beaker and register the instants when the liquid minutely sloshes over, splashes out, sprays in fine random mists. With all of its swaggering gravity and blowsy address—I'm thinking of Harold Ashby on Ellington's "Thanks for the Beautiful Land on the Delta"—Jarman's tenor sounds like the breath, even as it is being given to the horn, in the same gesture is being held back, nested in a sort of reserve.

Each time it makes an advance it's also retreating, retracting itself, as though it has turned around on its trail so many times its path has become a tangled, involuted thing, extricated and inextricable from a crowd of singular passes and recursions, wrapped in a texture that both encloses and exposes it.

In between songs, Jarman comments on the group's name, explaining its collaborative ideal. Equal interest: it might be a redundancy since interest means possessing a right, and a right by definition is equal to other rights. Yet the idea seems to be one of just apportionment, perhaps recalling that interest also means a being between, *inter-esse*, so that equal interest means no interest at all, but instead disinterestedness. I watch the shake, the fold of his white robe, the drop of a crease into shadow as the music swells. Back on the tenor, it seems he's walking in wind, such is the profusion of sound pouring forth. After a while, it's as though I'm not hearing so much as reading something off the air. Gusts stuff slots. Asterisks rain. And in the next fold: blotted flower, a blossoming gorgeous and engorged.

Jazz as ritual—a familiar concept from Ellington onward, jazz the American hybrid grafted upon the ring-shout of West African religion, that collective worship composed of staggered, syncopated patterns of call and response, song and dance in many voices and many rhythms. And closely linked to ritual, the act of sacrifice, ritual as oblation, offering, gift. The hagiography of jazz history is illuminated by images of sacrificial immolations, Bolden and Parker and Coltrane and so many others, burned by racism and hate, burned out by addiction and hard living. But they themselves generously consumed their powers, their lives devoted to the interest of an outpouring, a firing of silver and gold.

Ritual—those spontaneous Eucharists and interior glossolalias, those trackless meditations and mystic decompositions—wherever we're tripping, the intensities of ritual tend to be gathered back to the service of identity, our stepping out of the circle a means of reaffirming it. Yet hearing Jarman, now a Buddhist teacher who runs a school in Brooklyn, now a white-robed monk rather than an AEC member with his face painted in Asante colors, I learn how ritual is liable to go the other way around. Centrifugal rather than centripetal, not a matter of securing a place, not a matter of making a good bargain but of being caught up in a whirling that gives itself over. Suspended, abandoned, offering and offered, there's a wind and the sky's the limit, it flashes like the wings that ride it, it flashes a joy that thinks itself like a flocking in the air of bold souls.

In the *Tao Te King*, Lao-Tse speaks of the sage: "Opening and closing the gates of heaven, he will be like the mother-bird: bright, and white, and penetrating the four quarters. He quickens and feeds but claims not."

Eighty years old, my mother travels, along with my sister, nearly seven hundred miles by train from Chicago to Baltimore to visit us. She reads, talks to fellow passengers, makes friends with a man from Taiwan traveling the country. They have a photo taken together at one of the stops. The relatives back home will laugh, say it looks like they are holding hands.

At a motel in Massachusetts, my mother and my sister greet us in the morning carrying bagels and coffee, looking happy and refreshed. Outside the window of their room, they've just seen the season's first robin in the courtyard.

Back home in a Chicago suburb, my mother walks two miles around the lake and meets the birds—all sorts there, the ducks and geese on the water, the blackbirds and sparrows, the red-flashing cardinals. She travels amid light and air and the sounds that are calling her gaze to the positions, the motions of the birds, their casting off in all directions. The neighbors worry about her going out alone, and she is often accompanied by a lady friend, but no matter what, she has her outing, following the shore of the lake, at some points venturing on to the highway when the path gives out, tracing a broken circle back home where she'll be greeted by Peppy, the budgie, who pecks the food from her dish while she's eating her lunch, fluttering all around the table, and among his many voices sometimes a caressing growl and a pretty-bird whistling, long-remembered music of his old friend, my dad.

To think means to get up above, establish control by way of a bird's eye view. In *The Stones of Venice*, Ruskin follows the tour of an imaginary bird over a gorgeously illuminated mind-atlas of Europe, the vernal gold of Mediterranean lands highlighting the storms and crags of the north, the bird's flight writing in bold imprint Ruskin's dream of the Gothic. The flight of a high-riding bird serves Psyche in her fourth labor, when she is instructed to gather a vial of black waters from a hidden vent in a mountain rock guarded by dragons, the foul gushing stream whispering and singing all the while of despair and death. She can find no more tears to weep and she stands rigid as a stone, stripped of all will and mind. The eagle of Zeus rescues her, rising into the sky and then eluding the three-tongued dragons by tacking to the left and the right, its bright eye always on the prize.

Bold, thought rises above and wheels over and veers across the compass, comes down on its prey. Bolder yet, another thought flies and flies and when it lands doesn't settle down but soon lifts again, going off on another track, maybe coming back on itself, but by then no longer the same thought by virtue of its journey.

Bold—one can trace the word back to the Old Norse *balle*, which means dangerous, perilous. As in the waters of the sea, it is dangerous to lose one's form, perilous to partake of powers of the world which also partake of you. To don the head of a bear, the jaws of a hyena, the feathers of a bird may mean you will be carried off altogether. They were right when they said you would stay that way if you kept doing it—look, you can't turn back: Icarus's wings are melting and dripping and pouring off their substance like the sun to which he would mount.

The bold trickster Eshu on the road, the right side of him black and the left side of him white so you can't tell which direction he's heading; the bold trickster Coyote approaching the place where the maidens bathe, uncoiling the rope of his forty-foot phallus in the water and nobody able to say where he is or he isn't.

The bold one—the person who breaks out of the plane along which the others are assembled, shouts out the challenge, climbs on to the roof, strips off the clothes and dances, says out loud what everybody else knows but is afraid to say. The bold one—the one who says to hell with what I'm supposed to do, what's impossible, beyond me. The bold one steps forward, disregards consequence and history, forgets the past and meets the future. The bold ones run to defend the stranger being attacked on the street, the bold ones put themselves on the line, beyond prudence and self-interest, pumping with adrenaline, using themselves up . . .

Their thought is a step, a walk, a dance. Thoreau wandering the woods, Dickens in late-night perambulations from one side to another of London, teenagers walking nowhere and anywhere because the night is calling to them. Thinking with the trees, the streams, the rocks, the streets and the rooftops, finally coming back home the room looks different, the view out the window has changed, there's a space around everything that seems to finely vibrate as though the world has redoubled its motion. Peripatetic, the philosopher walking among the gardens: the overthrow of thought in the passions of leaves in the sun silvering over their shadows when he finds he has walked all the way back around to the place where he begun but for an instant fails to know it.

Eight Bold Souls—Edward Wilkerson Jr.'s ensemble, August 2002, at the Hot House in Chicago, Oliver Lake the guest soloist, Wilkerson the leader and tenor saxophone, Mwata Bowden, Bob Griffin, the other players whom he urges on, easily directs, swinging one arm, holding the sax at the ready with the other. From the second generation of the AACM collective and now in his forties, there's still a sense about Wilkerson of those early years when he must have been a young prodigy, the kid coming up whom everybody likes and predicts great things for and who remarkably fulfills that promise. In the early eighties, at a concert where his group opened for Pharaoh Sanders and the World Saxophone Quartet, I discovered the angularity and surprise of his music, the way he ranged across the tenor's sonorities with no strain, as if he were playing a big booming clarinet. Just looking at him on the stage tonight makes me happy—he seems primed for the show but relaxed, wearing a sports jacket with fine stripes in dark blue and gray, a variant on the pattern of a railroad engineer's cap. When he introduces the members of the band, his voice is surprising, not a bandleader's verbal strut but milder, softer and higher than you'd expect. His face maintains the air of youth, reminding me of a guy I knew in high school who was simply good, good at what he did, good in how he treated people, good in a way that made me feel the pressure and challenge of that good, a good that wasn't weak but instead was something strong, bold.

Over the years, Wilkerson's tenor work has been refined in other groups, especially the Ethnic Heritage Ensemble, a stripped-down trio where he's joined by Joseph Bowie on trombone and Kahil El'Zabar on percussion. Tonight, the horn is almost incidental to his directing the ensemble, but whenever he plays it's the rare thing that might be called composer's saxophone. The solo is no longer an issue. There isn't the staging of it in the conventional way, the saxophone dramatically coming forward, center stage. Instead it seems weighted with and drawn out of the composition, perhaps the piece to begin with having been built from it. Whatever the case, the horn lines pass in a flash, in marvelous compression, very fast strokes across them of other voices—Gene Ammons and Don Byas, Ornette Coleman and Coltrane, Mitchell and Jarman—and in those swift redactions an immense concentration that continuously studies its being liable to disruption, interruption, striking a path while at the same time letting it trail in a sonorous clouding, as if being lodged within itself entails its verging on becoming dislodged in turn, lost and found, found and lost.

How bold the voice, the cry, the call, bravely announcing itself! In doing so betraying its presence, its location, becoming liable to attack, question, displacement. As it impresses itself upon the world, so is it pressed in turn. Anaximander, as Nietszche remarked, believed everything that is is both just and unjust, the stutter of that *is* an echo of how being itself echoes and runs and scatters and is dispersed from itself.

One hand always touching the tenor, the other lifted and making passes through the air, Wilkerson running the train called Eight Bold Souls. The group is a labor of ten-plus years, so practiced there's no music on the stands though the section work is comparable to the best of Ellington and Basie and Mingus, the two saxes and trumpet joined with 'cello, trombone, and tuba, bass, and drums, the ensemble swinging, rocking, effortlessly managing far-stretched intervals, abrupt lyric excurses, cross-switched parts, Oliver Lake tunneling into the compositions with an immaculately hard alto that sounds like it's being tested and scored and scratched across its burnished, high-pressure tone, the construction of the solos rather like an orderly yet exquisitely unpredictable throw of birds into the air, suspended between converging and diverging, their paths catching and caught on the run.

Toward the end of the show the group plays a song called "Black Herman," Wilkerson prefacing the composition with a few words about its inspiration, the famous African-American prestidigitator and magician of the twenties. A richly echoing, time-shifting piece, in one place the tenor shadowing the changes, in another driving off those shadows, in another itself drenched, become a shadow of its own motions. Black Herman—he took over a magic show after the death of the proprietor, he the assistant becoming the main attraction, his act soon popular across the country, among large black audiences in Harlem and elsewhere, and, unusually for the time, among white audiences, too. Black

Herman said he was a descendant of the Zulus, a people who never could be enslaved, and who possessed a secret knowledge that made it possible for him to escape any chains. He demonstrated that he could even escape the prison of death and the grave, with great publicity having himself buried in a closed coffin and after several days being exhumed, reappearing warm and alive and well. When he died for real, in the middle of a performance in the South, no one believed it and assumed it was part of the act. And even at his wake, a public occasion for which tickets were sold, people poked and prodded at his body with needles and nails, still uncertain whether he'd played a grand trick on them all and might suddenly rise up and greet them in his slightly mocking voice, loud and booming and given to extravagant eloquence and bold claims.

Intuitive Research Beings

Chicago, 1973. A crowded, noisy space on Clark Street near Belmont, Mwata Bowden playing a looping feedback figure on the alto saxophone, an insistent incremental repetition that at first seemed wrong—the solo should have been going somewhere, journeying a road through peaks and valleys, soarings and glides and wheels, while this was an arrest in place, a stopped whirling—but then took hold by virtue of what was scared in it, what was brave in it, a defiance of forward tilt and skimming lift and mastering wing, a flight instead taking off by turning back round on itself, running over its track again and again until the notion of track was transformed, track become clue, clue become trace, trace become echo, out of the trembling bold of it a flash, an oscillatory quiver around the borders of its figure.

And the singer Rita Warford wearing something red and pushing the human voice to a point of glorious breakage—like Janis Joplin's voice, it sounded like it must hurt to sing that way, thrilling through a thicket of overtones richly harsh and piercing, a voice that as much as it pressed to break out and escape into song at the same time seemed to want to stay inside a secret place before any song, holding back an instant from the welling force of everything it must make so bold as to risk.

A short-lived group, an AACM band founded, I believe, by Bowden. Intuitive Research Beings: the name seemed outrageous—who in the world would propose themselves as such beings, and what would a thing called intuitive research be, other than moving round in circles, pursuing a knowledge that would be no more than an autodidactic rehearsal of itself?

All that exists is both just and unjust. Just, insofar as it has a claim to be, to persist in being; unjust, insofar as it holds to a place that some being other than itself could claim. To be or not to be is not the question so much as the mode of being, intransitive or transitive—being not positioned in an inertia in which it must persist or perish, but being as prepositioned, being with, between, among.

Plato dreamed a soul-bird that would ascend to the radiant knowledge of the Ideas, but in the cave of Lascaux, the shaman lies in trance with his head become a bird's head and beak, dreaming a second world among which the Ideas would be indistinguishable from the run and the dance of bright shadows in the dark.

The shadows of fires all over us, among those shadows yearning to become one of them, foreshortened and elongated, dancing and teasing and secondary. Delight of being no more than ruffled feather, minute trembling in the space between beats.

If jazz is essentially an abstraction of desire, endlessly generating figures, endlessly disseminating and squandering its powers, following its track might mean not so much loving jazz but loving the interval that it opens—so many notes running, sounding, the phrasings stacks of volumes, libraries of search and research, marginalia and annotations, suspensions and staggers and broken wheels approximating at the same time a sort of perpetual motion. What's happening not so much the content of it but the stretch of effort or the stung passivity, maybe, necessary to attend to it, follow it, and that passivity a trance of knowledge at the borderline of possessing something exquisitely detailed, complex and delightful, and of losing its possession, too, overwhelmed and possessed by it so you must forget, you must come back again for more, must return on your trail veering off it.

I can't touch the music on its run. I would shine a light, but really, I'm burning a candle, tending the flickering heart of its flame, its traffic with shadows. Like a flock of small birds in the room. Like the shadows of those birds.

Shadows on a brick wall, graffiti of hamadryads, those nymphs who spin and weave the green and the silver and the gold, sunlight and moonlight and the restless susurrus of the dancing leaves. On a warm day in May, the city feeling loose, indifferent, careless, the shadows of passing birds in the afternoon sunlight striking across the pavement. It seems among those shifting flickerings I could study for hours and years, reading and read by the drift and surprise of their unrepeatable combinations.

Or gathering decline, blighting, and death—the skull sockets, the guttering eyelights, the extinction of the day and its works—shadows attending the finish, casting back a history that blots up the life, its fine trembling, step of the walk, force of the voice, animus of the face composed and discomposed in the passion of its task. Look at the sweat pouring like rain off Coltrane's face, look at the golden hauteur radiating from Johnny Hodges's skin, look at the pop-eyes of Satchmo and his hand fluttering a white handkerchief. Then think of them dead, and how they shine even brighter.

Is it their traffic in passion, is it their passionate generosity that brights such an aura around their death? Who's gone, and for whom is the next tribute, the next memory of a never fully recognized greatness, as if jazz despite its flame of Eros is after all a martyrology, a cult of the dead—it's as if they're dead even when living, as if the hovering of death must attend their pouring out their powers, as if they're sacrificial victims igniting their own holocausts.

Hurry up and catch him live because he might not be around next time. Watch the shadows sway and leap and crawl behind the bandstand. Watch the shadow of your hand across the tablecloth, the thin lipping of your drink, the line of your mouth, the quiver of hunger, greed in it, as if you would snatch a breath out of the air.

Flip of a page in a book of sound, ghost encyclopedia, a script there whose words verse back and forth, like every book, in runs of shadows. That book is a volume of night where your eye tracking the page is blind to the writing because you're in the book, too, being searched as you search.

Bird of this music, this thought: it is your streaked wings I love because you live without comfort and without place, your life a parting of the air. I offer you a food of words: all that protects, all that welcomes, all that lifts and delves and rides boldly into its chances. All that slides, that bends, all that slurs and is slurred.

Shadows on a brick wall. Like birds, luminous omens, dark letters danced by souls who spin and weave, who stitch and knot and lace, who unspool and unwind and rip the thread.

Being learning the wrong of its right, the right of its wrong.

A dream where I float over the crowns of trees and the city rooftops, occasionally landing and then pushing off again as though the flying is a swimming through the air. Once in a while I take off by means of a running start, more rarely I find myself already at a great height in a space of bright sun. I see the word *ether*, and below me nothing of the world is visible. I'm inside the sky and my body is convulsing, twisting back round itself, coiling.

And then I see, far below on the earth, the flight of my shadow, something like a bird's high-riding wing, something like a dancing serpent across the ground.

A day in September, walking along the lake with my mother, we see the sparrows everywhere among the grass and the fences and the changing colors of the maples and oaks in the park. Sometimes they flock together, rise and fall in lowly scrimmages across the lawn. Toward sundown they collect by the hundreds inside the shrubberies along a path where the last daylight falls. Their evening song achieves a tremendous volume, far out of proportion to their size and their numbers.

Nearby is the ash tree we were allowed to plant here several years ago in memory of my father. It grows slowly, it isn't thick with leaf, but it has taken root and it seems strong.

In their gathering and their abandon, the sparrows all around us.

We stop for a minute and listen. It feels as though the cool air has opened wide. It feels as though whatever swells the sparrows into song carries us along in its gift.

discography

Gene Ammons
Boss Tenor (Prestige PRLP 7180), 1960.
Angel Eyes (Prestige PR 7369), 1960.
The Boss Is Back! (Prestige PR 7739), 1969·
Brother Jug! (Prestige PR 7792), 1969.
The Black Cat! (Prestige PR 10006), 1970.
You Talk That Talk! (Prestige PR 10019), 1971·

Fred Anderson
Destiny with Marilyn Crispell and Hamid Drake (Okkadisc 12003), 1995.
Chicago Chamber Music (Southport 0043), 1997.
Live at the Velvet Lounge (Okkadisc 12023), 1998.
On the Run (Delmark 534), 2001.
Back Together Again with Hamid Drake (Thrill Jockey 139), 2004.

Art Ensemble of Chicago
Phase One (Prestige 10064), 1971.
Tutankhamun (Freedom 40122), 1974·
Bap-tizum (Atlantic 1639), 1973.
Live at Mandel Hall (Delmark 432–33), 1974.
Coming Home Jamaica (Atlantic 83149–2), 1998.
Tribute to Lester (ECM 1808), 2003.

Ari Brown

Venus (Delmark 504), 1998.

Don Cherry
Mu First Part (BYG 1), 1969.

John Coltrane
My Favorite Things (Atlantic 1361), 1961.
The Complete Village Vanguard Sessions 1961 (Impulse 04–231), 1997.

Miles Davis
Collector's Items (Prestige 7044), 1959.
Sorcerer (Columbia CS 9532), 1967.

Wild Bill Davis (and Johnny Hodges)
Live in Atlantic City (RCA 3706), 1967.

Eight Bold Souls
Last Option (Thrill Jockey 071), 1999.

Duke Ellington
New Orleans Suite (Atlantic 1580), 1970.

Ethnic Heritage Ensemble
Dance with the Ancestors (Chameleon 6194–2), 1993.

Julius Hemphill
Coon Bidness (Arista AL1012), 1975.
Dogon A.D. (Arista AL 1028), 1975.

Andrew Hill
Point of Departure (Blue Note 84167), 1964.
Andrew! (Blue Note 4203), 1964.
Compulsion (Blue Note 4217), 1965.

Joseph Jarman
Equal Interest (OmniTone 12001), 2002.

Rahsaan Roland Kirk
I Talk with the Spirits (Limelight 82008), 1964.
Rip, Rig, and Panic (Limelight 82027), 1965.
Rahsaan, Rahsaan (Atlantic 1575), 1970.
The Case of the 3-Sided Dream in Audio Color (Atlantic 1674), 1975.

George Lewis
Voyager (Avan 014), 1993.

Jackie McLean
One Step Beyond (Blue Note 46821), 1965.

Charles Mingus
Pithecanthropus Erectus (America AM 6109), 1970.

Roscoe Mitchell
Nonaah (Nessa 9/10), 1977.
L-R-G / The Maze / S II Examples (Nessa 14/15), 1978.
The Flow of Things (Black Saint 0090), 1987.
Roscoe Mitchell and the Note Factory (Folio 20090), 1997.
Sound Songs (Delmark 493), 1997.

The Day and the Night (Dizim 4101), 1998.
Solo 3 (Mutable 17515–2), 2003.

Wayne Shorter
The Soothsayer (Blue Note LT988), 1965.
Speak No Evil (Blue Note 84194), 1965.

Sonny Stitt
Stitt Plays Bird (Atlantic 1418), 1961.
Burnin' (Argo/Cadet 629), 1962·
Soul Shack (Prestige 7297), 1963.
Constellation (Muse 5323), 1972.

Jimmy Smith
Back at the Chicken Shack (Blue Note 84117), 1965.
Monster (Verve 8618), 1967.

Sun Ra
Fate in a Pleasant Mood / When Sun Comes Out (Evidence 22068–2), 1993.
Fondation Maeght Nights 1 and 2 (Jazz View 006–007), 1970.
Space is the Place (Impulse 249), 1972.
Outer Space Employment Agency (Total Energy NER 3021), 1999.